MW00989348

PRAISE FOR

BRINGING OUT THE BEST IN EVERYONE YOU COACH

"For years, Ginger Lapid-Bogda has been in the forefront of Enneagram authors in bringing the Enneagram to the business world. With this book devoted to the art of coaching, she broadens her scope and goes deeper, while making the process of coaching with the Enneagram clear, comprehensive, and understandable to readers at all levels. She demonstrates that coaching is a subtle, person-to-person interaction and that the Enneagram can greatly clarify this process, bringing both coach and client to more understanding and precision in each situation. We are glad to see that Ginger has rightly used the Levels of Development as a primary framework for coaching effectively. We predict this book—clearly written, well organized, and practical—will quickly become the 'standard' Enneagram coaching book for years to come."

Don Richard Riso and Russ Hudson
Best-selling authors of *Personality Types* and *The Wisdom of the Enneagram*

* * *

"This book warrants a front-row place on the bookshelf of every coaching professional."

Helen Palmer
Teacher of intuition and author of *The Enneagram: Understanding Yourself and the Others in Your Life* and *The Enneagram in Love and Work*

* * *

"In *Bringing Out the Best in Everyone You Coach,* Ginger achieves yet another milestone. She has a deep understanding of the Enneagram and an outstanding ability to present it. Her work is practical, systematic, highly readable, clear, comprehensive, thoughtful, elegant, and compassionate. She honors process and method, levels of development, and all three centers of intelligence—head, heart, and body. This is a must-read for all varieties of helpers from coaches to managers to guides."

David Daniels, M.D.
Clinical Professor, Department of Psychiatry and Behavioral Sciences, Stanford University School of Medicine, and coauthor of *The Essential Enneagram*

"Ginger Lapid-Bogda has done a much-needed job of making coaching skills accessible for her Enneagram audience and of translating Enneagram information into the coaching arena. As an expert who knows both parties, Ginger is a good matchmaker. Her many concrete suggestions and examples provide a useful meeting ground or melting pot for blending coaching and Enneagram ingredients."

Jerry Wagner, Ph.D.
Author of *The Enneagram Spectrum of Personality Styles* and *The Wagner Enneagram Personality Style Scales*

* * *

"Highly recommended. An accessible, well-organized, at-a-glance guide that puts the Enneagram's wisdom at the fingertips of every coach."

Thomas Condon
Author of *The Enneagram Movie and Video Guide*

* * *

"Ginger Lapid-Bogda integrates the work of coaching and the power of using the Enneagram assessment in this important book. Coaches today need great training, years of experience, and a substantive tool kit—including assessments such as the Enneagram—in order to become masterful in this work. *Bringing Out the Best in Everyone You Coach* provides coaches with just such a resource as a coaching tool and for their own self-discovery on this path to mastery!"

Pamela McLean, Ph.D.
CEO, The Hudson Institute of Santa Barbara

* * *

"Ginger Lapid-Bogda has written a timely and authoritative book on using the Enneagram in coaching. The book is packed with information and tools … a valuable addition to any coach's bookshelf."

Karen Kimsey-House
President and cofounder, The Coaches Training Institute

* * *

"This is a great book, presenting the vital fact that potential comes in many forms, and a coach skilled in the techniques in *Bringing Out the Best in Everyone You Coach* can unlock the very best in each and every client. Rich in both explanation and precise coaching steps, this book is a must-read for coaches of all types."

Dave Logan, Ph.D.
Best-selling coauthor of *Tribal Leadership* and *Three Laws of Performance* and Professor, Marshall School of Business, University of Southern California

"I think of myself as a good coach, but Ginger's writing on coaching—even before the section on the Enneagram—was outstanding. I found a gold vein and would have been content not reading any more. Of course, I did and felt I found the mother lode. Even more, I was able to immediately apply what I learned. *Bringing Out the Best in Everyone You Coach* is a must-read for these competitive times in which the need for the people we coach to learn, develop, and transform is essential."

Teresa Roche
Vice President and Chief Learning Officer, Agilent Technologies

* * *

"I absolutely love this book. I found myself focusing in two ways: one as a frame to better understand myself so I can achieve greater progress toward high self-mastery and the other as a way to develop those I am coaching. Using the book's insights—and particularly the level of detail that differentiates the many ways individuals who claim the same Enneagram style can outwardly display different behaviors and emotions while at the core be so similar—will certainly help both me and others get the most out of the precious time with our boss or mentor relationships."

Nancy Brooks
Vice President, Customer Management & Operations, Best Buy Co., Inc.

* * *

"Ginger Lapid-Bogda's *Bringing Out the Best in Everyone You Coach* completes one of the most important trilogies in leadership and personal development. This book profoundly improved my versatility and effectiveness as a manager by combining the insights of the Enneagram with the skill of coaching. Every manager will benefit from understanding the distinction between managing and coaching. This book makes the art of coaching impactful and accessible by providing you with deeper awareness of how our unique ways of thinking, feeling, and behaving influence our path to greater performance. This book represents the most useful and important guide I have had in my search for how to be a more effective leader and manager."

Todd Pierce
Senior Vice President and CIO, Genentech, Inc.

"With her latest book, Ginger Lapid-Bogda has given coaches and leaders a methodology and approach that can unlock the powerful potential within each personality type as described by the Enneagram. Powerful coaching and leading are the essential ingredients of developing and sustaining a high-performance team. This book should be an essential resource for anyone who coaches others."

A. Gus Kious, M.D.
President of Huron Hospital, a Cleveland Clinic Hospital

●　●　●

"I could not put this book down! Ginger's unique way of intertwining the term 'coaching' leaves you convinced these tools can be helpful to anyone in your life. The Enneagram is very effective in our business, as leaders who want to assist employees with development, and we ourselves have changed because of Ginger's training and guidance. These challenging economic times demand quality in people, and this book is the road map for how to achieve this. A great read!"

Dalyn Schmitt
Executive Director/CEO of Heartland Regional Alcohol and Drug Assessment Center

●　●　●

"*Bringing Out the Best in Everyone You Coach* is an incredible tool for coaching in the workplace. As the CEO of Room to Read, a global nonprofit dedicated to improving educational opportunities for children in the developing world, I already use the Enneagram for understanding myself and enhancing communication among my executive management team. Now we have this easily digestible book, with great coaching tips and excellent development activities for each type, so we can coach ourselves as well as those who work for us."

Erin Keown Ganju
Cofounder and CEO, Room to Read

●　●　●

"I have found through the Enneagram that if you want to develop an effective team, start by developing yourself and use the tool to bring authenticity and constructive working relations back into your organization. This book takes you as a manager one step further, into the role of a coach that releases the power of your team."

Carolyne Coquet
Director, High Jewellery Development & Special Orders, Cartier

BRINGING OUT THE BEST IN EVERYONE
—— YOU COACH ——

BRINGING OUT THE BEST IN EVERYONE
——— YOU COACH ———

Use the
ENNEAGRAM SYSTEM
for Exceptional Results

GINGER LAPID-BOGDA, Ph.D.
Author of *Bringing Out the Best in Yourself at Work*

New York   Chicago   San Francisco   Lisbon   London   Madrid   Mexico City
Milan   New Delhi   San Juan   Seoul   Singapore   Sydney   Toronto

The **McGraw·Hill** Companies

Library of Congress Cataloging-in-Publication Data

Lapid-Bogda, Ginger.
    Bringing out the best in everyone you coach : use the enneagram system
for exceptional results / by Ginger Lapid-Bogda.
        p.   cm.
    ISBN 978-0-07-163707-7 (alk. paper)
        1. Enneagram.   2. Employees—Coaching of.   3. Employee motivation.
I. Title.

    BF698.35.E54L368   2010
    158'.9—dc22   2009025982

Copyright © 2010 by Ginger Lapid-Bogda. All rights reserved. Printed in the United States
of America. Except as permitted under the United States Copyright Act of 1976, no part
of this publication may be reproduced or distributed in any form or by any means, or stored
in a database or retrieval system, without the prior written permission of the publisher.

1 2 3 4 5 6 7 8 9 0   DOC/DOC   0 9

ISBN   978-0-07-163707-7
MHID   0-07-163707-9

McGraw-Hill books are available at special quantity discounts to use as premiums and sales
promotions or for use in corporate training programs. To contact a representative, please
e-mail us at bulksales@mcgraw-hill.com.

Contents

Acknowledgments

It has been stimulating and daunting to write a book on transformative coaching, one that is based on tested coaching practices, integrates the profound insights of the Enneagram, and can be easily used by all who coach. Those who coach come from a variety of backgrounds—for example, trainers, consultants, coaches, human resource personnel, managers, psychologists—and their coaching may involve short-term, crisis, or long-term coaching. In addition, individuals who coach may already subscribe to a particular coaching philosophy that works well for them and is based on personal experience, on a coaching certification program they have taken, or on a psychological framework they prefer. Given these factors, I have tried to write a book that is easy to use for everyone who coaches, makes a contribution to the field of coaching, and enhances the coach's ability to help clients achieve transformative results.

Although many people have influenced this work directly and indirectly, I want to mention those who have both inspired me and provided support. Natalie Toy has read every draft of this book, offering her most able feedback at every step. Claudine Prune, a consultant, coach, and Enneagram teacher from Paris, challenged me to write this book two years ago by saying, "Oh, but you must! It is part of the trilogy with the two other books." Dave Warner, an organization development colleague from Northern California, generously provided ideas when they were most needed. Todd Pierce, a vice president at Genentech, gave me unprecedented opportunity to create and field-test the material in this book with his high-level managers.

Several other individuals have also made significant contributions. Beatrice Chestnut helped conceive the "coaching approaches to enhance self-mastery" for the nine Enneagram styles and has influenced my understanding of the 27 Enneagram subtypes (Chapters 3 through 11). David Coleman, a coach from Washington, D.C., first introduced me to the power of the "Why would you want to do that?" challenge (described in Chapter 1 and tailored to each Enneagram style in Chapters 3 through 11). Don Riso and Russ Hudson have been generous in many ways, from colleagueship to advice; the self-mastery level information for each Enneagram style described in Chapters 3 through 11 has its genesis in their work on the levels of development. I am always in a state of gratitude for the Enneagram work of Claudio Naranjo. Finally, Helen Palmer and David Daniels gave me a wonderful foundation in the Enneagram system, and they continue to be special friends and colleagues.

My thanks also go to Jane Roberts and Muriel Nellis, my agents at Literary and Creative Artists, and to my longtime editor at McGraw-Hill, Donya Dickerson.

Foreword

Little did I know when Ginger knocked on my door in the summer of 1987 that someone special was entering my life, someone whose personal and professional interests would become intertwined with mine and who would also become a lifelong friend. Ginger had just moved to Los Angeles from the San Francisco area, where she worked as an organization development consultant. Before the days of Facebook and LinkedIn, a mutual friend suggested she call me. I told her to bring her walking shoes if she wanted to have a conversation with no distractions, and we took the first of our many walks, ones that always included truthful conversations about our lives, families, dreams, and losses.

My career development consulting and training practice was growing. I had completed my dissertation at UCLA and parlayed it into my first book, *Up Is Not the Only Way.* Ginger joined me on a number of early consulting projects in the career development arena and then led many on her own. Throughout that time, I recognized that Ginger was highly observant. I soon came to realize that she remembers everything I say, as well as what I don't say. She relishes in my success, as a good friend should, and when I have occasional misfires, she remembers those lessons too, and uses them.

Ginger is a versatile large-scale change consultant and brings this deep expertise to her work. More than 20 years later, I am not at all surprised that she has become a leader in bringing the Enneagram into organizations around the world. It combines her passion for people and systems. She's an honest, sincere, and insightful professional who is always finding new avenues to bring depth to her own growth and to help others do that too.

When I read her first book, *Bringing Out the Best in Yourself at Work,* I was impressed by her ability to describe the nine varieties of human behavior at work in intricate detail. After reading *What Type of Leader Are You?,* I was amazed at how much more she had to say—again in great detail. I also realized how integral her work was to employee development, retention, and engagement, areas that are a central focus of my current work. The more we know about ourselves and how to interact, network, and collaborate with others, the more we are able to advocate for our own workplace satisfaction. All of her work, especially her newest, is a superb guide for the savvy careerist.

The book you hold in your hands, *Bringing Out the Best in Everyone You Coach,* is one you can use as a wonderful guide, whether or not you have read the previous books. Managers, mentors, and coaches can delight in the fact that there is now a book that shows you precisely how to develop others—even providing models for short-term, crisis, and long-term coaching. Ginger brilliantly uses the profound and practical insights of Enneagram to do this. I was personally grabbed by the book when I went to my own Enneagram style and found that it described me perfectly. I marvel at how much she knows about her craft. Happily, we can all now know it and use it with our clients and ourselves.

Beverly Kaye, Ed.D.
Founder/CEO of Career Systems International

Introduction

Organizational coaching is a premier personal and professional development method in which the coach guides another individual toward the achievement of specific goals. In fact, coaching has become the fastest-growing human resource profession over the past two decades. A variety of people function as coaches—for example, managers, mentors, and "professional" coaches, such as certified coaches, human resource personnel, trainers, psychologists, and organizational consultants. With the proliferation of coaches worldwide, it is especially important that individuals who coach others understand what coaching is, how it works, and how to ensure that it actually produces results. The following story briefly illustrates both the potential challenges and dramatic benefits of coaching.

Louise had asked for executive coaching. However, each time she met with her coach, Maurice, she would either arrive late or leave early, and she frequently canceled her appointments altogether. Frustrated, Maurice developed a six-page document that compared Louise's coaching goals with information he had learned thus far about Louise's behavior. The data came from several sources: Louise herself; interviews with Louise's manager, peers, and subordinates; and Maurice's own observations. While Maurice had developed this document as a coaching tool for his own use, Louise desperately wanted to see it. After convincing Maurice to give her the document, Louise proceeded to defend her behavior and to argue over even the smallest details. Just one month later, however, Louise's manager and coworkers were stopping Maurice in the hallway to remark about the dramatic changes in Louise's behavior. All wanted to know not only how he had done it, but also how he had helped her change so dramatically in such a short period of time.

As this story suggests, it can be difficult to determine what really causes changes in someone's behavior or whether coaching actually achieves long-lasting results. At the same time, coaching has become the most effective method for increasing an individual's personal, interpersonal, and organizational effectiveness. Because coaching usually takes place as a one-to-one interaction between a coach and a client, it is a unique and highly individualized developmental experience.

Because a wide variety of people coach others, this book refers to any individual who serves in this capacity as the "developer" and to the recipient of coaching as the "learner." The developer provides knowledge, insight, perspective, and feedback to the learner in accordance with the coaching goals. These goals are developed collaboratively between the developer and learner, although others may also become involved—for example, the learner's manager or a human resource specialist.

This book provides a solid and practical grounding in basic coaching methodologies, approaches, and techniques, then integrates these with insights from the Enneagram in order to deepen the coaching experience and help developers and learners achieve far superior results than coaching without the Enneagram. Using the knowledge and skills gained from this book, developers can ensure that their chosen approach is tailored to the specific needs of the individual learner.

Coaching

Until the last decade, coaching was often reserved for three groups of people: senior executives, high-potential individual contributors, and employees with remedial needs. Companies offered their top executives the opportunity for coaching because members of this group tend to have neither the time nor the inclination to go through extended leadership development programs. Moreover, many executives appreciate having someone they trust and with whom they can discuss their concerns. Coaching was also offered to members of the second group, candidates deemed to have strong potential for management, as a way to launch and accelerate their leadership careers. A third group, individuals with extremely serious interpersonal or performance problems, received coaching either as a way to save their careers or as a last-resort effort prior to their being fired.

In recent years, however, companies have realized that many employees can benefit from coaching; unlike training programs, which typically cover generic knowledge and skills, coaching specifically targets individual developmental needs. For this reason, companies are hiring more external coaches, and human resource personnel are being asked to coach individuals. There has also been a proliferation of mentoring programs, and coaching subordinates is becoming a routine part of a manager's ongoing job responsibilities. In addition, individuals are electing to engage in coaching on their own and are paying for it themselves.

Coaching is increasingly becoming a best-in-class method for personal and professional development, but it can be said that there are as many coaching approaches as there are coaches. This is partly a result of the numerous types of coaching available—for example, performance coaching, executive coaching, and life coaching—as well as the wide array of psychological and experience-based approaches to coaching. In addition, there are several coaching organizations with explicit professional standards and certification processes. However, in reality, anyone can declare him- or herself a coach without being held accountable for upholding professional and ethical standards or achieving particular results. This book is intended to provide more clarity on all these issues and to bring depth to the coaching experience through the use of the Enneagram.

The Enneagram

The word *enneagram* comes from the Greek words *ennea* ("nine") and *gram* ("something written or drawn") and refers to the nine points on the Enneagram symbol. The nine different Enneagram styles, identified as numbers One through Nine, reflect distinct habits of thinking, feeling, and behaving, with each style connected to a unique path of development. Each of us has

Enneagram Symbol

only one place, or number, on the Enneagram; while our Enneagram style remains the same throughout our lifetime, the characteristics of our style may either soften or become more pronounced as we grow and develop. In addition to our core Enneagram style, there are four other styles that provide additional qualities to our personalities, which are discussed in Chapters 3 through 11.

The Enneagram's ancient history is uncertain, although the system first appeared in both Asia and the Middle East at least several thousand years ago. Since that time, it has evolved in various parts of the world, and the Enneagram's modern usage has been heavily influenced by three individuals. Two philosophers began working with the Enneagram on different continents: G. I. Gurdjieff in the 1930s in Europe, and Oscar Ichazo from the 1950s to the present in South America. Claudio Naranjo, an American psychiatrist born in Chile, initially studied the Enneagram with Ichazo and brought it to the United States in the 1970s. The contemporary use of the Enneagram has grown from the work of these three individuals and has been advanced by other teachers, among them Helen Palmer, Don Riso, David Daniels, Russ Hudson, Theodorre Donson, Kathy Hurley, Tom Condon, and Jerry Wagner. Currently, the Enneagram is being used in a continuously growing array of practical applications, as shown in the accompanying figure.

Enneagram: History and Applications

More than a personality typology, the Enneagram is actually a profound map that illuminates the nine different architectures of the human personality. It is also the most powerful and practical system available for increasing emotional intelligence, with insights that can be used for personal and professional development. Not only is the Enneagram highly accurate in its descriptions of how individuals of each style think, feel, and behave, it also explains the underlying drives and motivations for these patterns and provides precise development activities tailored to the specific needs of the nine styles. As such, the Enneagram is ideal for managers, mentors, and coaches who want to make a deep and lasting impact on those whom they coach.

Emotional intelligence is a combination of two factors: *intra*personal intelligence, which is the ability to understand, accept, and manage oneself, and *inter*personal intelligence, the capacity to work effectively with a wide variety of other people. Because the Enneagram is cross-cultural and highly accurate and has many work-related applications, it is currently being used by organizations worldwide to help employees and leaders in the following areas: communication, conflict, feedback, teams, leadership, strategy, decision making, self-mastery, coaching, and more. Fundamentally, the Enneagram helps individuals to develop greater self-awareness and self-acceptance and to take personal responsibility for their behavior, changing a pattern of holding others or circumstances accountable for their problems and difficulties to one of taking responsibility for the consequences of their actions. This enables employees at all levels to become actors in their environments rather than passive recipients.

The Enneagram also provides specific development paths and activities tailored to each Enneagram style, so that development time is spent more efficiently and results are clear and long-lasting. For example, Ones have exceedingly high standards and search for perfection, but developers do not help them when they coach Ones to become more perfect. Instead, developers need to coach Ones to become more relaxed and less self-critical and to appreciate the best in things rather than focusing on flaws and mistakes. Similarly, with Threes, who normally have a laser-like focus on goals and plans, developers only reinforce individuals of this style when the coaching emphasizes the development of more goals and plans. Instead, developers need to help Threes learn that they can be valued for who they are, not just for what they achieve or accomplish.

The Enneagram is not a quick coaching fix; rather, it is a powerful way to help people learn and grow, and it can make an enormous difference in their personal and professional lives. For example, Mary, an Enneagram style Seven, thrived on volunteering for any project that arose at work that she found stimulating. Although she desperately wanted to keep her commitments, she was juggling so many projects simultaneously that she was often late delivering her work product and never slept more than four hours at night. However, the Enneagram helped her to understand that this need for constant excitement was actually a way to not feel bored and an avoidance of her feelings of anger, anxiety, and sadness. When she learned to focus better at work and to say no to projects that interested her, she was also able to focus more on her family priorities and on taking care of herself.

More importantly, the Enneagram is an approach that allows learners to do a great deal of the development work on their own. This enables them to make greater strides at a faster pace, both because the coaching conversations are more focused and insightful and the development activities are tailored to their specific needs. Developers who use the Enneagram in their coaching work gain satisfaction from their efforts because they know they are making a difference in someone's life. In addition, organizations benefit, because well-coached individuals make a greater contribution to their organizations; they are more productive, work better with others, take responsibility for their behavior and development, are easier to manage, and become better leaders.

The Book's Structure

This book is structured with the developer in mind, although learners can also benenfit from reading it as a way to understand themselves better and to develop new skills. Logically sequenced and organized for easy use as a reference, this book provides explicit instructions, a wide array of stories and examples, and numerous development activities.

Chapter 1, Coaching Overview, provides a systematic overview of specific steps developers need to take to ensure that their coaching is effective and achieves results:

1. Assess and Enhance Your Coaching Competence
2. Optimize the Developer-Learner Match
3. Clarify Your Coaching Role
4. Select the Appropriate Coaching Methodology: Short-Term, Crisis, or Long-Term Coaching
5. Determine Coaching Goals and Learner Motivation
6. Assess the Learner's Level and Range of Self-Mastery, Then Use Level-Appropriate Coaching Approaches
7. Use Coaching Techniques That Challenge Growth
8. Accelerate and Sustain the Learner's Transformation

Chapter 2, The Enneagram and Coaching, explains the Enneagram's theoretical foundations and how these provide key insights into the underlying concerns of all learners.

Chapters 3 through 11 focus on the nine Enneagram styles; each chapter—one style per chapter—describes the thinking, feeling, and behavioral patterns of the style and explains how to tailor the coaching approaches and techniques from Chapter 1 to learners of a particular style, specifically Steps 5, 6, and 7.

Chapter 12, Transformation, provides three provocative activities, along with a development planning process, thus addressing Step 8: Accelerate and Sustain the Learner's Transformation.

A Personal Note

I have been an organization development consultant for more than 35 years. Over this time, I have coached hundreds of people, from CEOs of major corporations to individuals who caught me in the hallway on my way to a meeting and asked for a two-minute coaching session. When I studied the Enneagram in the early 1990s, I did so for my own personal development. However, my clients began to ask me how I understood others so well and could anticipate their reactions and behavior with such a high degree of accuracy. As I shared my knowledge of the Enneagram with them, I saw how easy it was for them to understand and use the system. This was the beginning of my work to bring the Enneagram into widespread use in organizations around the world.

Using the Enneagram in my coaching practice has enabled me to help my clients achieve deeper and longer-lasting results at a highly accelerated pace. Just as importantly, the process has infused them with a desire to engage in lifelong learning using the Enneagram as their major guide on this journey.

Certainly, there are excellent developers—managers, mentors, and coaches—who are not currently using the Enneagram as part of their work. However, great developers are always enhancing their capabilities, and once they discover the remarkable insights of the Enneagram, it becomes virtually impossible for them not to use it as part of their fundamental coaching approach. In addition, excellent developers are always working on their own development; they model the behavior they want to encourage in their learners. While this book is about how to coach for transformation, it is also my hope that it encourages all who coach to use the knowledge for their own development as well.

· ONE ·

Coaching Overview

To compete effectively in today's global marketplace, employees at all levels—leaders and individual contributors alike—must make a commitment to their ongoing personal and professional development. Expanding workforce capability and leadership bench strength has never been more important, and employees must be readily deployed to new value-producing activities so that their organizations can respond quickly and effectively to business challenges and opportunities. Coaching provides an incisive, customized, and effective way to develop both leaders and individual contributors, but it is also labor intensive, time consuming, and expensive. That is why it is so important that developers are highly skilled.

This chapter provides an overview of the steps that developers must take to excel as coaches. Listed in sequence below and described in more detail later in the chapter, these steps ensure greater quality and consistency in coaching. The remainder of this book shows you how to integrate the insights and wisdom of the Enneagram in tailoring steps 5 through 8 for those whom you coach.

EIGHT STEPS TO COACHING EXCELLENCE

1. Assess and Enhance Your Coaching Competence
2. Optimize the Developer-Learner Match
3. Clarify Your Coaching Role
4. Select the Appropriate Coaching Methodology: Short-Term, Crisis, or Long-Term Coaching
5. Determine Coaching Goals and Learner Motivation
6. Assess the Learner's Level and Range of Self-Mastery, Then Use Level-Appropriate Coaching Approaches
7. Use Coaching Techniques That Challenge Growth
8. Accelerate and Sustain the Learner's Transformation

EIGHT STEPS TO COACHING EXCELLENCE

Step 1 · Assess and Enhance Your Coaching Competence

Developers need to continuously assess and enhance their skills. This involves knowing their current strengths, identifying the areas in which they need to grow, and then making a commitment and developing a plan to increase their capabilities. The following Coaching Competency Model can guide the developer's skill development.

The Coaching Competency Model

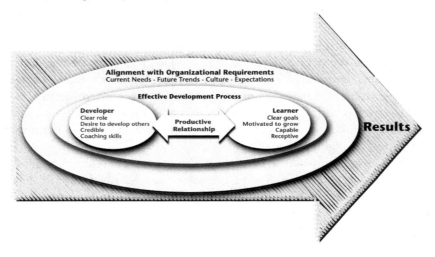

Having the ability to coach others effectively means that developers are skilled in the following six areas:

1. *Being an excellent developer of people.* Developers need to have a clear coaching role, honor their coaching agreements, have personal and professional credibility, possess a deep desire to develop others, have excellent coaching skills, and ultimately hold learners accountable for their own development.
2. *Knowing how to accelerate the learner's growth.* Developers need to focus learners on specific coaching goals that they are highly motivated to achieve, create a coaching environment that encourages learner receptivity, and accurately assess learner capability, including cognitive ability, emotional maturity, and work-related skills.
3. *Being able to create a productive relationship with the learner.* Developers need to create trusting and respectful relationships with learners that focus on individual development needs, are flexible and honest, and support the growth of both the learner and developer.

4. *Knowing how to implement an effective coaching process.* Developers need to use a systematic coaching methodology tailored to the learner's needs that includes an effective development process, a concrete development plan, and an ongoing feedback mechanism.
5. *Being able to align the coaching efforts with organizational requirements.* Developers need to make certain that the coaching goals and methodologies are aligned with the organization's needs, and that the organization's culture and political dynamics are factored into coaching conversations and recommendations.
6. *Being able to achieve lasting results.* Developers need to make sure that the coaching achieves effective results that can be sustained over the long run.

A complete skills assessment based on the Coaching Competency Model can be found in Appendix A.

REMINDER It is essential that you continuously enhance your coaching skills through increased knowledge, constant practice, and a commitment to your own self-development.

Step 2 · Optimize the Developer-Learner Match

A good match between a developer and a learner is just as important as the developer's coaching skills. The following information provides important guidelines when pairing developers and learners.

PAIRING DEVELOPERS AND LEARNERS

What developers should look for in a learner
- ✓ Honesty
- ✓ Willingness to learn
- ✓ A moderate to high degree of self-awareness
- ✓ Commitment to attend coaching meetings
- ✓ The learner should be someone the developer doesn't dislike.

What learners should look for in a developer
- ✓ Prior success as a coach
- ✓ Availability
- ✓ Credibility
- ✓ Good judgment
- ✓ Organizational savvy
- ✓ Excellent listening skills
- ✓ The developer should be someone the learner respects.

You may have noticed that *liking* the developer is not included on the learner's list of what to look for in a developer. While liking the developer can be beneficial, it is far more important that the learner *respect* the developer. With regard to what developers should look for in a learner, the phrase "someone the developer doesn't dislike" has been purposely chosen; the developer does not need to like the learner, only to have no adverse reaction to him or her. If the developer dislikes the learner, that individual would most likely sense the developer's negativity even if the developer tried to hide it.

When the learner respects the developer, the developer doesn't dislike the learner, *and* the coaching achieves tangible results, mutual positive regard and respect usually develop as the coaching progresses. Because most managers do not get to choose their learners—since coaching is often part of the manager's job—the coaching relationship can be severely compromised if unresolved tension exists between the two. Managers in this situation should try to repair the relationship before the coaching begins. If that is not possible, it is advisable to find an alternative developer for the learner.

The question is often asked whether learners and developers should be paired on the basis of a shared characteristic, such as gender, race, age, and/or personality. Individuals who are similar may understand each other better, and the developer may serve as a more viable role model, but these developers can also unintentionally reinforce the learner in ways that do not support growth. When paired with someone who is dissimilar to them, learners often benefit because the developer brings in a different perspective. With respect to the Enneagram, when the developer and learner are not the same Enneagram style, there are definite advantages; for example, the developer brings a different set of mental models, emotional responses, and behavior patterns from which to challenge the learner. If the developer and learner have the same Enneagram style, the match can still be beneficial, but *only if* the developer possesses a much higher level of self-mastery than the learner. When this is the case, the developer can do the following to optimize the process and results: fully understand the learner, serve as an excellent role model, challenge and inspire the learner to grow at an accelerated pace, and offer development activities that the developer knows will work from direct experience.

REMINDER   Make the best match possible, and plan in advance how to compensate for a less than optimal one.

Step 3 · Clarify Your Coaching Role

Even when developers have excellent coaching skills and the match between the developer and learner is a good one, problems can arise during coaching if either is unclear about the developer's role. At the very beginning of the coaching relationship, it is essential that both the developer and the learner understand whether the development interactions will be based on your being the learner's manager, mentor, or coach. Although managers, mentors, and coaches perform many of the same coaching functions, their roles in relation to the learner are different. The specific role you have directly affects the coaching expectations, subsequent relationship, and eventual success of the coaching. The following graphic shows the similarities and differences among and between the three roles.

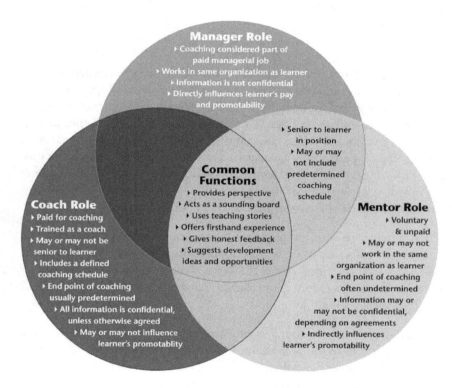

Manager Role
- Coaching considered part of paid managerial job
- Works in same organization as learner
- Information is not confidential
- Directly influences learner's pay and promotability

Common Functions
- Provides perspective
- Acts as a sounding board
- Uses teaching stories
- Offers firsthand experience
- Gives honest feedback
- Suggests development ideas and opportunities

- Senior to learner in position
- May or may not include predetermined coaching schedule

Coach Role
- Paid for coaching
- Trained as a coach
- May or may not be senior to learner
- Includes a defined coaching schedule
- End point of coaching usually predetermined
- All information is confidential, unless otherwise agreed
- May or may not influence learner's promotablity

Mentor Role
- Voluntary & unpaid
- May or may not work in the same organization as learner
- End point of coaching often undetermined
- Information may or may not be confidential, depending on agreements
- Indirectly influences learner's promotability

Three Coaching Roles

Manager

If the learner reports to you, you are coaching as a manager. The manager has the most firsthand information about the learner, as well as the most authority with which to influence the learner's growth and development. At the same time, because the manager directly affects the learner's income, current work responsibilities, and future promotions and is not bound by an agreement of confidentiality, learners may be more reluctant to share relevant information during the coaching process.

Mentor

You are coaching as a mentor if the following apply: The learner does not work for you and you are not responsible for his or her performance evaluation, you are not specifically paid to coach others or trained as a professional coach, and you have voluntarily agreed to coach the learner. Learners often perceive mentors as having the most organizational expertise and political savvy. However, because mentoring is usually voluntary and not part of the mentor's paid work, fewer mentors are available than are either managers or coaches. Also, while some mentors work in a strictly confidential manner, others do not.

Coach

If you are hired and trained to coach individuals and the learner does not work for you, you are a coach. Coaches usually have the most time and training for coaching and normally work under a complete confidentiality agreement with the learner. As a result, learners confide more in coaches than in managers or mentors. At the same time, coaches rarely have the same level of management experience as managers and mentors, and they often do not possess the same degree of organizational knowledge. However, because coaches are not directly involved in the organization's business, they are often perceived as the most objective or neutral type of developer.

NOTE   Human resource professionals who work inside an organization and coach others as a part of their job responsibilities normally function in the role of "coach" described above. However, some internal HR professionals function more as mentors than coaches and should use the mentoring role descriptions as their guide.

Although coaching arrangements can vary widely, all effective developers must perform specific functions. For example, coaching can be done in-person or by phone; developers and learners may have meetings as often as several times per week, as infrequently as once a month, or even on an as-needed basis; and coaching conversations can be as short as 15-minute emergency conversations or as long as several days.

All developers need to fulfill the following functions for learners:

- Offer a different perspective
- Serve as a sounding board so that learners can share and then reflect on their own thoughts, feelings, and behaviors
- Tell "teaching" stories that communicate important messages
- Share relevant firsthand experiences
- Give honest feedback
- Suggest development activities and provide other resources as needed

REMINDER Before you begin the development process, it is important that both you and the learner understand your role—including its strengths and limitations—and confidentiality boundaries.

Step 4 · Select the Appropriate Coaching Methodology: Short-Term, Crisis, or Long-Term Coaching

In addition to having a good match with the learner and a clear coaching role, the developer needs to reach agreements with the learner about the type of coaching that will best suit the learner's needs—short-term, crisis, or long-term coaching. This is important because each type of coaching requires a different coaching methodology, as described in more detail below.

Short-term coaching occurs over a short period of time—typically two to eight sessions, with the coaching process lasting anywhere from one to four months—and focuses on specific and limited topic areas that can be effectively addressed in a brief period of time.

Crisis coaching is needed when a learner is experiencing an acute crisis and is under severe duress as the result of a work or home problem or an external event.

Long-term coaching can be as short as four months or can extend over several years; this allows for outcomes that are larger in scale and deeper in impact than what can normally be achieved with short-term coaching.

Short-Term Coaching

Short-term coaching, sometimes referred to as "problem-solving coaching" or "solution-focused coaching," focuses on a specific problem or issue that can be quickly resolved. It is a particularly effective methodology to use when the coaching goal is sufficiently precise and narrow in scope and/or when the learner has a limited window of opportunity in which to achieve a result. However, short-term coaching is not effective when the learner is low in self-mastery or has insufficient skills and on-the-job experience to achieve the coaching goal within a limited time period.

The Change Strategy Formula[1] provides a coaching methodology that developers can use to assist learners in achieving the short-term development goal. This methodology is simple yet comprehensive and is best introduced during the first meeting with the learner, then used throughout the short-term coaching process. The formula has an implicit methodology, one that is ideal for short-term coaching.

---

[1]The Change Strategy Formula is an adaptation of the Formula for Change created by Dick Beckhard and David Gleicher in the 1960s.

Change Strategy Formula
D x V x P > R = C

D = desire and demand for the change; dissatisfaction with the status quo
V = vision for the change
P = plan and process for achieving the change
R = resistance to change
C = change the learner most desires, the goal to be achieved

In order for the learner to achieve his or her coaching goals (C), the learner needs compelling motivation to change (D), a clear and real vision of what his or her life would be like with the change in place (V), and a viable plan and process for achieving the change (P). For the change to occur, these three elements—that is, D, V, and P—must be greater than the learner's resistance (R). The coaching process involves defining the change desired (C), assessing the strength of the remaining four elements (D, V, P, and R), and then developing a change strategy based on the assessment.

A more detailed explanation of how to use the Change Strategy Formula is included in Appendix B.

Crisis Coaching

A learner who needs crisis coaching can best be described as (1) less stable than normal; (2) feeling highly threatened and anxious; (3) at a major life crossroads and experiencing a myriad of emotions; (4) having to examine newly revealed and disturbing feelings, relationships, and information; (5) finding that his or her normal functioning and primary defense mechanisms no longer work effectively; and (6) being uncertain about the outcome of the crisis but imagining that the worst may occur. Because of these factors, crisis coaching requires a different approach than short-term or long-term coaching, as seen in the box on the following page.

A more detailed explanation of the Crisis Coaching methodology is included in Appendix C.

Long-Term Coaching

Long-term coaching occurs over several months or years and requires an extended commitment from both the developer and learner. The developer must be able and willing to engage in coaching of this magnitude, and the learner must have a desire to learn, grow, and take advantage of the coaching experience. The best candidates for long-term coaching are learners with one or more of the following characteristics: (1) have serious performance issues

CRISIS COACHING METHOD

Respond to the urgent issues

1. Listen attentively.
2. Address immediate problems when possible; give advice carefully.
3. Be calm, compassionate, and clear.

Deal with the deeper dynamics

4. Identify root causes.
5. Deal with the learner's deeper concerns.
6. Provide hope and relief.

Create a sustainable action plan

7. Create a focused, concrete plan of action.
8. Design a support system.
9. Refer the learner to additional resources as needed.

that require more coaching than can be provided in short-term coaching; (2) have multiple coaching goals that require more extended coaching; (3) have a demonstrated commitment to and excitement about ongoing personal and professional development; (4) are high-potential candidates for future leadership jobs or high-impact professional positions; (5) are in highly stressful, high-pressure jobs for which having a coach as a sounding board and advisor can be extremely beneficial; or (6) are senior executives who need someone whom they trust to confide in.

Long-term coaching always involves unpredictable events and new opportunities—for example, the learner receives a promotion or gets fired, a new issue arises that provides a coaching opportunity, or an organizational change alters the coaching requirements. Because of these factors, effective long-term coaching must not only be emergent and spontaneous, but must also be predictable. The 5-C Coaching Method[2] provides this predictability because it ensures that the developer and learner are following a clear plan rather than an entirely open-ended process that may or may not lead to the intended results. A coherent coaching methodology, combined with enough flexibility to respond to emergent issues, dramatically increases the success of long-term coaching.

[2] I developed this five-stage coaching method over a 35-year period of working successfully with clients of all ages and from all industrial sectors, law and consulting firms, and non-profit agencies. It is an adaptation and refinement of the action research method, which was created by the physicist and behavioral scientist Kurt Lewin in the 1930s and developed further by National Training Laboratories (NTL).

5-C COACHING METHOD

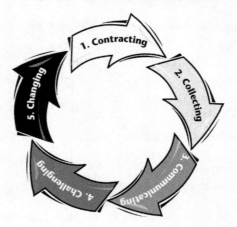

The 5-C Coaching Method follows five distinct stages:

 The developer and learner reach agreements about coaching goals, the methodology, and the premise of their relationship by discussing these questions:

- What are the coaching goals?
- Who else needs to be involved in this process?
- What is confidential?
- What coaching methodology will be used?
- What are the logistics and timetables?
- How will the coaching relationship work?

In order to gather information* related to the learner's coaching goals, these questions need to be addressed:

- What information will be needed?
- From whom will it be collected?
- What data collection methodology will be used to gather the information?
- When will it be collected?
- How will the data be analyzed?
- Who will see the information?

Information about the learner must be organized and delivered in ways that will have the most constructive impact on the learner. To accomplish this, developers must consider these questions:

- How will the data be organized?
- What is the data presentation strategy?
- When and where will the data be discussed?
- How will the data-feedback meeting be structured?

The developer needs to reexamine the learner's motivation by reidentifying the key development issues, then challenging the learner to grow. Developers need to reassess these areas:

- Based on the data, what development areas does the learner need to focus on, and how do these relate to the initial coaching goals?
- What goal adjustments should be made?
- Is the learner sufficiently motivated to grow in these areas?
- Which coaching techniques will increase his or her motivation?

Learners identify what to change and their motivation for making the change, then create an implementation plan by answering these questions:

- What is the learner truly committed to changing?
- Are these the right development areas?
- How will the learner and developer know when the change has been successful?
- Does the learner have both a plan and the support for the change?

*Long-term coaching almost always includes obtaining data from others in the organization.

The 5-C Coaching Method is both sequential and circular. Upon achieving the learner's coaching goals and completing the five-stage coaching cycle, the developer and learner may agree to re-contract—that is, discuss and negotiate the goals, the methodology, the relationship between them, timelines, and more—and begin the five-stage cycle anew. In addition, when new goals emerge during the course of long-term coaching, learners and developers need to re-contract for these (stage 1), then make adjustments to the other stages of the cycle as needed.

A more detailed explanation of the 5-C Coaching Method is included in Appendix D.

REMINDER It is essential to use a coaching methodology—short-term, crisis, or long-term—that best suits the developer's available time and skill set and the learner's specific coaching needs and goals. On occasion, developers may need to meet with learners before the methodology is selected, but developers and learners often know beforehand which approach will work best.

Step 5 · Determine Coaching Goals and Learner Motivation

After the appropriate methodology has been selected, developers need to help learners define concrete coaching goals that the learner is highly motivated to achieve. In fact, all effective coaching starts with one or more coaching goals that the developer and learner agree are the desired outcomes of the coaching experience. Not only do these provide direction and focus for the entire coaching experience, goals provide measures to determine whether the coaching has been successful. Without clear goals, the coaching discussion easily meanders on to a new topic every session, the developer and learner can lose interest in the coaching experience, and there is limited accountability for results. A simple question elicits a learner's coaching goals: "What do you most want to achieve as a result of coaching?"

Coaching goals must have a clear connection to the learner's most important motivations; people don't change and grow unless they have sufficient motivation to do so. Even when the link between goals and motivations seems obvious, it is important to make sure this is the case by asking the learner a simple question: "Why does this goal matter to you?" Chapters 3 through 11 describe the best ways to help learners of each Enneagram style define clear goals and how to link these to their most important desires and motivations.

REMINDER Make sure the learner has clear goals and sufficient motivation and that these are clearly linked.

Step 6 · Assess the Learner's Level and Range of Self-Mastery, Then Use Level-Appropriate Coaching Approaches

Once the coaching role has been clarified, the appropriate coaching methodology has been selected (short-term, crisis, or long-term coaching), and viable coaching goals have been defined and connected to the learner's key motivators, developers can tailor their coaching approach to the learner's self-mastery level to maximize results. The Self-Mastery Model illustrates the various components that comprise an individual's self-mastery.

Self-Mastery Model

- *Self-awareness* Conscious of own thoughts, feelings, and behaviors; realistic about strengths and weaknesses; understands impact on others
- *Responsive to feedback* Receptive to feedback and has the clarity to choose what is useful and actionable and what is not
- *Self-responsible and self-motivating* Fully responsible for self and has a problem-solving rather than blaming orientation
- *Self-managing and emotionally mature* Makes balanced and wise choices; receptive and flexible; encourages honest, respectful dialogue
- *Personal vision with integrity* Consistently trustworthy with constructive values and congruent behavior
- *Personality integration through lifelong learning* Dedicated to ongoing self-development with the ability to take effective, integrated action

The following chart describes how individuals behave at low, moderate, and high levels of self-mastery for each component.

Behavior at Different Levels of Self-Mastery

	LOW	MODERATE	HIGH
General Behavior	Exhibits reactive, unproductive behavior most of the time, with minimal personality integration demonstrated	May be aware of own inner experience, but responds out of habit more often than not; may demonstrate some degree of personality integration	Is highly aware of own inner experience and able to respond out of choice in productive and highly flexible ways, demonstrating a high degree of personality integration
Self-Awareness (NOTE: Self-awareness involves the capacity to be self-observing—that is, being conscious of one's own thoughts, feelings, and behaviors while these are occurring.)	Is unaware of own thoughts, feelings, and behaviors and/or dishonest about true motivations; not self-observing	Can be self-aware, although does not routinely put a high priority on this; has more difficulty being self-aware under duress; is intermittently self-observing	Routinely accesses and is honest about own thoughts, feelings, and behaviors; has realistic self-image; able to be self-observing almost always
Responsiveness to Feedback	Defends against, denies, and ignores feedback and/or blames others when criticized	Sometimes responds to feedback, but can also be under- or over-responsive to feedback	Welcomes feedback and uses it constructively; can distinguish between accurate feedback and opinion
Self-Responsibility	Has distorted perceptions of own motivations; sees others as causing his or her behavior; projects own thoughts and feelings onto others	Can act self-responsibly, but also has difficulty differentiating own responsibility from that of others	Takes full responsibility for own actions
Self-Motivation	Is either unmotivated or motivated by negative factors such as internal fears or external threats	Is partially self-motivated; often expects others to be the motivating force	Is highly self-motivated and self-determining

Self-Management		
Is overcontrolled or out of control; behavior is highly reactive	Sometimes makes conscious choices, but more often acts as if on automatic pilot	Is highly self-managing rather than reactive or acting out of habit; is in control without being overly self-controlled or controlling; makes conscious and constructive choices
Emotional Maturity		
Has low emotional maturity; perceives self as victim	Has moderate-to-low emotional maturity; fluctuates between personal reactivity and the ability to have perspective on self, others, and events	Has high emotional maturity in almost all situations; can rise above personal responses to understand multiple factors and perspectives affecting the situation
Personal Vision		
Has no personal vision or negative vision	Has unarticulated or oversimplified personal vision	Has clear, positive vision
Integrity		
Behaves and acts inconsistently with values or has destructive values	Generally has positive values, but behaviors not always consistent with values	Has positive values and "walks the talk"
Personality Integration		
Behavior reflects a low level of accurate self-knowledge and incongruity among thoughts, feelings, and behaviors	Behavior reflects intermittent self-knowledge and/or an overemphasis on thoughts, feelings, or actions; behavior not always congruent with feelings or stated intentions	Behavior demonstrates a high degree of self-knowledge and is congruent and integrated with thoughts and feelings
Lifelong Learning Commitment		
Has no commitment to self-development or lifelong learning	Has moderate-to-low commitment to self-development; engages in self-development under duress	Has high commitment to ongoing self-development, demonstrated through continuous action

The Enneagram authors who created and developed the Levels of Development, which can be applied to the issue of self-mastery in leadership, are Don Richard Riso and Russ Hudson in *Personality Types* and *The Wisdom of the Enneagram*. The material in this chart has its genesis in their work, which I am grateful to have their permission to use.

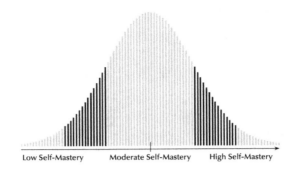

Low Self-Mastery   Moderate Self-Mastery   High Self-Mastery

There is also wide variation within each self-mastery level, indicated on the Self-mastery graph above. This is particularly true for the largest group, moderate self-mastery learners. Individuals at the high self-mastery level are the easiest to coach, while those who consistently function at low self-mastery can challenge even the best developers and cause serious problems within the organization, particularly if they are in leadership roles or other high-impact positions. In fact, chronically low self-mastery individuals are not good candidates for coaching and may need to be referred to outside specialists.

Different coaching approaches work best with different learners, depending on the learner's self-mastery level. For this reason, it is important for the developer to assess the learner's normal (or average) self-mastery level. The learner's range of self-mastery—that is, his or her highest and lowest levels—also provides important information. If the learner has a wide range of self-mastery, the developer can predict that this individual may have dramatic behavior swings during the course of coaching. If the learner's self-mastery range is limited, his or her behavior is likely to be very consistent, but the learner may also have more difficulty moving into a higher level of self-mastery. The chart below describes the three self-mastery levels and the coaching approach that works best with learners at each level.

Coaching Approaches to Enhance Self-Mastery

High Self-Mastery Learners
Coaching approach
Encourage the continuation of what they are doing; provide additional ideas and methods for enhancing their self-mastery.

Explanation
Self-motivating and committed to lifelong learning, these individuals are self-aware, take responsibility for their own behavior, and are easy to work with as long as developers are also at the high self-mastery level. If not, developers feel anxious and learners question the developer's guidance.

Moderate Self-Mastery Learners

(Most learners are at this level.)

Coaching approach

Stimulate their internal motivation and provide them with concrete development suggestions and activities.

Explanation

Because they are generally comfortable, most moderate self-mastery learners are not motivated to grow unless they are under pressure. Learners at the high end of this level grow at a faster pace than those at the low end, but developers need to challenge all to grow by stimulating desire and providing interesting activities with a great deal of follow-up.

Low Self-Mastery Learners

Coaching approach

Provide support, guidance, and clear boundaries.

Explanation

These learners are struggling and need support, guidance, and clear boundary setting so that they know what is acceptable and what is not. Because they are more defensive and fragile than other learners, coaching must proceed carefully and takes longer.

In Chapters 3 through 11, where you will learn how best to coach individuals of the nine Enneagram styles, you will find charts describing the specific behaviors exhibited by each style at the three levels of self-mastery and offering guidelines for customizing your coaching approaches to these individuals.

REMINDER   Knowing the learner's self-mastery level is important to being an effective developer, because the coaching approach differs fundamentally for each level. As a developer, make your best guess, and then revise your assessment as new data and patterns emerge during the coaching process.

Step 7 · Use Coaching Techniques That Challenge Growth

Coaching is essentially a human experience. If developers forget this and either employ too many techniques or use techniques at the wrong time, they become more coaching technicians than developers who can make a difference in the lives of learners. The most important thing a developer can do for a learner is to listen in an active way. This includes hearing not only what is said, but also how it is said and what it means; recognizing, then encouraging or challenging, the learner's patterns of thinking, feeling, and behaving, particularly those that support or detract from the learner's goals and ultimate growth; and having the experience, intuition, and wisdom to know when to just listen and when to say or do something.

In addition, there are four coaching techniques that, when used at the right time, can make a big difference in the pace and depth of the learner's development. These techniques, described below, are actually supportive challenges and target the three Centers of Intelligence: the Head Center (mental), Heart Center (emotional), and Body Center (action). These are discussed in greater detail in Chapter 2, The Enneagram and Coaching.

Head Center Challenges: "What if?" Questions

"What if?" questions work well in situations in which the learner makes assumptions that something is absolutely true and inviolable. These assumptions are part of the learner's mental models; unexamined mental models limit a learner's understanding of what is truly possible and therefore reinforce current behavior.

After hearing the learner express an assumption, the developer poses a relevant "What if?" question.

> During a coaching meeting, Hannah tells her manager that she is completely frustrated working with a specific client, whom she perceives as being overly opinionated and having poor listening skills and a belligerent attitude. Hannah says, "I'll never find a way to work well with this person."
>
> **DEVELOPER'S "WHAT IF?" CHALLENGE**
> *"What if you could find a way to work effectively with this person, even if you still don't like the interactions?"*
>
> Before Hannah can develop a way to work effectively with this individual, she has to first believe that this is both possible and she is capable of doing so. After Hannah responds to the "What if?" challenge with a statement that implies she recognizes that working effectively with someone like this is possible, the developer can then work with her on alternative tactics.

Specific assumptions associated with learners of each Enneagram style are listed in Chapters 3 through 11, along with effective challenges to these mental models.

Heart Center Challenges: Recognizing and Leveraging Defense Mechanisms

Defense mechanisms are unconscious psychological strategies used by individuals to deal with uncomfortable and difficult situations. These mechanisms work to reduce a person's anxiety, sadness, and/or anger and to maintain his or her self-image.

Developers need to recognize and learn to leverage the learner's defense mechanisms for two important reasons. First, the learner's defense mechanisms appear primarily when the learner is avoiding something. Thus, uncovering what lies beneath a defense mechanism is almost always a key to unlocking what the learner most needs to examine. Second, the defense mechanism is often the most obvious manifestation of a learner's resistance to growth. When resistance is left unchecked, the progress of coaching will be severely compromised. Once a learner exhibits a defense mechanism, the developer can use either an indirect or a direct challenge, both of which are designed to highlight the defense mechanism and to explore the learner's avoidance or resistance. Indirect challenges are more subtle and less intrusive, but they may have less impact; direct challenges get the learner's attention faster, but they can heighten resistance and may be too strong for some learners.

Defense Mechanism

Distortion is a clearly incorrect and flagrant reshaping of external reality to meet a person's internal needs.

> When Nathan spoke with his coach about his failure to garner approval for the new website vendor he had been asked to recommend, he was full of fury. Blaming his boss for not supporting his choice of vendor—claiming the boss had given him the authority to make this decision—Nathan also blamed the team he had created for refusing to advocate on his behalf. After listening to Nathan for half an hour, his developer, Erin, became concerned. Nathan's furor and explanations were in direct conflict with prior information he had given her about how supportive his boss had been and how well the team had functioned. Because she perceived that Nathan was distorting what had really occurred, Erin decided to challenge Nathan's defense mechanism.
>
> **DEVELOPER'S INDIRECT CHALLENGE**
> *"To help me understand better, can you remind me of the original agreement you had with your manager about this, conversations you've had since then, the role of the committee you created, how often they've met, and how they have functioned? My memory of this doesn't match exactly what you're telling me now."*
>
> **DEVELOPER'S DIRECT CHALLENGE**
> *"I know you are very, very upset by this, and this may be causing you to distort some of what actually occurred. Let's talk about your feelings, then what actually transpired."*

Individuals of all Enneagram styles use a variety of defense mechanisms at different times; however, specific defense mechanisms are strongly associated with each style, and these particular coping strategies are most obvious when the learner is dealing with difficult issues. The Enneagram style–specific defense mechanisms and how to challenge these are described in Chapters 3 through 11.

Body Center Challenges: "Why would you want to do that?" Challenges

Although learners may say they both want and plan to change something, they may possess neither a deep desire to make the change nor the necessary will and endurance. Learners usually expect the developer to respond by saying, "That's great. How will you go about doing it?" Consequently, a "Why would you want to do that?" question, *stated in a neutral voice*, constructively challenges learners to reflect more deeply on their wishes and intentions. As a result of the "Why would you want to do that?" question, the learner either changes his or her course of action or becomes more deeply committed to the original plan.

> In a coaching meeting with his mentor, Michael says, "I've decided what to do about the promotion I want. I'm going to get a degree—one that is not required but is suggested for the job."
>
> **DEVELOPER'S "WHY WOULD YOU WANT TO DO THAT?" CHALLENGE**
> *"Why would you want to go back to school for a degree?"*

The "Why would you want to do that?" challenge is also useful when learners articulate a plan of behavior that could be counterproductive to their goals or best interests. For example, if the learner says to the developer, "I'm going to walk into my coworker's office and tell this person that the work he/she produces is the lowest quality I have ever received," the developer would say, *"Why would you want to do that?"* After listening to the response, the developer can help the learner explore his or her anger and realize that there are alternative ways to communicate with the coworker about the issue.

Examples of "Why would you want to do that?" challenges for learners of each Enneagram style are provided in Chapters 3 through 11.

Transformative Challenges: Paradoxes

Paradoxes, or apparent contradictions, pose frustrating yet motivating dilemmas for learners. The learner's paradox is this: The learner truly wants something and believes that his or her behavior is designed to achieve that result. However, more often than not, the learner's own behavior is the primary impediment to the achievement of the desired goal. After developers issue a paradoxical challenge, they need to remain silent so that learners feel compelled to resolve the paradox themselves. Developers who are learning the paradoxical challenge technique can use the following structure: "Although you say you want X, your behavior actually creates Y."

The following example illustrates how to use the paradox technique to stimulate learners to change.

Jake desperately wanted recognition and influence in his firm. However, he was regularly late for staff meetings, and he often had not read the pre-meeting materials that had been assigned as preparation. As a result, he often asked questions during the meetings on topics that had already been covered in the pre-meeting materials or discussed at the meeting prior to his arrival.

PARADOX

Jake deeply desires recognition and influence; however, his lateness and lack of preparation create the impression that he does not take the work seriously, thus undermining both the recognition he receives and the amount of influence he wields in the firm.

DEVELOPER'S RESPONSE

"Jake, let's examine your behavior both before and during staff meetings, and then let's analyze how this behavior may actually be affecting your degree of influence and the extent to which you get recognition."

The paradoxical challenges for each Enneagram style described in Chapters 3 through 11 are deep-level paradoxes that should be used only with moderate or high self-mastery learners. Low self-mastery learners are not in a psychological state to handle the complexity and ambiguity inherent in the resolution of this level of paradox, and deep-level or complex paradoxes can increase their anxiety. While less powerful paradoxes can be used with these learners, developers should do so with caution.

SUMMARY: THE COACHING TEMPLATE

The following summary can serve as a coaching template and may be used for short-term, crisis, or long-term coaching.

Determine Coaching Goals and Learner Motivation

Make sure the goals can be accomplished in the time available and are linked to one or more of the learner's key motivators.

Assess the Learner's Level and Range of Self-Mastery, Then Use Level-Appropriate Coaching Approaches

- Determine the learner's normal (average) level and range of self-mastery.
- Select the development approach(es) from the corresponding Self-Mastery Levels and Coaching Approaches to Enhance Development chart (see Chapters 3 through 11) that would be most effective with the learner, and experiment with these.

Use Coaching Techniques That Challenge Growth

Plan how you will use each of the four coaching techniques from this section, and use them at appropriate moments during the coaching process.

Head Center Challenge: "What if?"

What have you heard the learner say or imply that reflects a mental model or assumption you can challenge? How will you phrase this "What if?" challenge to the learner?

Heart Center Challenge: Recognizing and Leveraging Defense Mechanisms

When have you observed the learner use a particular defense mechanism? Would a direct or an indirect challenge be more effective? How would you phrase this defense mechanism challenge to the learner?

Body Center Challenge: "Why would you want to do that?"

What behavior has the learner stated that he or she plans to do? Do you think this is a wise course of action? How would you phrase this "Why would you want to do that?" challenge to the learner?

Transformative Paradoxical Challenge

What paradoxes have you observed in the learner? Select the most significant one. How would you phrase this paradoxical challenge to the learner?

When customized for individuals of the nine Enneagram styles, the four coaching techniques described above have an enormous impact on the speed, depth, and change of the learner's development. The Enneagram style applications of these techniques are explained in Chapters 3 through 11.

REMINDER   Using an effective coaching challenge at an opportune moment stimulates the learner to grow at an accelerated pace. However, using too many techniques can interfere with excellent coaching, which is essentially an interaction between two human beings. Listening attentively, conveying respect for the learner, and being committed to the learner's growth are far more important than any technique.

Step 8 · Accelerate and Sustain the Learner's Transformation

Ultimately, developers want learners to grow. However, some learners show little real growth from coaching because they have no real desire to change, although they may use coaching to get advice or to express and release pent-up frustration. Other learners make incremental changes—for example, learning new approaches for dealing with conflict, being able to lead with greater clarity and conviction, and being able to make important and wise decisions in a timely way. While these are valuable outcomes of the coaching process, the greatest value of the coaching experience is in the learner's making transformational change.

Transformational change requires learners to examine their fundamental patterns of thinking, feeling, and behaving. They need to assess what they truly want, realize that the fundamental obstacles to achieving these desires are often rooted in their own thoughts, feelings, and behaviors, and recognize that they have real choices that are within their control. In addition, learners who make transformational changes continue to grow and develop throughout their lives.

Chapter 12, Transformation, contains four transformation activities that have a profound effect on learners of all nine Enneagram styles, as well as a development planning process that promotes sustained change.

REMINDER   The learner may appear committed to change, but it is important to clarify whether the intended change is incremental or transformational. Always make sure the learner has a plan for change, or the growth will be difficult to sustain.

TWO

The Enneagram and Coaching

HOW TO IDENTIFY YOUR ENNEAGRAM STYLE

To use the Enneagram for coaching, the learner must first identify his or her Enneagram style. Some people recognize their Enneagram style easily and relatively quickly, while others need more time to do so. A number of factors influence this, including self-awareness level, experience in identifying and understanding patterns of response, and the complexity of the individual. However, the amount of time needed is not a major issue; self-reflection and self-discovery are as important and valuable as identifying one's Enneagram style, and both are essential for a learner to be effectively coached.

The most accurate way to identify one's style is to learn the Enneagram system through an individual coaching session with someone who knows the Enneagram well, to attend an introductory workshop, to read an excellent Enneagram book, or to take an Enneagram typing test used in conjunction with one of these other methods. Although there are several Enneagram tests available both online and in hard copy, none have sufficient stand-alone reliability and validity to consistently type people accurately.

It is important that people take time in discovering their Enneagram style and that they are careful not to prematurely type themselves. They need to remember that the Enneagram describes a person's internal character structure and motivation, not merely his or her visible character traits and behavior. In fact, several Enneagram styles exhibit similar behavior, but each does it for fundamentally different reasons.

This chapter, an overview of Enneagram theory and how it relates to coaching, provides a context for understanding the nine Enneagram styles. Each style is then described in greater detail in Chapters 3 through 11.

THE THREE CENTERS OF INTELLIGENCE: HEAD CENTER, HEART CENTER, AND BODY CENTER

To understand the Enneagram as a system, it is helpful to start with the three Centers of Intelligence. Each of the nine Enneagram styles is rooted in one of three Centers—the Head Center, the Heart Center, or the Body Center. Although every person has all three Centers of Intelligence, each of us has a primary Center, a secondary Center, and a tertiary (or third) Center. We rely on our primary Center as a way of orienting to and experiencing the world. This includes both how we take in and interpret information, and how we express ourselves. Our secondary Center is one most of us use less often, although there are a few individuals who rely on their primary and secondary Centers of Intelligence almost equally. Our tertiary Center is far less active, and for some individuals this Center is nearly dormant. Most people have clear primary, secondary, and tertiary Centers.

The concept of the three Centers of Intelligence emphasizes that intelligence is not solely a mental function; in fact, each Center has a special type of intelligence, serves a specific function, and has productive and unproductive uses. The real purpose of working with the Enneagram is actually threefold: (1) to gain greater access to all three Centers of Intelligence, (2) to be able to use each Center as productively as possible, and (3) to use all three Centers in an integrated way—that is, not relying on only one or two Centers but rather using all three at work, at home, when making decisions, and more. The three Centers of Intelligence are described below, with a brief explanation of the three Enneagram styles that are formed in each Center.

The Head Center

Individuals of all nine Enneagram styles utilize the Head Center in the following ways:

HEAD CENTER FUNCTIONS

Gather information · Generate ideas · Mental processing · Rational analysis · Planning

Productive Uses	Unproductive Uses
Objective analysis	Overanalysis
Astute insight	Projection*
Productive planning	Overplanning

Projection is imagining that someone else is thinking, feeling, or doing something that is actually true of oneself.

Three of the nine Enneagram styles are called Head Center styles—Fives, Sixes, and Sevens. They engage in extensive mental analysis; value facts, information, and ideas; and share a common concern about safety and trust in response to the emotion associated with the Head Center—fear, the imagining that something negative could happen.

Head Center Enneagram Styles

Three Personality Styles Formed as a Response to Fear

Five   Withdraw from fear of intrusion and loss of energy by trying to depend solely on their own resources; gather abundant information to analyze for the purpose of understanding how everything works

Six   Develop continuous anticipatory scenarios in order to overcome potential problems and reduce their fear that something could go wrong, and/or go headlong into fearful situations to prove their own courage

Seven   Move away from fear of pain, sadness, and discomfort by imagining positive future possibilities and by generating exciting ideas rather than feeling fearful or uncomfortable

The Heart Center

Individuals of all nine Enneagram styles utilize the Heart Center in the following ways:

HEART CENTER FUNCTIONS

Experiencing feelings · Emotional relating · Sensitivity to others

Productive Uses	Unproductive Uses
Empathy	Emotional manipulation*
Authentic relating	Playing roles
Compassion	Oversensitivity

Emotional manipulation is using emotional information to get an individual to do something he or she might not otherwise agree to do.

Three of the nine Enneagram styles are called Heart Center styles—Twos, Threes, and Fours. They want others to respond to them in very specific ways and create an image to get the desired response. With a common focus on creating an image and being concerned about how others perceive them, the Heart Center styles end up feeling not valued for who they really are, and this gives rise to the emotion associated with the Heart Center—sorrow.

Heart Center Enneagram Styles

Three Personality Styles Formed to Create an Image

Two   Create an image of being likable, generous, and concerned for other people, then look to others for affirmation of their self-worth

Three   Create an image of self-confidence and success, then seek the respect and admiration of others for what they accomplish

Four   Create an image of being unique, special, and different, then use their emotional sensitivity to avoid feeling not good enough

The Body Center

Individuals of all nine Enneagram styles utilize the Body Center in the following ways:

BODY CENTER FUNCTIONS

Movement · Physical sensations · Action or inaction · Control

Productive Uses	Unproductive Uses
Effective action	Excessive action
Steadfastness	Passivity
Gut knowing	Reactivity*

Reactivity is responding both immediately and hastily, without making a conscious choice to behave in this manner.

The three Enneagram Body Center styles—Eights, Nines, and Ones—primarily trust their guts and instincts and have different ways for dealing with control that arise from the emotion associated with the Body Center—anger.

Body Center Enneagram Styles

Three Personality Styles Formed as a Response to Anger

Eight   Readily express anger starting from the gut, believing that anger is simply energy that needs release; exert control by taking charge

Nine   Avoid both their own and others' anger, seeking instead to mediate differences and create harmony; do not let others control them

One   Manifest anger as irritation and resentment, believe anger is a negative emotion that must be kept under control, and exert control by being self-controlled and highly structured

THE CENTERS OF INTELLIGENCE AND COACHING

Even though each Center contains three Enneagram styles, all of us have a Head Center, a Heart Center, and a Body Center. Understanding the Three Centers of Intelligence is fundamental to the success of coaching, because learners of all nine Enneagram styles share common, often implicit, coaching concerns that are directly related to the emotions associated with each Center. These subsurface coaching issues, briefly described in the chart below, are explained in more detail throughout this chapter.

Implicit Coaching Issues—Learners of All Enneagram Styles

CENTER OF INTELLIGENCE	CENTER-RELATED EMOTION	WHY THIS OCCURS DURING COACHING	IMPLICIT COACHING ISSUES
Head Center	Fear	Fear arises from concerns that negative things may occur during or as a result of coaching.	All learners experience some degree of *anxiety,* become concerned about *trust* in many forms, and engage in *overanalysis.*
Heart Center	Sorrow	Sorrow emerges from having one's self-image and self-worth potentially threatened as a result of coaching.	All learners pay attention to the *coaching relationship* and to the *value and prestige* of the coach and the coaching, and are attuned to the *reactions of others.*
Body Center	Anger	Anger appears in a variety of forms, based on the learner's not feeling in control of what happens to him or her in relation to others and the environment during and after coaching.	All learners want coaching to result in *direct action* that they influence or *control,* and they expect *honesty* from the developer and *clarity* throughout the coaching process.

In most coaching interactions, these implicit concerns are not discussed, because learners are either unaware that they are feeling these emotions or are uncomfortable discussing them directly. However, these concerns usually become apparent through direct observations of the learner's behavior. For example, learners who ask repetitive questions or display signs of nervousness are likely feeling fearful; learners who are highly defensive and appear hurt are probably feeling sorrow and are concerned that their self-worth is at risk; and learners who constantly try to direct the coaching meetings and regularly challenge the developer's perspective or suggestions are probably frustrated or angry and trying to gain control over the coaching process.

Although these tacit emotional concerns may resolve themselves without discussion, often they do not. Without resolution of these concerns, invisible barriers arise between learners and developers that become obstacles to the success of the coaching experience. For example, coaching meetings become tense, developers become frustrated, and learners stop being honest or receptive to suggestions. However, when developers become keen observers and are attuned to the learner's concerns, they can use opportune moments to initiate constructive conversations that invite dialogue. For example, a developer can say, "I've noticed you've asked the same question several times, and I'm wondering what you might be concerned about."

The rest of this chapter details the implicit coaching issues that affect learners of all Enneagram styles, then focuses on the specific responses of the three Head Center styles to the Head-based concerns; the specific responses of the three Heart Center styles to the Heart-based concerns; and the specific responses of the three Body Center styles to the Body-based concerns.

Head-Based Coaching Issues: Anxiety, Trust, and Overanalysis

Anxiety

All learners experience anxiety at some point during the coaching process and feel particularly worried when they are receiving data-based information that pertains directly to them, whether this is direct feedback from the developer or data collected from other people. When the information is from others and learners perceive the data as negative, they almost always focus their concerns on the accuracy of the data, how the information has been interpreted, or on the rigor of the data collection methodology—that is, who contributed to the data and who did not, when the information was collected, and what questions were asked. Moreover, learners also worry about what the developer may be thinking as a result of the data and about his or her subsequent inferences and conclusions.

Individuals of the Head Center styles (Fives, Sixes, and Sevens) often have more palpable fear and trepidation about these issues. While it is true that information is always subject to interpretation—that is, inferences are made from data, and these may or may not be accurate—the Head Center styles are most acutely aware of this. To help address their anxiety, developers can contact Fives, Sixes, and Sevens via phone or e-mail to provide periodic updates about the progress of the data collection process, to share some of the developer's thoughts about what was discussed during coaching, or to ask the learner whether he or she has any questions. This type of short, intermittent contact between coaching meetings provides opportunities for the discussion of additional issues that may be on the learner's mind and for the developer to implicitly or explicitly communicate what he or she is thinking. This sort of clarity from the developer usually reduces the learner's anxiety, even when the information from the developer is more negative than positive. Fives, Sixes, and Sevens often have vivid and highly active imaginations and can create scenarios about the coaching that are often far worse than the reality. As a result, truthful information, even if it is not entirely positive, is reassuring to them.

> Gail had eight coaching clients from the same organization. Two of these clients had told Gail during separate coaching meetings that a third client, Miles, had made some negative remarks to them about the coaching process. They reported that Miles had indicated that while he liked and respected Gail, he did have some concerns—for example, was Gail collecting accurate data from the right people, and would she be able to maintain objectivity during the data collection process and not give too much weight to what was said by certain people she was interviewing?
>
> Gail could not tell Miles what she had heard from these other two individuals because of her confidentiality agreements with all clients, so she thought about how she might elicit this information from Miles himself. During their next coaching meeting, Gail made the following statement to Miles: "Because I'm right in the middle of collecting data about you for the coaching, I wondered if you had any questions or concerns about this stage of the process."
>
> Miles looked startled by this comment and responded, "Wouldn't anyone? After all, why should I think you're going to be objective about what you hear when my boss is paying your bill?"
>
> Gail answered, "Yes, he pays the bill, but my work continues only as long as you are satisfied with the coaching and both you and your boss perceive the coaching to be effective. So, even though he actually pays the bill, I treat this process as though you are paying me to get accurate information that will help you reach your coaching goals."

Trust

Trust between the developer and learner is crucial to the success of the development experience, and trust-related issues need to be discussed at the earliest stages of coaching with individuals of all Enneagram styles. Learners must have trust that the developer will do the following:

- Maintain confidentiality agreements
- Possess impeccable integrity and not have side conversations with others in the organization related to the coaching
- Be reliable in the coaching relationship—that is, the developer will be available to the learner when needed

The learner must also trust the organization—for example, the learner must believe that there is no ulterior motive behind the development process, such as an impending demotion, or that anyone in the organization will pressure the developer to reveal confidential information. To calm the learner's mental agitation, developers and learners need to make very clear confidentiality agreements as soon as coaching begins regarding the content of coaching conversations and any data that may be collected. Developers must adhere to these agreements even if pressured by others to disclose information. In addition, the developer needs to be aware of potential hidden agendas in the organization that relate to the particular learner, proceeding with the coaching only if this seems to be in both the learner's and the organization's best interests. Although organizations almost always have some reason for wanting an individual learner to receive coaching—they would not authorize the resources for coaching otherwise—hidden agendas erode the learner's trust in the process and, therefore, the success of the coaching experience.

These trust issues will be chronic and more worrisome for Head Center Enneagram styles Five, Six, and Seven. Not only are issues of trust and doubt central qualities of these personality styles, but all three styles have hyperactive minds, particularly when anxious. For example, Head Center styles may imagine a variety of scenarios that they believe could be occurring behind the scenes, or they may want to know what might occur in the future in far greater detail than is possible at the current time. Developers need to be patient in addressing these concerns, at the same time helping learners recognize that it's not possible to know everything in advance.

> Sheila engaged the services of David, an executive coach. Although David came with excellent recommendations from colleagues she trusted, Sheila spent half of the contracting session asking him an endless array of questions. In fact, she had brought three typed pages of questions to the meeting.
>
> The following represent only about 10 percent of the questions she asked: How long had David been a coach? What kinds of clients had he worked with? How did he know that coaching worked? How was he planning to work with her? Who had given him information about her prior to this meeting? What was he going to tell her boss about how the coaching was going? How was he going to handle confidential information she might give him about the company? What would happen if she missed a session? How would David handle being on vacation? Would she receive a promotion as a result of development sessions? What if the coaching produced no tangible results? What if the company no longer wanted to provide coaching services?
>
> Because David was very experienced as a developer of people, none of Sheila's questions surprised him. He had heard them all before. He was, however, amazed by the number of questions she asked at this stage of their relationship. As Sheila proceeded to ask one question after another, David reflected for a moment and asked her, "Sheila, may I stop you for a moment and ask you why you are asking me all these questions? What is it you think you will learn from the answers?"
>
> Sheila answered without hesitation, "I want to know if I can trust you."

Overanalysis

Every learner tends to overanalyze the data he or she receives during the coaching experience—data collected from others in the organization as part of the coaching, as well as feedback from the developer based on his or her observations. This is particularly true when the information is new to the learner or is something with which the learner disagrees. Although learners are more likely to overanalyze data they perceive as negative, they may also do this with positive information.

The three Head Center styles tend to overanalyze data even more than other learners. This is a result of their data-driven, mental-processing orientation, as well as their tendency to analyze information as a means of intellectual stimulation and of avoiding or preparing for fearful situations. While they respect concrete, verifiable data, Fives, Sixes, and Sevens also resist most information unless it is presented logically and in a well-organized manner. When they receive negative information, the Head Center styles will analyze, challenge, and produce counterarguments, then analyze and reanalyze the data again and again.

When communicating data to the Head Center styles, it is also important that developers use anonymous anecdotes, quotes, or direct observations to supplement any thematic information collected from other people about the learner. Some Fives, Sixes, and Sevens may use their own logic to invalidate the themes, downplay their importance, or discount the importance of others' perceptions in general. As a result, integrating factual information with anecdotal data makes them more receptive.

Kevin and his manager, Andrea, had spent many hours reviewing and confirming what type of data would be collected and who would be asked for input for Kevin's 360° feedback. However, during the meeting to discuss the actual information, Kevin began questioning the entire process even before he had received any data, saying things such as this: "We really should have asked this person rather than that person. You really should have asked this question rather than that question. I don't know if people were entirely honest. And I had an argument with one of the people you spoke to, so they had to have said something very negative about me."

Andrea responded to Kevin by saying, "There's always some uncertainty in the 360° feedback process, and that's very unsettling. If you second-guess the process, it will be really hard to move forward. Do you think you can go with what we have, imperfect as we know it always is?"

Andrea's comments seemed to relax Kevin. However, when he reviewed the feedback that Andrea had collected, he began to debate many of the items she presented. In some instances, he would agree with a specific issue—for example, that he frequently canceled meetings with his peers and subordinates—but would then disagree with the conclusion that many people found him unavailable. In other cases, Kevin would agree with the general point made—for example, that he tended to both overrate and underrate his own abilities, and that he often undercut his own credibility within the organization—but he would disagree with a specific example, such as the fact that he would regularly take personal calls on his cell phone during meetings. In Kevin's mind, making plans with his wife about who would pick up the children or arranging his weekend golf game in full earshot of those in the meeting did not undercut his credibility.

"Kevin," Andrea said, "can you stop just a moment so I can ask a question? Can you move a step beyond critiquing the details of the data and tell me this: What in the data is useful to you?"

Heart-Based Coaching Issues: The Coaching Relationship, Value and Prestige, and the Reactions of Others

The Coaching Relationship

The quality of the relationship between the developer and the learner is important in every coaching relationship. Mutual positive regard is essential because it creates an environment in which the learner is more likely to feel comfortable about being open. If the learner perceives a lack of positive regard from the developer, the coaching meetings typically have an underlying tension that makes both uncomfortable. In addition, learners want a positive relationship with developers, believing that the developers will then offer more useful coaching information, provide them with more professional contacts, and suggest developmental opportunities both within and outside the organization.

Heart Center learners—Twos, Threes, and Fours—pay even greater attention than other styles to the emotional nuances of the coaching relationship. They often read meaning into how the developer acts when they are together, reading the developer's body language, tone of voice, and other cues during the interaction. Twos, Threes, and Fours are highly invested in the image they have of themselves, and when developers don't respond to them in a way that reinforces this, their self-esteem is at risk. In fact, they can become so unsettled that it becomes difficult for them to focus on the coaching itself. They feel hurt or confused and wonder what they can do to repair the relationship.

Developers need to pay attention to the nonverbal cues they give so they don't unintentionally communicate negativity. However, when they are working with learners who seem overly focused on the coaching relationship, developers can help learners recognize that they may overinterpret body language and overemphasize the importance of how others perceive them.

Mary liked to keep in touch with Warren, her manager, at regular intervals between their face-to-face meetings. She would e-mail Warren with updates on her progress, and she would sometimes call him just to check in. When the data collection period for her 360° feedback process was complete, however, Mary's calls to Warren increased threefold, because she knew Warren would see the results before she did. During these phone conversations, Mary never raised any of her concerns directly. Instead, she would ask Warren questions such as "How are you?" and "Is everything going okay?"

After several weeks of receiving these calls, Warren finally decided to use this change in Mary's behavior as a way to surface any specific concerns she might have. At their next coaching session, Warren said, "I've noticed you've been calling me more to check in, and I wondered if there might be something specific you wanted to ask me."

"Not really," Mary responded. "Talking with you just gives me a sense of how the data collection is going—you know, whether it's good, bad, whatever."

Value and Prestige

Value refers to the perceived advantages and benefits to the learner that are possible outgrowths of the development relationship. During coaching meetings, learners of all Enneagram styles may silently consider whether or not there are sufficient benefits to justify the time and energy involved in development work. Factors in the value equation include the level of respect and credibility the developer commands in the organization (the *prestige* factor) and the competence and credibility of the developer with regard to achieving the development goals.

The Heart Center styles place an even greater emphasis than other styles on the value and prestige of the developer and the coaching. A developer who lacks high visibility and recognition in the organization is going to have a more difficult time establishing credibility with Heart Center learners. Similarly, an external coach hired by the organization to work with individuals who are volunteering to be coached is unlikely to find Twos, Threes, and Fours among the first volunteers.

Most developers have to establish initial credibility with learners, but this typically dissipates as learners experience the direct benefits of coaching. If learners persist in challenging the developer's credibility and credentials, it may mean they are not satisfied with how the coaching is proceeding. It is more likely, however, that the learner is preoccupied with external factors such as status and prestige rather than being fully engaged and committed to the coaching. Whatever the cause, developers need to initiate a discussion about the issue.

Don was a director for a large insurance company and had agreed to be coached at the request of his boss. During the first meeting, Don and the coach, Richard, reviewed the development goals and process. Right after this, Don said, "Let me ask you a question. Who else have you worked with successfully in the coaching capacity that I might know by reputation?"

The Reactions of Others

All learners are sensitive to how others respond to them and feel hurt when they receive negative feedback, whether or not they admit it. In addition, most learners realize that how they are perceived in the organization affects their work effectiveness, ability to influence others, and likelihood of being promoted. In fact, communicating feedback collected from others is one of the most delicate and complex parts of the coaching process, requiring not only honesty but also subtlety and kindness from the developer. However, not everyone is sensitive to negative feedback to the same degree.

The Heart Center styles—Two, Three, and Four—are the most likely of the Enneagram styles to be concerned about how they are seen by others and to feel distressed when the information is negative. When developers communicate information collected from other people, the Heart Center styles want to learn as much as they can—for example, how many people share a given perception, whether or not there is a wide range of perceptions, how intensely the perceptions are held, what in their behavior has caused these perceptions, what the consequences might be of others having these perceptions, and what can be done to change these.

During the coaching process, Twos, Threes, and Fours may become so concerned with how others are reacting to them that they may lose sight of how they actually feel about the issues raised in coaching, how they perceive themselves in relation to these issues, and what development goals are most important. While it is important for every learner to accept and respond to feedback in a constructive way, it is equally important that the learner does not lose his or her sense of self in the process.

As a result of their sensitivity to negative feedback, it is important that developers state the feedback in an objective yet supportive way. For example, when the feedback refers to how the learner displays his or her anger, it is better to say "When tense or stressed, you tend to appear more on edge, causing others to be more cautious around you" than "People don't want to be around you when you are angry."

Ashley felt anxious about her upcoming data-feedback meeting with her coach, Jon. Although Ashley believed that the people who reported to her would make mostly positive comments about her management style, she also had concerns, thinking, "You never know how people really feel!"

The feedback Jon gave Ashley was quite positive for the most part, although he did mention a few development areas—for example, Ashley's tendency to withdraw from people with whom she had had a conflict, and her extremely high expectations of others.

When Ashley became very quiet, Jon asked her, "So, what are you thinking?"

Ashley gave a lengthy response: "I wish I knew who said these things. I do stay away from people who have upset me, but only so I can regroup and heal. What do they want from me? I'm only human! I feel terrible if I've hurt someone. I do have high expectations. Shouldn't I? Am I making people miserable?"

Jon listened closely and said, "Ashley, yours is some of the most positive feedback I've ever heard. Why did you hear only the negative, when that was only about two percent of the data?"

Body-Based Coaching Issues: Direct Action, Control, and Honesty and Clarity
Direct Action

Most learners expect direct action and hope for a positive result from the coaching experience; otherwise, they would not have engaged in coaching. Although most learners don't expect any actionable results until they have had several coaching sessions, they still want to feel that something productive has occurred at each coaching meeting.

However, the Body Center styles—Eight, Nine, and One—expect concrete, direct action very early on in the coaching process, even if these are small action steps, and they want assurance that the coaching results will yield productive action. Although developers can give verbal reassurances that concrete action will result from the coaching, Body Center styles primarily trust what they experience. For this reason, developers need to build action into every coaching meeting. At the end of every meeting, the developer can ask, "What have you learned from today's conversation?" and "What actions will you take as a result?" Then, at the start of the next meeting, the developer can ask, "What has taken place since we last spoke, and what actions have you taken during this time?" Taking the time to assess progress and action steps at regular intervals is important for individuals of all Enneagram styles, but especially for the Body Center styles.

Ron ran into his coach, Marilyn, in the hallway and said, "Do you have a minute to talk? There's something I want to ask you."

Marilyn could tell something was on Ron's mind and agreed to accompany him to his office. Before she even had a chance to sit down, Ron closed the door and asked her, "So, are you getting anything good from the interviews you're doing regarding my leadership style?"

"What do you mean by 'good'?" Marilyn asked. "Positive data?"

Ron replied, "You know ... good! Information I can act on."

Control

Issues of control often appear early on in the development process for all Enneagram styles and usually continue throughout the coaching process. Such control issues include who sets the agenda and time for the meetings, who prevails in the event of a difference of opinion or a disagreement about the direction of the coaching, and even power issues stemming from differences in personal and organizational power between the developer and learner. For example, if the learner has an assertive personal style and the developer is more relaxed, the learner may try to assert a disproportionate amount of control during the coaching meetings. Similarly, if the learner is the company president or a high-ranking company executive and the developer an externally hired professional coach, the learner may attempt to take control of the meetings, particularly if the coach offers feedback he or she does not want to hear.

When coaching the Head Center styles—Eights, Nines, and Ones—developers need to be acutely aware that these learners want to feel in control of the coaching experience. If they do not, they feel disoriented and vulnerable, and their response to these feelings may be anger, unresponsiveness, and intransigence. However, developers cannot afford to give primary control of the coaching process or content to the learner, because doing so disempowers developers from having sufficient influence to guide the learner's development, offer constructive feedback, and challenge the learner when needed.

Developers can, however, offer learners reassurance through words and actions about how best to proceed, what the learner will change, and that the most effective development actions to take will be decided on with the learner's full participation. While verbal reassurances help, collaborative planning and decision making throughout the coaching process are also needed.

> Marianne agreed to be coached by her manager, but she had some hesitations. Although she was appreciative that the company was showing interest in her development, she wasn't convinced that she would benefit from the experience. In addition, she wondered where she would find the time for the development meetings. When she met with her manager, Susan, to discuss how they would proceed with the development process, Marianne became more relaxed. She found Susan to be easy to talk to and believed that Susan knew what she was doing. For her part, Susan enjoyed Marianne and was pleased that she seemed so cooperative.
>
> However, when they began to schedule the development meetings, their relationship shifted dramatically. Susan became frustrated when Marianne seemed unable to find any time to get together in the coming two weeks. Susan wondered, "Does Marianne really want to do this?"
>
> Marianne, on the other hand, felt that Susan had suddenly turned insistent. Marianne felt frustrated and thought, "Isn't the coach supposed to accommodate the client? If I'm busy, then I'm busy!"

Sensing that the relationship was going awry, Susan said to Marianne, "Something shifted when we began to discuss the development schedule. Is there something about the scheduling that would be helpful for us to talk about?"

Marianne answered, "I'm just so busy right now that finding the time is hard." What she was thinking, however, was this: You're pressuring me.

Honesty and Clarity

Honesty between developers and learners and clarity about the direction of coaching are the cornerstones of effective coaching. Developers must offer honest feedback, and the data they collect and communicate to learners must be accurate and truthful; otherwise, both the developer and the coaching process have little credibility. Developers must also be clear and transparent with learners about how they are proceeding and why they are doing so. Without clarity and transparency, developers and learners may have different assumptions and expectations, and the coaching can proceed—albeit unintentionally—in two different directions.

Honesty is a particularly important value to the Body Center styles, and they instinctually sense truthfulness in others. Because the primary sensing mode of Eights, Nines, and Ones is more visceral than cognitive or emotional, these learners most trust what they directly experience. Developers who coach Body Center styles need to be especially straightforward and truthful, while at the same time being respectful. In addition, Body Center styles like even more clarity than other styles about the process and future direction of the coaching; knowing this information gives them more assurance that they can influence both the process and the outcomes of the coaching.

It is important for developers to be both honest and clear with all learners. When developers are honest, they not only build trust with learners, but they also encourage the same behavior from the learners. It is almost impossible for coaching to be successful unless conversations and data are based on truthfulness. Clarity in coaching is complex, because the outcomes of coaching can't be known in advance and because some of the most valuable coaching moments emerge spontaneously. At the same time, developers can make a concerted effort to provide clarity about a number of issues that *are* known—for example, roles, expectations, confidentiality issues, the coaching methodology, and the coach's availability.

Samantha was startled when her manager, Ken, told her during a coaching meeting that some of her peers had reported that her behavior sometimes interfered with her effectiveness and credibility with senior management. Incredulous, Samantha asked for examples, and Ken cited several, including an incident that had taken place while Samantha was waiting with several colleagues for a meeting with the company president. As they walked into the waiting room of the presidential suite, one of Samantha's colleagues, Nancy, had noticed that Samantha was holding a plastic cup containing iced tea from a fast-food restaurant. Nancy had whispered to Samantha, "Dump that cup. You're not supposed to bring drinks into the executive suite. The president's assistant will offer us something to drink."

Samantha had been visibly irritated by Nancy's remark and had, indeed, carried the cup with her into the actual meeting. When the president's assistant offered Samantha and her colleagues something to drink, Samantha had declined, saying, "I already have something." Samantha's colleagues had been embarrassed by her behavior, particularly when they were served coffee and tea in fine china.

Ken was surprised by Samantha's anger at his using the cup incident as an example. Samantha told him, "I know what's appropriate and what's inappropriate."

Ken waited several seconds before responding, then said, "You know, Samantha, I've been to the executive suite, and no one ever brings in their own drinks or food. I'm wondering why you are having such a strong reaction to this incident."

Samantha answered quickly, "I don't care what anyone else says! I'm right and I can do what I want."

Ken responded, "So, maybe we should talk about the choice you may be making between being right and being effective."

Although Samantha initially resented being told that she had behaved ineffectively, Ken's honesty and clarity made her reconsider her insistence that she was right.

THE NINE ENNEAGRAM STYLES AND COACHING

Chapter 1 explained the steps that developers need to take to ensure that their coaching is of excellent quality, while Chapter 2 has described the three Centers of Intelligence, the Center-specific coaching concerns of all learners, and the ways in which the three Enneagram styles formed in each Center react even more strongly to particular coaching concerns. The chapters that follow will explain how developers can apply the information from the first two chapters to the coaching of each of the nine different Enneagram styles.

Chapters 3 through 11 provide the following: (1) in-depth descriptions of each Enneagram style; (2) an overview of how to coach learners of each style; and (3) information on how to use the coaching approaches and techniques from Chapter 1 with learners of each style.

The in-depth discussions include the following information about each Enneagram style:

- Basic description
- Core beliefs
- Emotional patterns
- Workplace behaviors
- Quotes from famous people of the style
- Subtypes: three variations of the style
- Wings and arrow lines: four other styles related to the style
- Three type-based questions

Subtypes are three variations (self-preservation, social, and one-to-one) of Enneagram styles. They reflect three different ways in which individuals of a style express their basic needs. Self-preservation subtypes focus on safety and security issues, social subtypes focus on the group, and one-to-one subtypes emphasize relationships with other people on an individual (one-to-one) basis. Subtypes are important in helping people identify their Enneagram style more precisely, because the three subtypes of the style can behave quite differently, even though their essential motivation and patterns of thinking and feeling are similar.

In addition to your core Enneagram style, there are four related styles that may add additional characteristics to your personality. Wings are the two styles on either side of your core style. Arrow lines refer to the two styles connected by the arrows that point toward and away from your core Enneagram style. Individuals may have access to both wings and both arrow styles, none of the four styles, or some combination in between. Individuals of the same Enneagram style can also behave somewhat differently, depending on their use of their wings and/or arrows.

THREE

Coaching
Enneagram Style One

Ones seek a perfect world and work diligently to improve both themselves and everyone and everything around them.

Center of Intelligence · Body Center

HOW TO IDENTIFY ONES

Thinking   Feeling

CORE BELIEFS

- If it's not worth doing right, it's not worth doing.
- Most people don't seem to take their responsibilities seriously, but those who do are people you can count on.
- No one is perfect, including me; what matters is that you are constantly working to improve things.

EMOTIONAL PATTERNS

- Have strong emotional reactions that may not be verbalized but usually show in their body language
- Express irritation and resentment regularly but try to control their deeper anger

Behaving

WORKPLACE BEHAVIORS

Lead by example · Have highly discerning minds · Relish organizing and structuring work · Have difficulty relaxing at work · Delegate reluctantly

The "Controlled Body"

By being self-controlled and highly structured, Ones feel as if they are in control of situations. As individuals who pursue perfection, trying to make everything as correct and error free as possible, Ones monitor what they say, how they say it, the timing of delivery, and more. They try to live up to the internal standards of what they believe to be behavior beyond reproach, including not expressing anger directly. By living structured lives and highly organizing their work, Ones strive to do the best job possible, down to the smallest details.

Emotional Patterns of Ones
Have strong emotional reactions that may not be verbalized but usually show in their body language

Ones are a reactive Enneagram style, experiencing strong immediate responses that include thoughts and opinions and quick emotional reactions. Although some Ones express most of what they think and feel, others try hard to keep the intensity of their responses from being obvious. However, this becomes nearly impossible, since Ones have very expressive body language (e.g., a tightened jaw, a frown of disapproval or smile of appreciation, and a quick backward movement when they dislike something).

Express irritation and resentment regularly but try to control their deeper anger

Ones try to be exemplary in their behavior, including not exhibiting behavior they perceive as negative. Ones perceive the direct expression of anger as negative—that is, in the One's view, exemplary people do not get angry. Since Ones actually experience anger quite frequently, they attempt to control its outward expression. Their anger gets displayed as frequent irritation that arises from feelings of resentment about any number of things—for example, others being irresponsible, dishonest, and not living up to the One's standards and expectations.

Workplace Behaviors of Ones
Lead by example

Working hard to be impeccable in areas they deem important, Ones try to keep their behavior beyond reproach. As a result, they lead by example, trying to set a standard of behavior for others to emulate. This includes being well-mannered and gracious, even when they are feeling ill-tempered and inhospitable. At times, these real feelings are expressed through humor, which may be amusing but may also contain an edge of anger imbedded in the joke or comment.

Have highly discerning minds

Ones continuously critique themselves and others, and they react strongly to mistakes or infractions. However, they also take pleasure when excellence is achieved. Adhering to a set of explicit or implicit rules of conduct and behavior they have learned from their family backgrounds and/or have developed over time, Ones have strong opinions that they verbalize quickly in an effort to affirm what they believe to be true, to correct misinformation, and/or to make suggestions for improvement.

Relish organizing and structuring work

Ones like to have multifaceted, unorganized work that they can transform by creating a clear structure with defined processes and top-quality deliverables. Organizing and structuring stimulate and satisfy Ones, and they do this with an emphasis on practicality, responsibility, and consistency.

Have difficulty relaxing at work

When there is work to do, Ones feel responsible for giving it their full attention and for achieving the best possible result. In addition, they typically have an abundance of work, because they often volunteer so that tasks will be done correctly. Ones place a priority on making certain all work they undertake is error free. As a consequence, most Ones need to be completely away from work responsibilities in order to fully relax and enjoy themselves.

Delegate reluctantly

Ones enjoy the day-to-day work, and there are certain tasks they enjoy so much or believe are so important that they are reluctant to delegate this work to others. In addition to wanting things done as well as possible, Ones often assume they are among the few who can accomplish this.

FAMOUS ONES

Jerry Seinfeld	"A bookstore is one of the only pieces of evidence we have that people are still thinking."
	"See, the thing of it is, there's a lot of ugly people out there walking around, but they don't know they're ugly because nobody actually tells them."
Mahatma Gandhi	"Indolence is a delightful but distressing state; we must be doing something to be happy."
	"A man who was completely innocent offered himself as a sacrifice for the good of others, including his enemies, and became the ransom of the world. It was a perfect act."
Hillary Clinton	"Probably my worst quality is that I get very passionate about what I think is right."
	"In the Bible it says they asked Jesus how many times you should forgive, and he said 70 times 7. Well, I want you all to know that I'm keeping a chart."

Subtypes: Three Variations of One

Although all Ones seek perfection, avoid mistakes, and experience anger as chronic dissatisfaction and irritation with the many things in life and work that are not as they should be, there are three distinct ways in which Ones manifest these characteristics, called subtypes.

Self-Preservation Subtype Ones focus on getting everything structured and organized correctly and experience anxiety, worry, and irritation when they think this may not occur. Wanting to make sure that everything is under control, they emphasize precision and extreme accuracy as a way to make certain that everything is done right.

Social Subtype Ones perceive themselves as role models who represent the right way of being and behaving. In their view, they set the standard for their particular reference groups. Teaching by example, social subtype Ones also focus their efforts on social institutions, often critiquing them as a way to perfect them.

One-to-One Subtype Ones have a driving need to perfect others, particularly those who matter to them, as well as to perfect society in general. They perceive reforming others as both their right and their responsibility, and they go about this with intensity and passion.

Wings and Arrow Lines for Ones

Because they seek perfection and avoid mistakes whenever possible, Ones can be extremely serious and single-minded, incessantly driven to work hard, and highly critical of themselves and others, especially when their expectations are not met. They become quickly reactive when others say or do things that the One disagrees with or dislikes. Access to

their wings (styles Nine and Two) and arrows (styles Four and Seven) can counterbalance these qualities in Ones.

Wings for Ones

NINE WING   Ones with a Nine wing have a greater ability to relax and unwind without having to go on vacation, are less reactive when they disagree with someone, and are more likely to solicit the opinions of others rather than relying primarily on their own judgments or those of others whom they respect.

TWO WING   Ones with a Two wing are more consistently generous and people-focused, in addition to being more gregarious and displaying more consistent warmth to others.

Arrow Lines for Ones

ARROW LINE TO FOUR   Ones who have a strong connection to style Four pay more attention to their own inner experiences and are therefore more introspective and aware of their own feelings. In addition, a link to Four adds originality and creativity to the ways in which Ones approach work, life, and any aesthetic interests that they may have.

ARROW LINE FROM SEVEN   Ones who have a strong connection to Seven are far more flexible, spontaneous, innovative, and lighthearted, and they have more fun.

Three Typing Questions for Ones

1. Do you have an inner voice—akin to a tape recorder in your head—that continuously criticizes you (90% of the time or more) for what you do wrong and sometimes applauds you when something goes exceedingly well?
2. Do you have a constant need for self-improvement, while knowing that no one will ever be perfect, not even you?
3. Do you have a very hard time relaxing, having fun, and getting away from your responsibilities unless you are on vacation?

HOW TO COACH ONES

Areas of Strength
- Strive for quality
- Organized
- Perceptive
- Honest

Areas for Development
- Reactive
- Critical
- Opinionated
- Impatient

COACHING OVERVIEW

Although most Ones like being coached because they embrace self-improvement and appreciate development ideas that are practical, logical, and concrete, they are also very sensitive to feeling criticized and can react to even neutral statements as though these were harsh judgments. On one hand, Ones want developers to be straightforward and honest with them. On the other, because Ones tend to be self-recriminating, developers must be especially careful and kind when offering them verbal or written performance feedback that directly or indirectly implies that a performance issue exists. Otherwise, One learners can become reactive and angry or self-blaming in a way that can spiral downward.

At the same time, Ones can't help but notice mistakes they and others make, and they are more prone to doing so when they feel stressed or anxious. For this reason, it is very important that developers make certain that any documents they provide Ones as part of the coaching process contain no grammatical, punctuation, or typographical errors and that any stories they share include information that is 100 percent accurate. When Ones read a poorly executed document or hear a factually flawed anecdote, they start to doubt the validity of all further written and verbal information from that person and will even begin to question the developer's professional competence. It is not uncommon during coaching meetings for Ones to take a pen to the page of a document and edit it as they read or to aggressively challenge the developer's information if they believe it is flawed.

Finally, Ones like to act quickly. They believe it is their responsibility to fix problems, and feel compelled and eager to check off items on their extensive to-do lists. Although these qualities have likely contributed to the One's prior successes, they can also cause difficulties. For example, One learners in management positions can become obsessed with "fixing" a problem employee whom they believe can change, thus spending an inordinate amount of time and energy trying to solve a problem that they cannot control. Similarly, One learners may present developers with a course of action that they plan to take without consideration of other alternatives. A developer can support One learners by helping them do the following:

- Realistically assess what they can and cannot control
- Identify multiple courses of action rather than assuming that the plan they've come up with first is the "best" one
- Take the time to be more deliberative and less reactive

First, Determine Coaching Goals and Learner Motivation
Goal Identification: What to Ask Ones

Ones like coaching goals that are pragmatic and lead to effective action, but they also want to feel that they are in control of both creating these and determining the actions they will take to get there. While goal setting can be the easiest aspect of coaching Ones, because they usually come prepared with a very clear idea about what they want to accomplish, it can sometimes be the most challenging. While Ones are usually precise in what they want, they tend to define goals that are narrow in scope, thus limiting what they can gain from the coaching experience. As a result, developers may need to work with Ones to help them be more expansive in their aspirations and more open and flexible regarding how the coaching will proceed. For example, One learners may proceed immediately to how the coaching work should be structured—and coaching is work to them—without always understanding that the value of coaching is as much in the exploration as it is in a concrete end result. The following questions can be useful for helping Ones be involved in the goal-setting process and expand their thinking:

- *What specific goals do you have for yourself as a result of this coaching?*
- *What additional long-term desires do you have that would also be useful to pursue?*

After they have answered these two questions, Ones should be asked this question about their motivations:

- *What makes each of the goals you have mentioned important?*

When discussing the One learner's goals, developers should help Ones clearly connect the key development motivators listed below to specific coaching goals. This link may be obvious to learners as they discuss why each coaching goal is important, but if it is not, developers can do one of two things: (1) Ask One learners, *"What personal and professional benefits will you gain when you achieve this goal?"* or (2) explain the connection between the goal and the motivator directly by saying, *"This could help you put less pressure and be less hard on yourself. Is that important to you?"*

Key Development Motivators for Ones

- To be able to continuously improve themselves without feeling that they have done something wrong when they identify an area needing development
- To be more consistently compassionate and attuned to others
- To be less critical of themselves on such a continuous basis
- To relax, have more fun, and feel more serene, especially when mistakes are made and/or things feel out of control

Second, Assess the Learner's Level and Range of Self-Mastery, Then Use Level-Appropriate Coaching Approaches

The best way to determine the self-mastery level of the learner is to read the behavioral descriptions for all three levels in the chart on pages 50–51 and answer these questions:

1. What is this person's normal (average) level of self-mastery?
   ☐ Low ☐ Moderate ☐ High
2. What do I know and what have I observed that leads me to this conclusion?
3. What is this person's range of self-mastery—that is, the individual's highest and lowest levels?
4. What do I know from my own observations or other data that leads me to this conclusion?

Ones: Self-Mastery Levels and Coaching Approaches to Enhance Development

High Self-Mastery · The Serene Acceptor

Core understanding

Everything, including imperfection, is as it should be

Enneagram Ones who demonstrate high self-mastery take their self-development work seriously and understand, befriend, and diminish the influence of their inner critic. While still focused and discerning, they also exhibit dignity, patience, and a peaceful acceptance of the idea that they and everyone else are perfect even with their imperfections. They observe their negative responses before they express them, then make the choice of whether or not to share their reactions. They are lighthearted, and they know how to have fun and let their humor emerge spontaneously.

Coaching approaches to enhance the One's self-mastery

Provide encouragement and additional methods for expansion.

- Emphasize the positive, but more importantly, commend Ones when they themselves emphasize the positive, particularly in situations that contain both positive and negative elements.
- Appreciate and reinforce their humor, levity, and lightheartedness, especially when they are using these in the workplace and not just in their personal lives.
- Provide suggestions for them to balance work and play even more than they already do.
- Suggest relaxation techniques, meditation, or physical activity such as aikido or daily walks to help them enjoy themselves more.
- Have Ones purposely make mistakes—for example, putting things on their shelves in the wrong place—and learn to both laugh at themselves for needing such order and to practice accepting something that's not exactly right.

Moderate Self-Mastery · The Teacher

Core concern

Making a mistake, being imperfect

Ones with moderate self-mastery can be discerning and judgmental, opinionated and reactive, highly organized and methodical, witty and wry, and easily irritated and resentful. Events that suggest mistakes on either the One's part or another's—particularly mistakes that violate the One's values, high standards, or sense of himself or herself as being beyond reproach—cause Ones to react with strong negativity. Although they are often aware of their critical thoughts and feelings and try to hide them from others, Ones often convey their reactions through body language, or they may erupt angrily at a later time over something that is of little consequence. They can also become so enamored of excellence in others that they overlook dysfunctional behavior in these individuals.

Coaching approaches to enhance the One's self-mastery

Stimulate motivation and provide concrete development actions.

- Emphasize the positive in the One, others, situations, and the environment. Guide Ones to see the positive as well as things that are not right.
- Help them recognize and internalize the positive things they do, even when these are not completely error free.

- When Ones become discouraged and self-recriminating, provide insight about how harsh they are being on themselves and give them permission to show themselves more compassion.
- Help them see that underneath their resentment lies a deep level of anger toward others and situations. Encourage them to explore these deeper issues and to recognize how their quest for perfection contributes to these issues.
- Be available to discuss the One's difficulties at length; encourage them to express their needs.

Low Self-Mastery · The Judge

Core fear
Being bad or malevolent; having something deeply, intrinsically wrong with them

Ones with low self-mastery can be intolerant, tightly wound, inflexible, volatile, unstable, and punishing. Judgmental and unforgiving, they become prosecutor, judge, and jury all rolled into one. These reactions can be aimed either at others or at themselves and can be provoked by even minor perceived infractions.

Coaching approaches to enhance the One's self-mastery
Offer support, guidance, and boundaries.

- Frame your constructive feedback in positive terms, if possible; emphasize positive actions they can take.
- Encourage them to take a lighter approach to tasks and relationships through your use of a lighter tone, humor, and an easygoing attitude.
- Provide positive reinforcement for any signs of flexibility on the One's part.
- When Ones become excessively critical of others, encourage their understanding, compassion, and a broader perspective.
- Gently mention their desire to punish someone else for mistakes this person has made; explain that while this reaction is understandable, it may not be necessary or productive in this situation.

Once you have an initial assessment of the One learner's self-mastery level, read the recommended approaches appropriate to that level and select those you believe will be most effective for the learner.

Third, Use Coaching Techniques That Challenge Growth

As you read the following four coaching techniques, it can be helpful to think about several Ones you know and how you might use the techniques with those individuals. Although all Ones have striking similarities, they are also very different based on factors such as self-mastery level, empathy, use of wings and arrows, subtype, experience, age, gender, and culture. In particular, self-preservation subtype Ones display far more anxiety and worry about making sure everything is under control and working right. As a result, developers who coach Ones of this subtype need to help them become more aware of this nervousness and concern, how it functions in their lives, and what they can do to relieve some of this pressure on themselves.

Head Center Challenge: The "What if?" Question

"What if?" challenges work well in situations in which the learner makes assumptions that something is important and inviolate—that is, a mental model. These assumptions are part of the learner's unchallenged beliefs and paradigms. After hearing the One learner express an explicit or implicit assumption, the developer poses a relevant "What if?" question. The following chart lists three common mental models for Ones, the question the developer should ask to challenge each assumption, and the ways in which the developer should respond once the One has answered the challenge.

Developers should be aware that even though Ones like the "What if?" challenge, they can also take it as an affront to what they believe are their correct opinions and right way of thinking. Although it may initially appear that the technique is not working effectively, it may in fact be the most effective technique developers can use with Ones. The more neutrally the developer communicates the "What if?" question, the more receptive the One will be.

"What if?" Challenges for Ones

Common Assumption No. 1

"Most people are not very responsible."

Developer's challenge

"What if others are responsible and don't demonstrate it the same way you do?"

Developer's follow-on response

- If the One says, "That's not true," or something similar that discounts the challenge entirely, respond by saying: *"Please define what you mean by 'responsible' so we can discuss this in more depth."* Then follow the One's response by asking questions such as the following: *"Do you always do these things? What are the ways in which you are not always responsible? In what ways have others shown responsibility that is different from the way you do?"*
- When the One can acknowledge that there are multiple ways to demonstrate responsibility and/or recognize that he or she may be overly responsible, say: *"Good, now let's talk about what causes you to be so responsible, the price you and others may pay for that, and how you can relax more and still feel good about yourself and the work you do."*

Common Assumption No. 2

"It's not worth doing if it's not done right."

Developer's challenge

"What if events don't allow work to be done in a way that guarantees no errors?"

Developer's follow-on response

- If the One says, "Circumstances always allow for error-free work," give an example of when good enough was good enough, and perfect but late would have been a mistake. Then let the One respond.

- When the One can also offer examples of this, ask questions to help the One move to greater depth and insight, getting the One to talk about how he or she ultimately felt about the work and how this understanding can be useful going forward.

Common Assumption No. 3

"I can't delegate to anyone who's not better than I am; otherwise, I should do it myself."

Developer's challenge

"What if you could delegate to people who can do the task at least as well as you can?" or *"What if you could delegate to people who can do the work 80% as well as you can, and then you coach them on how to do the remaining 20%?"*

Developer's follow-on response

- If Ones refuse to consider delegating work to someone unless it is done as perfectly as they think they could do it, ask: *"When you believe this so strongly, how is someone else going to learn and grow, and how are you going to learn to relax?"*
- When Ones respond in a way that indicates they are considering delegating, say: *"Let's look at different things you do that could be delegated, and identify the individuals who could do it 80% as well as you could."*

Heart Center Challenge: Explore the Learner's Defense Mechanism
The One's Primary Defense Mechanism: Reaction Formation

Reaction formation is a defense mechanism by which individuals reduce or try to eliminate anxiety caused by their own thoughts, feelings, or behaviors that they consider unacceptable by responding in a manner that is the exact opposite of their real responses. The One's active inner critic dictates what is acceptable based on social mores, contextual expectations, and moral principles, and reaction formation becomes a defensive remedy when the One learner has what he or she deems "unacceptable" reactions.

At one level, reaction formation is unconscious and automatic. At another level, however, Ones usually know that this behavior is the opposite of the real truth, but this realization usually happens after the fact rather than while it is occurring. In addition, and perhaps surprisingly, Ones who acknowledge that they've behaved in a way diametrically opposed to their true feelings, thoughts, and desires rarely exhibit embarrassment or negative self-judgments about having done so. A subtle example often seen in Ones is when they dislike someone yet are especially nice and polite to this person. A more blatant example—one that is not exclusive to Enneagram style Ones—is an individual who crusades against corporate corruption, only to be discovered later as having embezzled money from the organization.

From the developer's perspective, working with the One's defense mechanism of reaction formation can be difficult. First, it may not be obvious that

REACTION FORMATION

A One is furious at his manager for not providing clear directions and concrete performance feedback, yet continuously interacts with the manager in a cordial and gracious manner, even becoming overly solicitous toward this person in both public and private interactions—for example, frequently complimenting the manager. From an outside observer's perspective, the two would appear to have an excellent relationship, perhaps even being close friends.

this is occurring, because the developer may not know the One's true feelings. For this reason, developers need to listen closely to Ones when they describe others, then remember this information for later comparison. For example, a One learner may express intense, ongoing disapproval of someone, then later share a situation in which the One voluntarily agreed to work on an extended project with that individual. Similarly, a One learner may discuss a list of attributes that are essential in a productive working relationship, then later describe someone with whom they appear to work well who has none of the listed qualities. In both cases, it is probable that the One's reaction formation is operating. These two examples are actually symptoms or manifestations of reaction formation that often hide or defend against the following deeper developmental issues for Ones:

• Becoming accepting, calm, and serene rather than trying so hard to make everything perfect—themselves, others, and the environment
• Letting go of being so intensely attentive to details and needing to have everything under constant control
• Becoming more flexible and relaxed rather than judging everything and being highly reactive mentally, emotionally, and behaviorally

To work with the One's defense mechanism of reaction formation, developers can use either an indirect or a direct challenge. It is often better to start with the indirect challenge, because it elicits more responsiveness and less resistance. However, because the reaction formation defense strategy is so complex, many Ones may miss the power and impact of a challenge unless it is delivered in a direct way. Developers need to accomplish two tasks: (1) Help Ones realize that their behavior is the opposite of their real reactions (which is the easier part), and (2) get Ones to recognize that although this may be polite or correct behavior, it is essentially a mask or ruse, which is a problem. Developers need to be patient, kind, honest, and persistent in helping Ones grow in this area.

INDIRECT CHALLENGE TO REACTION FORMATION
"You told me at the last session that you have no respect for this person personally or professionally, yet you act overly polite and friendly when you interact with him. Can you help me understand this?"

DIRECT CHALLENGE TO REACTION FORMATION
"You pride yourself on being a very honest and forthright person, and you act as if you like this person immensely, but this is the opposite of what you actually feel. What is your behavior covering up that you need to examine?"

Body Center Challenge: The "Why would you want to do that?" Question

When One learners say they want to change something about themselves, asking them this question works effectively as a way of supportively challenging their desires. As a response to this technique, the One learner either changes his or her course of action or becomes more deeply committed to the original plan. This technique is especially useful in two situations: (1) The One learner articulates an intention to take action that sounds productive, or (2) the One learner expresses an intention to take action that might be risky or could be counterproductive to his or her best interests.

This technique is especially useful for Ones, who move to action so swiftly. Because they are often so sure they are right, Ones may not take the time for self-reflection or for considering other alternatives, unless the situation is highly complex. The "Why would you want to do that?" challenge slows them down long enough for them to be more considered and deliberate in their actions.

"Why would you want to do that?" Challenges for Ones

A One's Productive Intention to Act
"I want to be less critical and feel less resentful."

Developer's challenge
"Why would you want to be less judgmental and angry?"

Developer's follow-on response
- If the One cannot think of an answer or gives an unconvincing answer, say: *"It doesn't sound like you really want to do this. Have you considered that you like being critical and resentful more than you dislike it?"* Then wait for the response.
- When the One gives a convincing response, say: *"It sounds like this is very important to you. What would you be like if you were less critical and more accepting?"* Follow the answer with this statement: *"Let's talk about how you can learn to do this more."*

A One's Counterproductive Intention to Act
"I'm simply going to control myself and keep my thoughts to myself."

Developer's challenge
"Why would you want to be more self-controlling?"

Developer's follow-on response
- If the One gives you a reason that also makes sense to you, this is fine, but you need to probe to determine whether the One is saying he or she needs to be more self-controlling rather than self-managing. Control suggests the One is still highly reactive but just doesn't share these reactions. Self-managing refers to the One's learning not to be as reactive, so there is no need to control. Ask the One: *"Do you mean self-controlling or self-managing? Are you willing to work on actually being less reactive, which is what self-management is all about?"*
- When the One gives a response that shows he or she recognizes that increasing self-control would be counterproductive, because Ones are already self-controlling rather than relaxed and responsive, say: *"Good. Let's discuss how you can learn to relax your reactions more, not control them."*

Transformative Paradoxical Challenges

Most Ones enjoy and understand intricate puzzles such as paradoxes, but they are so experience-based that the paradoxical challenge needs to be used when the One is in the throes of the paradox. Otherwise, the paradox will seem like an abstract commentary or even a criticism. For example, Ones may interpret a developer's paradoxical challenge as a condemnation that means *All your problems are your own fault.* The developer can minimize this reaction by stating the paradox with warmth and compassion; if the One becomes defensive upon hearing the paradox, the developer can gently say, *"I'm paraphrasing what you've already told me,"* and then wait for the response.

THE ONE PARADOX

Nick worked as a high-level manager for a public utility company. The work in his division required precise attention to detail, and Nick was determined to have his group not only meet but exceed the company's standards of excellence. He engaged the help of a mentor because he was overwhelmed with work, felt frustrated because his subordinates' work did not measure up to the standards he had set for them, and had received negative feedback from his boss that the subordinates were feeling anxious and undermined by Nick's constant criticism.

During the development sessions, Nick told the mentor that he felt extremely anxious and was having difficulty sleeping. He described his dilemma this way: "I don't seem able to do anything right. When I attempt to get my staff to do higher quality work more quickly, they criticize me to my boss. When their work product is below par, I receive enormous pressure from peers as well as from my boss, and the boss starts to micromanage me. He says he supports me, but I don't believe him."

Paradox Explanation

Ones want to be accepted and valued without criticism, reservations, or conditions; however, they act so critically toward others that they push people away, and they are so self-critical that they would not really believe that someone else could value them without also judging them.

Developer's Paradox Statement

"Nick, this issue is clearly causing you stress. It actually provides an opportunity to explore the role of judgment and criticism in your own behavior. For example, there's your desire for acceptance—from your boss, your subordinates, and fundamentally from yourself—and then there's the way you judge and criticize so many things in your life, including your boss, those who work for you, and especially yourself. You seem to want something from others that you have trouble giving to them or to yourself."

> NOTE Use the paradoxical challenge only with moderate to high self-mastery Ones; low self-mastery individuals may not be psychologically stable enough to handle the ambiguity inherent in paradoxes.

ONE COACHING CASE STUDY SUMMARY: KATHRYN

Determine Coaching Goals and Learner Motivation

Make sure the goals can be accomplished in the time available and are linked to one or more of the learner's key motivators.

> Because Kathryn often feels overwhelmed by the quantity of work she has and is chronically exhausted, she wants to find a way to be less stressed and still get everything done. When asked why this matters, she states, "I'd enjoy life more and would probably be a better manager, although I think I'm pretty good already."

Assess the Learner's Level and Range of Self-Mastery, Then Use Level-Appropriate Coaching Approaches

Determine the learner's normal (average) level and range of self-mastery.

> Kathryn functions at the mid-point of moderate self-mastery most of the time, but when she gets overworked and feels tired, she sometimes exhibits behaviors at the lower end of moderate self-mastery. Although she rarely operates

much higher than the midpoint, Kathryn has moments when she feels thrilled by a work product's excellence, stimulated by her team's responsiveness to challenging issues and by her own ability to master a difficult task. When this occurs, Kathryn feels internally satisfied but confuses this with being at the high level of self-mastery. For this reason, her estimation of herself is somewhat higher than her actual level, and this discrepancy needs to be uncovered during coaching in a way that doesn't demoralize her.

Select the development approach(es) from the chart on pages 50–51 that would be most effective with the learner, and experiment with these.

Kathryn definitely requires encouragement to talk more about her concerns and needs, but the needs discussed must be at a level deeper than just relief from the workload and more sleep. It is possible Kathryn is extremely angry about the amount she sacrifices in order to believe that she is a highly responsible person and that her performance is beyond reproach. She needs to bring more fun and pleasure into her work setting, but she also needs to find the work and the people more enjoyable. Being able to integrate some fun or relaxation into the workday would be beneficial for Kathryn, so discuss what she is doing already, then explore additional ideas with her.

Use Coaching Techniques That Challenge Growth

Plan how you will use each of the four coaching techniques from this section, then use them at appropriate moments during the coaching process.

Head Center Challenge: "What if?"

What have you heard the learner say or imply that reflects a mental model or assumption you can challenge? How will you phrase this "What if?" challenge?

All of the following challenges would be effective with Kathryn.
"What if you didn't do all the work yourself to make sure it's done right?"
"What if you could have real fun at work? How would you do that?"
"What if you actually enjoy the burden you carry at work?"

Heart Center Challenge: Recognizing and Leveraging Defense Mechanisms

When have you observed the learner use a particular defense mechanism? Would a direct or an indirect challenge be more effective? How would you phrase this defense mechanism challenge?

It's possible that Kathryn's intense commitment to work and her apparent pleasure in doing it is partly a reaction formation to her deeper desire to be free and spontaneous. This may or may not be true, but it is worth exploring. A possible tactic is to introduce the concept of reaction formation as a defense mechanism for Ones, explore how she might recognize when she is engaged in reaction formation, then discuss how her overcommitment to work may be a reaction formation to something deeper that she desires. If she can recognize what this might be and try to fulfill that need more directly, the reaction formation behavior should lessen dramatically.

INDIRECT CHALLENGE

"You seem to be so committed to work. Are there also ways in which you may not like having to be so responsible?"

DIRECT CHALLENGE

"Each Enneagram style has a specific defense mechanism that individuals of that style use most often to mask their real feelings and needs. For Ones, it's reaction formation—doing the opposite of what you truly think, feel, need, and so on. An example of this is being overly nice to someone you detest. Can you think of instances when you engaged in this kind of opposite behavior?" [Have discussion. If Kathryn clearly acknowledges she does this, then proceed with the next question.] *"Can you see any way in which your intense need to be responsible at work and to do everything with absolute diligence could be a reaction formation to something deeper that you really want?"*

Body Center Challenge: "Why would you want to do that?"

What behavior has the learner stated he or she plans to do? Do you think this is a wise course of action? How would you phrase this "Why would you want to do that?" challenge?

"Why would you want to be less stressed?"

Transformative Paradoxical Challenge

What paradoxes have you observed in the learner? Select the most significant one. How would you phrase this paradoxical challenge to the learner?

"You say you want to be less stressed, yet you don't talk much about giving up what you currently do or changing your approach to work so you can relax more."

NOTE Paradoxical challenges should be used only with moderate or high self-mastery learners. Low self-mastery learners are not in a psychological state to handle the complexity and ambiguity inherent in the resolution of this level of paradox, and deep-level or complex paradoxes can increase their anxiety. While less powerful paradoxes can be used with these learners, developers should do so with caution.

DEVELOPMENT ACTIVITIES FOR ONES

Developers can suggest the following activities to One learners.

Core Issue: Learn to appreciate what is positive in everything.

Whenever you have negative reactions, add an equal number of positive ones. If you try to erase or submerge your negative feelings or thoughts, they are likely to become stronger or else go underground temporarily, only to re-appear more strongly at a later date. However, if you also add positive reactions, you will begin to neutralize some of the negativity and build up your ability to see the positive.

Expansion Through Wings and Arrows
NINE WING   Learn to relax.

Because you push yourself hard and engage in self-reflection and self-recrimination, learning to relax at work is essential, especially when you are under pressure. Take 20 to 30 minutes each day to do something pleasurable and relaxing. This will be easier to do when you set a time limit on this activity; during that time period, enjoy yourself completely. You may want to practice this at home first, but it is especially valuable when you do this at work.

TWO WING   Focus on people.

When you begin a new task that involves other people, switch your normal orientation and experiment with focusing on the people first and the task second. Rather than moving directly into the task, spend some time engaging people in a social conversation. Instead of offering a way to organize the work, first ask others for their ideas.

ARROW LINE FOUR   Become more fluid in your working style.

Ask yourself the following questions at regular intervals: *What do I feel like doing right now? What is my deeper personal experience, and how am I responding to that? What is it that would give me meaning?* When you ask yourself these questions, it can help free you from what you think you ought to do and help move you into a less structured, more spontaneous way of organizing your life.

ARROW LINE SEVEN   Explore possibilities.

When you begin to think that there is only one best way to organize work and/or you start to discount ideas or alternatives because they seem too impractical, challenge yourself to do the following: Think of at least three very different ways to organize the same work, and articulate the value of what may appear on the surface to be an impractical idea. To take this even further, ask other people how they think the work could be organized, trying to elicit as many ideas from others as possible.

Communication: Pay attention to your "right/wrong" language.

Notice the language you use that implies judgment—for example, words such as *should, ought, right, wrong, correct, mistake,* and *error.* After you become more aware of the frequency with which you use critical words and phrases, substitute words that imply flexibility and receptivity—for example, *might, could,* and *possible*—rather than categorical or emphatic thinking. Experiment with language that encourages the sharing of alternative points of view and acknowledges the input or reactions of others, even if you don't agree with these.

Conflict: Use your feelings of resentment as a clue to your deeper-seated anger.

Whenever you feel irritated or resentful, ask yourself these questions: *Am I really angry about something else that has little to do with this person or situation? Is there some core value I hold that I believe has been violated? Is there something in how I see myself or how I want to see myself that has been threatened?*

Teams: Emphasize relationships as much as tasks.

Add a strong relationship focus to your current task focus by suggesting that team members introduce themselves and get to know one another. Show more patience during times of team conflict, encouraging yourself and other team members to express feelings and opinions in a constructive manner.

Leadership: Honor your leadership gift of pursuing excellence and enhance your capacity to truly delegate.

Delegate work to others more often than you do now, and remember the following: Delegate the *whole task* rather than only part of a project; initiate a discussion of the goals, time frames, deliverables, and process so the person knows what's expected; check in periodically but don't micromanage; and give plenty of positive reinforcement. In addition, practice delegating work that you enjoy as well as work you do not. Remember that when you continue to do work that someone else could do, you are not doing something more important and more strategic that is awaiting your attention.

FOUR

Coaching
Enneagram Style Two

Twos want to be liked by those they want to like them, try to meet the needs of others, and attempt to orchestrate the people and events in their lives.

Center of Intelligence · Heart Center

HOW TO IDENTIFY TWOS

Thinking

Feeling

CORE BELIEFS

- *You can intuit what others need if you just pay close enough attention.*
- *Relationships are what matters most.*
- *People like people who are as generous and thoughtful as I am.*

EMOTIONAL PATTERNS

- *Focus more on the feelings and needs of others than on themselves*
- *Become sad when feeling unappreciated, unwanted, or unvalued*

Behaving

WORKPLACE BEHAVIORS

Empathize with others · Focus on relationships · Want others to feel motivated and well treated · Can become surprisingly angry and aggressive · Act as if they have no needs

The "Warm Heart"

Twos use their Heart Center to focus on the feelings and needs of individuals and groups. They tend to be consistently warm, although this does not mean they exhibit the same level of warmth with everyone or that they are warm all the time. Appearing warm makes Twos feel as though they are considerate and thoughtful, and it also draws others to them.

Emotional Patterns of Twos

Focus more on the feelings and needs of others than on themselves

By focusing on the feelings and needs of others, Twos become adept at reading other people and understanding intuitively what they need. This helps Twos provide others with resources such as attention, time, advice, referrals, and more, but it also distracts them from paying attention to their own real feelings and desires. In fact, Twos repress their own responses and often have difficulty identifying their own deeper feelings. Although they do emerge, these emotional responses are often less intense than Twos actually feel. As a result, their repressed feelings accumulate, and when they are finally expressed, they may appear to be an overreaction.

Become sad when feeling unappreciated, unwanted, or unvalued

Because Twos base their sense of self-worth on other people appreciating their good intentions and generosity, Twos become sad and angry when they feel others do not respond to them in this way.

Workplace Behaviors of Twos

Empathize with others

The Two's focus on others—paying close attention to what others say, how they say it, and their patterns of response over time—and sensitivity to other people's feelings allow the Two to recognize and often experience the feelings of others as if these were his or her own. This ability to read the emotional states of others enables Twos to be compassionate and caring.

Focus on relationships

Because Twos place such a strong emphasis on relationships and most have highly developed people skills, they believe they can develop good relationships with whomever they want to. They are often surprised if someone dislikes them—that is, unless they don't like the other person either, in which case they don't care. Because Twos are generous with their time and resources, often at their own expense, they can easily become overcommitted and overworked.

Want others to feel motivated and well treated

Twos take great pleasure in helping others live up to their potential by motivating them and giving abundant advice in a variety of areas—for example, how to resolve emotional, interpersonal, work-related, and life issues. They are equally persistent in their efforts to make sure that people are treated well by coworkers, bosses, and the organization.

Can become surprisingly angry and aggressive

Although Twos are primarily cordial, warm, and easy to get along with, they become agitated, insistent, and even aggressive when they feel someone is taking advantage of or undervaluing them. When Twos perceive that someone else is being treated unfairly, they rise to the other person's defense.

Act as if they have no needs

Because Twos focus primarily on other people's needs, they are often unaware of their own needs, frequently acting as if they have none. When asked what they themselves want and need, Twos are often confused by the question. Although Twos rarely ask for assistance directly, they appreciate it when help is spontaneously offered. At the same time, most Twos are not fully aware of the degree to which they give to others in order to gain appreciation, approval, and a sense of being valued in return.

FAMOUS TWOS

Gloria Estefan "Whatever it is your heart desires, please go for it, it's yours to have."

"I am privileged to help in some way."

Bill Cosby "I'm still waiting for some actor to win, say, an Oscar ... and deliver the following acceptance speech: 'I would like to thank my parents, first of all, for letting me live.'"

"I'm here for a friend. I brought a couple of boxes of chocolate Jell-O."

Sally Field "I was raised to sense what someone wanted me to be and be that kind of person. It took me a long time not to judge myself through someone else's eyes."

"I can't deny the fact that you like me! You like me!"

Subtypes: Three Variations of Two

All Twos have their sense of self-worth, personal pride, and importance integrally linked with how others respond to them and want to be viewed as appealing individuals who are valued for helping others and for being able to influence things in a positive direction. There are three distinct ways in which Twos manifest these characteristics, called subtypes.

Self-Preservation Subtype Twos deny their own needs for protection while at the same time trying to attract others who will provide exactly that for them. Drawing others to them in the same way that children do—that is, by being appealing and appearing to be without guile—self-preservation Twos are also ambivalent about close relationships and less trusting than social subtype or one-to-one subtype Twos.

Social Subtype Twos focus on helping groups more than individuals and are more intellectually oriented and comfortable being in visibly powerful positions than individuals of the other two subtype variations. Social subtype Twos are less concerned with how specific individuals respond to them and more focused on group-level reactions, which is a result of their desire to stand above the crowd in some way.

One-to-One Subtype Twos are primarily oriented to individual relationships and meeting the needs of important people and partners. They try to attract specific individuals as a way of getting their needs met—that is, they feel they have value when chosen by someone important—but they are also highly motivated to meet the needs of these individuals as a way of developing and sustaining the relationship.

Wings and Arrow Lines for Twos

Because Twos seek to be appreciated and needed as a way to avoid feeling unworthy, they become so other-focused that they lose touch with their own needs. Twos can be unaware of their own true drives and motivations, using their ability to relate to and read other people in ways that can be counterproductive both for themselves and for those around  them. Access to their wings (styles One and Three) and arrows (styles Eight and Four) can counterbalance these qualities in Twos.

Wings for Twos

ONE WING   When Twos have access to their One wing, they balance their focus on people with a dedication to task, are more discerning about situations and people, pay more attention to detail, and have an increased ability to be firm and to say no, with far less worry about how others will react to them when they assert themselves in this way.

THREE WING   Twos with a Three wing are far more comfortable being visible, such as holding a high-profile leadership position. In addition, these Twos feel more comfortable acknowledging their desire to be successful; in fact, they often pursue being respected as much as being liked.

Arrow Lines for Twos

ARROW LINE TO EIGHT Twos with a strong link to Eight have a far deeper sense of their own personal power, tend to be bolder and more candid, and are more in touch with their energy and the power of their anger.

ARROW LINE FROM FOUR Twos who are strongly connected to Enneagram style Four have increased emotional depth, because they focus on their own emotional reactions as much as on the feelings of others. They also tend to be more creative and original.

Three Typing Questions for Twos

1. Do you intuitively know what someone else needs but have a hard time articulating your own needs, even to yourself?
2. If you're completely honest, do you believe that you can get almost anyone to like you if you really want to?
3. Do you feel really good when others respond to you in the way that you most want, but particularly deflated when this does not occur?

HOW TO COACH TWOS

Areas of Strength	Areas for Development
• Empathic	• Accommodating
• Supportive	• Indirect
• Motivating	• Feeling unappreciated
• Warm	• Tend to overextend

COACHING OVERVIEW

Because focusing on themselves makes them uncomfortable, Twos may have difficulty making the time for coaching sessions. They often get so busy or feel overwhelmed with helping others at work that they don't have the emotional reserves to engage in their own development. In addition, Twos want people to like them, and the idea that they may hear something critical or negative about themselves during coaching is unappealing.

The location of the coaching meetings matters to Twos and contributes dramatically to its effectiveness. In general, Twos prefer meeting in places where there are no distractions, and because Twos make an effort to help others feel comfortable, they appreciate it when someone else takes the time to think about what *they* might want. Many Twos respond well to meeting at an attractive restaurant that serves excellent food, while others prefer the beach, the mountains, or the golf course. What matters most is to get Twos away from the work environment, where people may need them for a variety of reasons, and into an environment where they are the primary focus.

Finally, unless they are extremely angry, anxious, or sad, Two learners are aware that they feel or need something but can't identify exactly what that is. Because these deeper reactions get submerged, Twos may overreact to something that occurs later, similar to a pot of hot water that has begun to boil over. An effective developer helps them uncover their deeper feelings, needs, and truer responses.

First, Determine Coaching Goals and Learner Motivation
Goal Identification: What to Ask Twos

Although Twos like to be asked what they really want from the coaching, they may have difficulty identifying their goals. Developers need to be patient with Twos as they search for answers to this question. Often, their first answer may not be what they truly want, and developers may need to probe several times and listen closely. The following questions can be effective.

- *If you could name three things you most want from coaching, what would they be? You can think in terms of feelings, skills, or anything that comes to your mind. What would make you feel satisfied with the time we spend together?*

When discussing the Two learner's goals, developers should help the Two clearly connect the key development motivators listed below to specific coaching goals. This link may be obvious to learners as they discuss why each coaching goal is important, but if it is not, developers can do one of two things: (1) Ask Two learners, *"What personal and professional benefits will you gain when you achieve this goal?"* or (2) explain the connection between the goal and the motivator directly by saying, *"This will help you feel less depleted and be more focused on what is best for you."*

Key Development Motivators for Twos
- To feel less exhausted and depleted
- To better help and serve others
- To develop relationships in which they can truly count on others
- To be able to say *no* without feeling guilty, anxious, or angry
- To be less dependent on the responses of others and more reliant on their own sense of real inner strength and solidity

If Two learners talk only about helping and serving others better, it is important to tell them that while this is a valuable intention, they also need to find some reason to engage in coaching for themselves. Coaching rarely creates fundamental changes in learners when the primary motivation to change is solely to benefit other people; when Twos do this, the coaching reinforces their over-focus on the needs of others. Their real development comes when Twos realize that they also have developmental needs that they need to address.

Second, Assess the Learner's Level and Range of Self-Mastery, Then Use Level-Appropriate Coaching Approaches

The best way to determine the learner's self-mastery level is to read the behavioral descriptions for all three levels in the chart below and answer these questions:

1. What is this person's normal (average) level of self-mastery?
   ☐ Low ☐ Moderate ☐ High
2. What do I know and what have I observed that leads me to this conclusion?
3. What is this person's range of self-mastery—that is, the individual's highest and lowest levels?
4. What do I know from my own observations or other data that leads me to this conclusion?

Twos: Self-Mastery Levels and Coaching Approaches to Enhance Development

---

High Self-Mastery · The Humble Servant

Core understanding

There is a profound purpose to everything that occurs that is independent of one's own efforts.

Enneagram Twos with high self-mastery do not give to get, and they do not feel a need to reinforce their self-worth by getting others to like them and orchestrating other people's lives. Gentle, generous, humble, inclusive, and deeply compassionate, they give simply to give and express their own deeper needs directly. Their sense of well-being and warmth draws others to them.

Coaching approaches to enhance the Two's self-mastery

Provide encouragement and additional methods for expansion.

- Provide guidance for Twos in developing their personal and professional vision and goals, focusing on what they want for their own lives.
- Affirm Twos when they maintain their equilibrium after experiencing something that would normally inflate or deflate their sense of self-worth.
- Provide positive reinforcement when they express their own needs, opinions, and preferences, especially when these go against the preferences of others.
- Encourage them to spend extended time alone without engaging with others—including phone calls, e-mails, and casual interactions with strangers—so they can explore their feelings, reflect on their experiences, and engage in activities they can do and enjoy by themselves.
- Affirm them every time they access and utilize their mental and physical intelligence as much as their emotional intelligence.

Moderate Self-Mastery · **The Friend**

Core concern

Feeling valuable, liked, needed, appreciated, and worthy

Twos with moderate self-mastery often have many friends and/or are at the center of social groups or institutions. They read people well and tend to engage others through flattery, giving attention, doing favors, and engaging in other forms of interpersonal behavior—such as showing warmth—that are sometimes sincere, but sometimes not. They may also be emotional, aggressive, and hovering. Having difficulty saying no, they often orchestrate interpersonal dynamics behind the scenes. They can be compassionate and helpful, often offering useful advice that they expect others to take.

Coaching approaches to enhance the Two's self-mastery

Stimulate motivation and provide concrete development actions.

- Encourage Twos to say no more often, especially when they do not have a good reason for saying yes.
- Help them explore their true motivation for helping others so often, reviewing each situation in detail. Suggest that each time they are about to agree to do something for someone, they ask themselves why before agreeing.
- Probe for their real feelings and help them recognize the depth of their emotions.
- When Twos seem either overly helpful or resentful, look for hidden needs and invite the expression of their true desires and preferences.
- Notice their pattern of focusing on other people rather than themselves; bring this to their attention on a regular basis.

Low Self-Mastery · **The Manipulator**

Core fear

Being unwanted, discarded, and deemed intrinsically unworthy

Twos with low self-mastery can be master manipulators, using guilt, blame, or shame to control others. These Twos fall into psychological despair, then try to make the other person feel responsible. When their efforts are thwarted, these Twos will use full force to get what they want, but will take no responsibility for their unproductive behavior.

Coaching approaches to enhance the Two's self-mastery

Offer support, guidance, and boundaries.

- Start with positive feedback and appreciation; be gentle but direct when offering critical feedback.
- Challenge Twos in a kind, compassionate way when they engage in manipulative behavior, and encourage them to express real feelings, needs, and personal goals more directly.
- Help them identify ways to take care of themselves and their own real needs that do not rely on someone else's behavior.
- Consistently invite their concerns and opinions so that their fears and needs don't remain below the surface.
- Regularly ask about their needs and preferences. If Twos say they have no needs, leave this as an open question; don't accept having no needs as an answer, but challenge them later, once it is obvious that this is a repeating pattern.

Once you have an initial assessment of the Two learner's self-mastery level, read the recommended approaches appropriate to that level and select those you believe will be most effective for the learner.

Third, Use Coaching Techniques That Challenge Growth

As you read the following four coaching techniques, it can be helpful to think about several Twos you know and how you might use these techniques with those individuals. Although all Twos have the same basic personality architecture and motivations, there are variations in how these manifest in their behavior. For example, some Twos are intellectual while others are less so, and there are vast differences in their levels of assertiveness and degree of ease in being in visible roles rather than orchestrating behind the scenes. In addition, there are also differences based on factors such as self-mastery level, empathy, use of wings and arrows, subtype, experience, age, gender, and culture.

Head Center Challenge: The "What if?" Question

"What if?" challenges work well in situations in which the learner makes assumptions that something is important and inviolate—that is, a mental model. These assumptions are part of the learner's unchallenged beliefs and paradigms. After hearing the Two learner express an explicit or implicit assumption, the developer poses a relevant "What if?" question. Twos typically have a large number of beliefs and assumptions about how they and others should behave. They hold these rules of interpersonal engagement so strongly that they may initially resist having them challenged.

The following chart lists three common mental models for Twos, the question the developer should ask to challenge each assumption, and the ways in which the developer should respond once the Two has answered the developer's challenge.

"What if?" Challenges for Twos

Common Assumption No. 1

"I can't really refuse to do this."

Developer's challenge

"What if you did say no to this?"

Developer's follow-on response

• If the Two says, "I just can't," answer: *"What if you could?"* If there is still no concrete answer, ask: *"Do you always say yes to everything others ask of you? Can you lend me some money?"* This last question is meant as a joke to jar the Two.

- When the Two can say what would happen if he or she said no, ask: *"And what would be the benefit to you of doing that?"* After the answer, ask: *"How can you set guidelines for yourself about when you can refuse and when you choose not to say no?"* This wording affirms that it is the Two's choice, not an obligation, to agree to do something.

Common Assumption No. 2

"My ability to get things done is based on my relationships with others."

Developer's challenge
"What if you could accomplish things on some basis other than relationships?"

Developer's follow-on response
- If the Two cannot think of such a situation, tell a relevant compelling story, then ask: *"Have you ever seen or experienced something similar?"*
- When the Two can express what would happen if he or she could accomplish things on a basis other than relationships, ask questions to elicit more depth and insight.

Common Assumption No. 3

"I have to be available to this person even though I'm exhausted."

Developer's challenge
"What if you took care of yourself as much as you take care of others?"

Developer's follow-on response
- If the Two cannot think of such a scenario, ask: *"At what point do you fall apart from exhaustion as a way to be unavailable?"* After the Two's response, ask: *"Is that what you want?"*
- When the Two gives a concrete and positive response, ask: *"How important are you to yourself? Are others really more important to you than you are?"* Follow the answer with this: *"Let's talk about the price you pay for putting other's needs and demands above your own needs and resources. You must get more from doing this than you lose, or else you wouldn't continue this behavior."*

Heart Center Challenge: Explore the Learner's Defense Mechanism
The Two's Primary Defense Mechanism: Repression

Repression is a defense mechanism by which individuals hide information about themselves from themselves—for example, feelings, desires, wishes, aversions, fears, and needs—that are too difficult to acknowledge consciously. However, the repressed information doesn't disappear; instead, expression of the repressed data is controlled or held down while it continues to influence the individual's behavior. For example, Twos may feel anxious and need reassurance, but they may be only minimally aware of this. Instead of exploring these feelings or seeking comfort, the Two reassures another person who appears to be in distress.

Twos repress so often that it becomes readily apparent during the coaching process. However, because the repressed information is not easily avail-

REPRESSION

A Two has been working excessively on behalf of the team, putting in long workdays for over a month and engaging in constant worry about the success of the project and the overwork of other team members. Although it is obvious that the Two is exhausted and is likely frustrated and angry about being the primary team member who is working so hard to keep the team together and the project from failing, the Two mentions nothing about this and focuses only on the impact of the workload on other team members.

able or accessible to Twos themselves, developers must gently call it to their attention. The best way to do this is to ask Twos about their feelings on an ongoing basis. Examples of repression include focusing on the needs of the developer rather than on their own needs; having an explosive reaction—for example, anger, deep hurt, or high anxiety—about an incident in which the feelings seem appropriate but the intensity of them seems extreme; and appearing more withdrawn or more manic (hyperactive) than normal. These examples are actually symptoms or manifestations of repression that often hide or defend against the following deeper developmental issues for Twos:

- Acknowledging that they have needs and desires, and knowing the importance of taking care of themselves rather than always catering to the needs of others
- Finding an internal basis for their self-esteem rather than making their self-worth dependent on the reactions of others
- Integrating their need to depend on others and also be autonomous in both personal and professional relationships, rather than being overly independent and/or overly dependent in their relationships

To work with the Two's defense mechanism of repression, developers can use either an indirect or a direct challenge. It is often better to start with the indirect challenge, because it elicits more responsiveness and less resistance. However, if the learner is ready or you have an excellent relationship with this person, a direct challenge may have a bigger impact. With Twos at the lower level of self-mastery, an indirect challenge is more effective because these Twos are more sensitive, fragile, and easily hurt. However, Twos at the higher levels of self-mastery respond best to a direct challenge.

INDIRECT CHALLENGE TO REPRESSION
"I think you may be having more feelings about this than you've actually discussed with me. Are you willing to explore these in more depth?"

DIRECT CHALLENGE TO REPRESSION
"I know you actually have much stronger feelings about this than even you are allowing yourself to realize. When you repress your feelings, they build up and then explode. It will be far healthier for you to talk about what you feel and how deeply you feel these things."

Body Center Challenge: The "Why would you want to do that?" Question

When Two learners say they want to change something about themselves, asking them this question works effectively as a way of supportively challenging their desires. As a response to this technique, the Two learner either changes his or her course of action or becomes more deeply committed to the original plan. This technique is especially useful in two situations: (1) The Two learner articulates an intention to take action that sounds productive, or (2) the Two learner expresses an intention to take action that might be risky or could be counterproductive to his or her best interests.

When working with Two learners using "Why would you want to do that?" challenges, developers need to be alert to anxiety reactions Twos may exhibit when asked this question—for example, laughing out of nervousness or becoming slightly angry as a way to avoid answering the question. In addition, developers need to gently challenge Twos whose answers indicate that they want to take action for the sake of others rather than for themselves. For example, a Two may say he or she wants to be more assertive about something but offers the following reason: "This will help the other person change his or her behavior." The developer needs to say, *"And why would you want to do this for yourself and not just for the other person?"*

"Why would you want to do that?" Challenges for Twos

A Two's Productive Intention to Act
"I want to find out what I really want to do rather than always focusing on helping others figure out what they want to do."

Developer's challenge
"Why would you want to clarify your own vision rather than assisting others in finding theirs?"

Developer's follow-on response
- If the Two cannot think of an answer or gives an unconvincing answer, say: *"It doesn't sound like you really want to do something for yourself,"* then wait for the response.
- If the Two gives a convincing response, say: *"It sounds as though this is really important to you. Please tell me more about this and what you would gain from giving more attention to your own needs and desires."*

A Two's Counterproductive Intention to Act

"I'm just going to go along with what my coworker wants to do rather than confronting this person."

Developer's challenge

"Why would you want to acquiesce rather than be honest?"

Developer's follow-on response

- If the Two gives you a reason that makes sense to you, say: *"It sounds as though you're convinced this is the best choice, but let me ask you this: Are there alternatives for you to consider other than either acquiescing or confronting this person?"*
- If the Two realizes that this is not a productive action to take, say: *"It's great that you realize this is not truly in your best interests. Let's discuss other alternatives and their potential positive and negative consequences."*

Transformative Paradoxical Challenges

Although some Twos like paradoxical challenges, others may initially perceive them as overly complex. Twos who have the latter reaction may not be accustomed to being self-reflective in this way—in other words, some Twos have difficulty accepting challenges to their thinking habits, emotional patterns, and behaviors. Because of this, it is best to use the paradoxical challenge after Two learners have acknowledged the need to grow and are willing to examine their own behavior.

After the developer states the paradox, it is particularly important to allow Twos to ponder the implications of it. Twos may want to discuss some of their feelings and thoughts, or they may ask that the paradox be restated several times, but these discussions may be distractions from self-examination.

THE TWO PARADOX

Todd had been the acting dean at a university for more than a decade. Each time the university found a viable candidate for the permanent dean's role, the person didn't work out, and Todd was asked to continue in the role until a suitable permanent replacement could be found. After years of going through this repetitive cycle, Todd felt exhausted, frustrated, and furious. He expressed his feelings to his mentor this way: "Why does it always come back to me? I kill myself for this university and have to keep bailing them out of terrible situations, but there's no one else who can do it. What I really want to do is write a book, but I have no time or energy to do it. I want to quit, but the program would fail, and I can't let my colleagues down."

Paradox Explanation

Twos want to have their own desires materialize—for example, their desire to be appreciated and supported, to get rest, and to follow their own dreams. However, they spend so much of their time and energy on helping other people that often they are either unaware of what their own needs truly are or else downplay their desires, giving little indication to others that they, too, want something.

Developer's Paradox Statement

"You seem to be clear that your need for rest and creative pursuits is being super-seded by your unwavering commitment to the university, but who is the person making that decision? Let's talk about what you really want and how your own behavior is getting in the way of your ability to take care of yourself and follow your own dreams."

NOTE Use the paradoxical challenge only with moderate to high self-mastery Twos; low self-mastery individuals may not be psychologically stable enough to handle the ambiguity inherent in paradoxes.

TWO COACHING CASE STUDY SUMMARY: LESLIE

Determine Coaching Goals and Learner Motivation

Make sure the goals can be accomplished in the time available and are linked to one or more of the learner's key motivators.

Although Leslie is a talented and smart marketing consultant, she feels highly anxious when she thinks about marketing herself. Her stated coaching goal is to feel confident and comfortable doing activities that give her high visibil-ity—for example, giving speeches to large groups, and taking her business to the next level by promoting herself as a person rather than just promoting the work she does. When asked why this matters to her, she laughs nervously, hesitates, and says, "I think I'm good. I want other people to know this, too."

Assess the Learner's Level and Range of Self-Mastery, Then Use Level-Appropriate Coaching Approaches

Determine the learner's normal (average) level and range of self-mastery.

Leslie believes she is at the higher range of moderate self-mastery, even pos-sibly in high self-mastery. However, she is usually at the middle of the moder-ate self-mastery level, with a range that begins near the bottom of moderate self-mastery (when she becomes unstable and volatile, often when someone she cares about responds to her in a negative way) and extends to high self-mastery (when she spends time alone and engages in self-reflection).

Select the development approach(es) from the chart on pages 69–70 that would be most effective with the learner, and experiment with these.

> Although Leslie does engage in self-reflection at periodic intervals when she is alone, she needs to do far more self-exploration on a regular basis. During every coaching meeting, ask her extended questions about her feelings, needs, and desires, particularly at times when she does not want to explore them. Probe for her deepest responses at these times, not just the responses that come most easily to her. Help her explore all the resentment and hurt she feels when others do not perceive her as she wants them to or when she feels unappreciated or overlooked (another way in which Leslie feels not appreciated enough).

Use Coaching Techniques That Challenge Growth

Plan how you will use each of the four coaching techniques from this section, and use them at appropriate moments during the coaching process.

Head Center Challenge: "What if?"

What have you heard the learner say or imply that reflects a mental model or assumption you can challenge? How will you phrase this "What if?" challenge?

> All of the following challenges would be effective with Leslie.
> *"What if you are already excellent at giving speeches—in fact, just as good as you are at facilitating discussions?"*
> *"What if you are actually appreciated by this person but he or she has a different way of showing it?"*
> *"What if you didn't need the affirmation of others to know you are talented?"*

Heart Center Challenge: Recognizing and Leveraging Defense Mechanisms

When have you observed the learner use a particular defense mechanism? Would a direct or an indirect challenge be more effective? How would you phrase this defense mechanism challenge?

> Leslie doesn't realize that she represses her real feelings. She is highly emotional, but she lets her feelings build up and then tries to control them. Eventually, she has a volcanic eruption that surprises both herself and those around her. In addition, some of Leslie's feelings may be masking deeper emotions. For example, she becomes angry when she's actually hurt, and she becomes hurt when she's actually anxious. When Leslie is functioning at her normal moderate self-mastery level, an indirect challenge would be best. When she is functioning closer to high self-mastery, a direct challenge would have the most impact on her.

INDIRECT CHALLENGE
"You talk about being hurt by this incident, and I can understand why. Might you also have other feelings about this, in addition to the hurt?"

DIRECT CHALLENGE
"I know you are a feeling person, but have you ever considered that you are actually repressing, or holding down and controlling, the depth and array of your real feelings?"

Body Center Challenge: "Why would you want to do that?"

What behavior has the learner stated that he or she plans to do? Do you think this is a wise course of action? How would you phrase the "Why would you want to do that?" challenge?

"Why would you want to be more visible?"

Transformative Paradoxical Challenge

What paradoxes have you observed in the learner? Select the most significant one. How would you phrase this paradoxical challenge to the learner?

"How ironic that you are so effective at helping others market themselves and become visible, yet don't put the same intention, effort, and care into marketing yourself and making yourself visible."

NOTE   Paradoxical challenges should be used only with moderate or high self-mastery learners. Low self-mastery learners are not in a psychological state to handle the complexity and ambiguity inherent in the resolution of this level of paradox, and deep-level or complex paradoxes can increase their anxiety. While less powerful paradoxes can be used with these learners, developers should do so with caution.

DEVELOPMENT ACTIVITIES FOR TWOS

Developers can suggest the following activities to Two learners.

Core Issue: Examine the ways you give in order to get something in return.

Make a list of everything you have done for other people in the last week, whether it was bringing someone home from the hospital or listening to someone for a longer time than you may have desired. Next to each item, write down what you wanted in return. Continue this list for several weeks. You may find that your behavior changes simply as a result of becoming more aware of your giving to get something in return. If not, then reflect on the price you pay for continuing this behavior.

Expansion Through Wings and Arrows
ONE WING   Learn to discern.

Because you place such a high value on people's feelings and their reactions, you likely feel anxious when you need to take action that may affect others adversely. When you struggle to make a tough decision, one that you know is correct but may negatively affect someone you care about, ask yourself: *For the greater good of the organization and our work, what is the best thing to do?*

THREE WING   Seek respect.

Although you want to be liked, being respected is equally important; in fact, the respect you need most is respect from yourself for who you are, regardless of the perceptions of other people. The questions to ask are these: *Do I really respect myself? What must I do to gain the self-respect that is entirely independent of what others think of me?*

ARROW LINE EIGHT   Care less about how others react to you.

Because you are attuned to an invisible "audience" when you react to something or contemplate taking action, you limit your freedom of action. You likely consider the reactions of others more often than you know. Whenever you contemplate an action and begin to think about the reactions of others, or whenever you feel guilty about something you've done, thought, or felt, gently confront yourself with these questions: *What do I really want? What do I really think is the best thing to do or to have done? What are my real feelings about this?*

ARROW LINE FOUR   Go deep inside yourself.

Ask yourself at regular 15-minute intervals: *How do I feel about this? Am I getting what I need, or is something missing here?* Taking stock of yourself in this way gives you an ongoing report and trend analysis of your feelings and needs.

Communication: Be explicit about your true intentions.

Before you ask someone a question, ask yourself what is behind your question. *Is it really a statement formulated as a question?* If so, make the statement instead. *Is it really a way to get to know the person better in order to form a relationship?* If so, tell the person something about yourself instead. Questions are fine, but it is also important that you have more variety in your interactions and that your intentions match what you say.

Conflict: Focus on what you need to learn from the situation.

When you are upset or in conflict with someone else, focus on yourself rather than on the other person. This way, the issue is not what the other person needs to learn but what you need to examine about yourself. Ask yourself these questions: *What do I need to learn from this? What is my responsibility in this conflict? Even though this person did something I didn't like, what do I believe is my part of the dynamic between us if I am being completely honest?*

Teams: Pay as much attention to the team's task as you do to its purpose.

Add a strong task focus to your current relationship focus by stating what you believe is the team's central purpose so that others can agree or disagree with you. Learn to be as comfortable with disagreement as with agreement.

Leadership: Honor your leadership gift of motivation and service to others, and enhance your comfort and willingness to be a visible leader.

It is important for you to claim both the authority that goes with the leadership role and the personal influence you can have. Doing so makes it easier for others to follow your lead; it also creates more respect for the leadership role, and this increased level of recognition is important both for the team's success and for your own professional growth. In public settings, refer to yourself as the leader of the team. Run your own team meetings rather than having someone else facilitating them for you. Pay attention to ways in which you minimize your leadership role.

FIVE

Coaching
Enneagram Style Three

Threes organize their lives to achieve specific goals and to appear successful in order to gain the respect and admiration of others.

Center of Intelligence · Heart Center

HOW TO IDENTIFY THREES

Thinking   Feeling

CORE BELIEFS
- *The world values winners and ignores or ridicules losers.*
- *Who and what you know is important, but how you're known is more important.*
- *Stay focused on your goals; everything else falls into place.*

EMOTIONAL PATTERNS
- *Maintain a demeanor of self-confidence*
- *Keep most strong feelings to themselves and even from themselves, particularly fear and sadness*

Behaving

WORKPLACE BEHAVIORS
Focus intensely on goals and plans · Have well-developed interpersonal skills · Become abrupt and short-tempered under stress · Become angry when obstacles block their goals · Enjoy competition

The "Other-Directed Heart"

Threes use their Heart Center to focus on how other people are responding to them in terms of the Three's gaining their respect and admiration. Because most Threes read their audience adroitly, they are able to change their persona—specifically, what they are saying and how they are saying it, as well as their nonverbal behavior—in order to elicit the response they desire. For this reason, Threes are called the "chameleons" of the Enneagram.

Emotional Patterns of Threes
Maintain a demeanor of self-confidence

Threes want to appear successful, and in their view, successful people look confident. As a result, Threes almost always appear focused, positive, somewhat serious, and as if nothing really bothers them much; they believe that confident people don't feel or display anxiety, and they certainly don't show the kind of sad feelings that vulnerable individuals do. Threes learn to mask the outward signs of anxiety, sadness, or anger while still appearing to be involved in what they are doing. However, when a Three is under extreme duress for a period of time, his or her public persona becomes more difficult to maintain, and small events can evoke strong emotional responses in him or her.

Keep most strong feelings to themselves and even from themselves, particularly fear and sadness

Although most Threes can sense that they have feelings, they may not know exactly what these are or how deeply they are feeling them. When Threes have emotions they prefer not to feel, they most often dive into work as a way to avoid them. Anger and frustration are usually easier for Threes to acknowledge than sadness or anxiety, although many Threes have difficulty allowing themselves to feel fully angry with people who are deeply important to them.

Workplace Behaviors of Threes
Focus intensely on goals and plans

Threes base their success on defining and achieving specific goals they believe will enable them to gain the respect and admiration of others. After selecting goals based on the context in which they want to be seen as successful, Threes develop what they consider to be an effective and efficient plan for reaching their objectives, and then focus on execution with laser-like intensity. In addition, because Threes avoid failure, they limit their involvement in situations where this might occur and/or reframe failures as "learning opportunities."

Have well-developed interpersonal skills

Most Threes adapt well to individuals and groups, trying both to engage others in conversation and to make them feel comfortable. For example, Threes might remember someone's area of interest, and then ask this person a question about the topic as a way to start the conversation. In a group setting, Threes may make comments to or ask questions of certain individuals who are not yet participating in the interaction. They reduce the pace of their conversational rhythm when talking with someone who has a relatively slow style of speech, and they become more energetic when discussing a topic with someone who is highly animated.

Become abrupt and short-tempered under stress

Threes' effective social skills abruptly disappear when they are stressed, fatigued, overworked, or anxious about the potential failure of something—for example, a work project, a promotion, or a personal concern—and they become irritable, short-tempered, and even angry. This can take others by surprise, because there is often no forewarning. Threes under chronic stress may exhibit these qualities on an ongoing basis, in which case their social skills may not be apparent for long periods of time.

Become angry when obstacles block their goals

Once Threes have set their goals and developed a workable plan, they go into action according to the operational rules as defined by the organization. However, they become highly frustrated when the rules change arbitrarily or unnecessarily or when insurmountable obstacles block their path to goal achievement.

Enjoy competition

Because Threes enjoy winning as much as they abhor failing, they are highly competitive in most situations. They enjoy solo competition as well as being on a winning team, whether at work or in recreational activities.

FAMOUS THREES

Tom Cruise	"I disagree with people who think you learn more from getting beat up than you do from winning."
	"I've learned to relax more. Everybody feels pressure in what they do—maybe mine is just a little different because there don't seem to be enough hours in the day to accomplish what I want to."
Oprah Winfrey	"The big secret in life is that there is no big secret. Whatever your goal, you can get there if you're willing to work."
	"I always knew I was destined for greatness."
Kobe Bryant	"I'll do whatever it takes to win games, whether it's sitting on a bench waving a towel, handing a cup of water to a teammate, or hitting the game-winning shot."
	"Everything negative—pressure, challenges—is all an opportunity for me to rise."

Subtypes: Three Variations of Three

All Threes feel they must appear successful in order
to gain the admiration and respect of others, and
they avoid failure in any form by hiding parts of
themselves that do not conform to their image of
success, deceiving not only others, but also themselves as they come to believe that the image they
create is actually who they are. There are three dis-
tinct ways in which Threes manifest these characteristics, called subtypes.

Self-Preservation Subtype Threes try to be seen as self-reliant, autonomous, and hardworking, thus portraying an image of being a good or ideal
person. They may even create an image of having no image.

Social Subtype Threes want to be seen as successful and admirable in
the context of specific reference groups—that is, the groups in which they
want to be seen as successful. They like to be around other successful people,
because this proximity reinforces both the Three's image and status.

One-to-One Subtype Threes want to be viewed as successful by people
who are very important to them, partly by appearing attractive to these people in some way, but also by helping them achieve success.

Wings and Arrow Lines for Threes

Because Threes seek admiration and respect and
avoid failure, they can become extremely driven, fix-
ated on goals and plans, and so over-identified with
their work that they forget who they are underneath
all their accomplishments. As a result, they cannot
feel valued—by themselves or others—for who they
are. Access to their wings (styles Two and Four) and
arrows (styles Nine and Six) can counterbalance these qualities in Threes.

Wings for Threes

TWO WING   Threes with a Two wing are far more sensitive to the feelings of
others and more generous with their time and resources, and they often focus
on helping others in their professional and/or personal lives.

FOUR WING   Threes who have a Four wing are far more in contact with their
own feelings, are willing to engage in emotional conversations with others,
have a deeper personal presence, and may engage in some form of artistic expression or refined level of artistic appreciation.

Arrow Lines for Threes

ARROW LINE TO NINE   When Threes have a strong connection to arrow line
Nine, they use this to relax, slow down their pace, and engage in activities

simply for the pleasure of doing them. Being able to access style Nine also helps Threes be more mellow and easygoing.

ARROW LINE FROM SIX   Although many Threes are smart, accessing their arrow line Six augments their normal intelligence with an enhanced analytical capability and insightfulness. In addition, Threes with a link to style Six tend to be more aware of their own true reactions rather than engaging in work as a way to avoid their feelings.

Three Typing Questions for Threes

1. Do you do the things you do to impress others so that they will value and respect you?
2. Are you so busy "doing" things that you don't even know what simply "being" means?
3. Do you avoid failure by engaging only in activities you will be good at, focusing on goals and making sure you achieve them, and reframing failure by calling it "a learning experience"?

HOW TO COACH THREES

Areas of Strength	Areas for Development
• Energetic	• Competitive
• Entrepreneurial	• Abrupt
• Confident	• Overly focused
• Results oriented	• Selectively disclosing

COACHING OVERVIEW

Threes often look forward to coaching meetings, particularly if these highlight their accomplishments and contain actionable ideas that will help them become even more successful. Because the word *failure* is not in their vocabulary, Threes prefer negative feedback that is straightforward, kindly delivered, and framed as an opportunity for them to become more effective.

Once Threes think they understand an issue, they are ready to take action immediately, even before the coaching meeting is over. They like to solve problems quickly and then move on. The challenge for the developer is to help Threes slow their pace and take some time to reflect and examine their deeper feelings and desires before making a decision to change. An effective way to do this is to ask a question such as this: "Can you slow down before you decide what actions to take, so that you can be certain what problem you are solving and what you really want to do?"

While most Threes have many friends, with some of these friendships going back for decades, they often have few true confidants. There are two reasons for this. First, most Threes have extremely busy lives, leaving little time for the development of deeper relationships. Second, Threes are often reluctant to share their deeper emotions, particularly those related to their self-perceived shortcomings and failures. The developer often becomes a confidant and advisor to the Three—a sort of surrogate friend—particularly if the Three respects the developer and feels respected in return. Developers who have this type of reciprocal relationship with a Three are in a position to have an enormous positive impact.

Developers can most assist Three learners by helping them understand the extent to which they overidentify with their work (including goals, plans, and activities) and understand the personal price they pay for this. Because Threes have their self-worth so interwoven with what they do and accomplish, they lose touch with a sense of self that is based on who they are as a human being.

First, Determine Coaching Goals and Learner Motivation
Goal Identification: What to Ask Threes

Threes expect to have a clear discussion and a firm decision about their coaching goals at the earliest stage of coaching. Without concrete goals, most Threes feel directionless, which makes them feel anxious and disoriented. While some Threes may have put a great deal of thought into their goals for coaching, some may need more help to determine the coaching outcomes that would be of most benefit to them. Because Threes are generally successful at work, a coaching experience that focuses only on becoming more successful in terms of status, reputation, and image does not help the Three grow and develop. However, Threes who come to coaching because they are failing at something have a prime opportunity to work on their most significant development areas.

Because Threes think in terms of goals on an ongoing basis, a direct question such as one of those below is used to start the conversation about the Three's coaching aspirations. However, the second question—why each goal matters so much—is the most important one. Once Threes have answered that question for each goal, they may think of additional goals that are also important to them.

- *What are your goals for the coaching?*
- *What made you select each of these?*
- *Are there additional goals that you think would be beneficial?*
- *What would be the benefit of these?*

- *Taking into consideration all the goals you've mentioned, which ones are the most important to you?*

When discussing the Three learner's goals, developers should help the Three clearly connect the key development motivators listed below to specific coaching goals. This link may be obvious to learners as they discuss why each coaching goal is important, but if it is not, developers can do one of two things: (1) Ask Three learners, *"What personal and professional benefits will you gain when you achieve this goal?"* or (2) explain the connection between the goal and the motivator directly by saying, *"This can help you be just as successful as you desire, or even more so, but in a more relaxed, less pressured way."*

Key Development Motivators for Threes

- To feel more successful without feeling the pressure of always having to prove themselves
- To have better, more meaningful, and longer-lasting relationships
- To be able to relax and just *be,* without feeling the need to constantly impress others
- To experience themselves at a deeper level
- To find out what they really want for themselves, apart from what they believe their goals should be, based on their work or social context

As a note for developers coaching Three learners, most Threes will automatically try to define and confirm a coaching plan as soon as the goals are agreed upon. While this makes sense, because Threes move immediately from goal to plan, this step is premature at this point in the coaching relationship. The developer and learner have not yet discussed the developmental issues related to the learner's goals, how often and for how long they need to meet, and how to make the coaching relationship work best for both of them.

Threes usually want everything they do to be efficient and effective, and they easily merge efficiency (achieving something in the shortest possible time) with effectiveness (achieving the desired outcome). In coaching, the process may not always feel efficient, as new topics, themes, issues, and goals emerge that may actually be more significant for the development of the learner than the initial goals. In addition, it is not possible to predict exactly how long a certain aspect of the coaching may take. Much of this depends on the learner's receptivity, the complexity of the issues, the developer's skill, and the relationship between the learner and developer. Thus, if Three learners try to get total clarity about how the coaching will proceed at this stage, the developer can use the learner's insistence to raise an important coaching issue for Threes: their addiction to goals and plans.

Second, Assess the Learner's Level and Range of Self-Mastery, Then Use Level-Appropriate Coaching Approaches

The best way to determine the self-mastery level of the learner is to read the behavioral descriptions for all three levels in the chart below and answer these questions:

1. What is this person's normal (average) level of self-mastery?
   ☐ Low   ☐ Moderate   ☐ High
2. What do I know and what have I observed that leads me to this conclusion?
3. What is this person's range of self-mastery—that is, the individual's highest and lowest levels?
4. What do I know from my own observations or other data that leads me to this conclusion?

Threes: Self-Mastery Levels and Coaching Approaches to Enhance Development

High Self-Mastery · The Believer

Core understanding

Everyone has intrinsic value, and there is a natural flow and order to everything.

Threes with high self-mastery have looked inside themselves to find out who they really are (apart from what they accomplish) and what they truly feel (instead of masking their emotions). Willing to admit that they don't always feel on top of things and that they have foibles like everyone else, these Threes possess a contagious enthusiasm, genuineness, and confidence. Moreover, they are deeply spontaneous, because they understand that it is not their responsibility to make sure everything happens efficiently and effectively.

Coaching approaches to enhance the Three's self-mastery

Provide encouragement and additional methods for expansion.

- Invite their complete authenticity and honesty, and warmly acknowledge this when it occurs for items both big and small.
- Continuously reinforce their expression of deep feelings, of strongly held opinions, and—especially—of their failures.
- Encourage Threes to slow down in every way, reassuring them that they will be even more effective and happier, then helping them recognize this when it occurs.
- Give them a continuous stream of new ways to experience *being* rather than *doing;* have them practice these between meetings and report on their progress.
- Help them identify and engage in activities that they enjoy for the pure pleasure of doing them rather than for the prestige or competitive nature of the activity.

Moderate Self-Mastery · The Star

Core concern

Feeling successful, avoiding failure, and gaining the respect of others

At the midlevel of self-mastery, Threes focus on goals and work, usually at the expense of their relationships. Driven and competitive, they seek recognition and have a need to outdistance their rivals. Although Threes at this level often appear friendly, they are most often motivated by their desire for success. Many times, what looks like an emotional response from them is more the kind of response that they believe a person in their situation should have, not an authentic reaction. At times, even they wonder who they really are.

Coaching approaches to enhance the Three's self-mastery
Stimulate motivation and provide concrete development actions.

- Be continuously authentic and honest yourself as a way to model the behavior; remember that Threes mirror the behavior of others when they think it's effective.
- Help them explore and express their feelings on a far more sophisticated and nuanced level than they do normally. Encourage them to discuss these at length, exploring feelings that may be masking other emotions—for example, anxiety may be masking issues of low self-esteem, or anger may be covering sadness.
- Encourage them to slow down—for example, in their rate of speech and in their need to be constantly engaged in activities.
- Affirm Threes when they define success in broader terms than just work; explain why this is so important for their continued growth, asking about their interests, outside life, convictions, and feelings.
- Reinforce the idea that a positive image includes being genuine and honest, including admitting shortcomings, and acknowledge Threes when they behave this way.

Low Self-Mastery · The Calculator

Core fear
Extreme fear of failure, since failure would make a Three feel that he or she has no value

At the lowest level of self-mastery, Threes may be described as phony, self-serving, opportunistic, and a variety of other adjectives that are often used to depict people who go after whatever they want (usually, the external trappings of success, for example, money, status, and fame) with little regard for anyone or anything that stands in their way. Although they become extremely isolated, these Threes hide their inner emptiness by believing that they actually are the image or façade they have created. However, that image is only a shell masking a hollow interior.

Coaching approaches to enhance the Three's self-mastery
Offer support, guidance, and boundaries.

- Mirror back to them a positive view of their real selves by identifying what they are good at that is not purely work-related; recognize and affirm these qualities.
- Frame critical feedback in terms of behavior that is an obstacle to their goal achievement and, therefore, their success.
- Differentiate between intention and impact. For example, help Threes realize that their behavior may be viewed as opportunism, even if this is not their intention.
- Explore their feelings of competitiveness without implying that this is a negative quality. Help them differentiate between healthy, productive competitiveness and that which is destructive, both for themselves and for others.
- Explore their feelings at a basic level. Do not accept "I don't know" as an answer, but be gentle as you challenge them.

Once you have an initial assessment of the Three learner's self-mastery level, read the recommended approaches appropriate to that level and select those you believe will be most effective for the learner.

Third, Use Coaching Techniques that Challenge Growth

As you read the following four coaching techniques, it can be helpful to think about several Threes you know and how you might use the techniques with those individuals. Threes can be very different from one another, particularly with regard to their level of access to their own feelings. These differences are based on factors such as self-mastery level, empathy, use of wings and arrows, subtype, experience, age, gender, and culture.

Head Center Challenge: The "What if?" Question

"What if?" challenges work well in situations in which the learner makes assumptions that something is important and inviolate—that is, a mental model. These assumptions are part of the learner's unchallenged beliefs and paradigms. After hearing the Three learner express an explicit or implicit assumption, the developer poses a relevant "What if?" question.

The chart below lists three common mental models for Threes, the question the developer should ask to challenge each assumption, and the ways in which the developer should respond once the Three has answered the developer's challenge.

"What if?" Challenges for Threes

Common Assumption No. 1
"I can't allow myself to fail at this."

Developer's challenge
"What if you could allow yourself to fail?"

Developer's follow-on response
- If the Three says, "I can't possibly fail," answer: *"What if you did fail?"* If there is still no concrete answer, ask: *"What does failing mean to you?"*
- When Threes identify what could occur if they failed, such as losing a job, ask: *"And how likely is that?"* After the answer, ask: *"What if there were some benefits to allowing yourself the possibility of failing?"* Then explore what these might be, following the Three's lead.

Common Assumption No. 2
"I can't slow down; everything will stop, and the project won't work."

Developer's challenge
"What if you could actually work better if you slowed down a bit?"

Developer's follow-on response

- If the Three can't consider the possibility, tell a relevant compelling story, then say: *"You must have a similar story. Can you tell me about it? You must have had an experience of a time at work when you were not in overdrive, and the work was actually more successful."*
- When the Three offers several benefits of slowing down and tells a real story, ask: *"How can you expand this experience to more situations?"*

Common Assumption No. 3

"I have to do this work myself; it takes too much effort to give it to someone else."

Developer's challenge

"What if you could give it to someone else to do instead of doing it yourself?"

Developer's follow-on response

- If the Three can't think of such a scenario, ask: *"What if something happened to you, and you had no choice but to give the work to someone else? What would you do then?"*
- When the Three gives a concrete and positive response, say: *"Good. How can you do this more? How would you, the other person, and the organization benefit from this?"*

Heart Center Challenge: Explore the Learner's Defense Mechanism
The Three's Primary Defense Mechanism: Identification

Identification is a defense mechanism in which a person unconsciously incorporates attributes and characteristics of another person into his or her own personality and sense of self. Identification is a way of bolstering one's self-esteem by forming an imaginary or real alliance with an admired person, then taking on that person's characteristics. When Threes model their own behavior after someone else or the idea they have of someone, they are usually not aware of doing so. Thus, it becomes complicated for them to untangle who they really are from this image. In particular, Threes identify most with images of persons who are admired in the Threes' desired social context, and the image with which Threes identify often changes as their context changes.

IDENTIFICATION

A Three feels quite nervous before making a presentation at a big meeting. Rather than reveal this outwardly in any way, the Three has a convincingly self-confident manner, appearing to be composed and self-assured. Although some Threes may be aware that they are feeling anxious and covering this over, others may be totally convinced that they are just fine even when this is not the case. In this situation, the Three has an internalized image of what a successful presenter looks like and acts like, and she then plays this role.

Threes also identify with what they *do* as a way to generate the admiration they want from others. Examples of this identification for Threes include the following:

- Being hypersensitive to criticism of what they do (their work product, hobbies, and behavior) as if it is a personal criticism of them
- Becoming very different people to various groups ("shapeshifting")
- Joining clubs, forming friendships, and seeking memberships to organizations and institutions just because these have prestige
- Overworking and going into hyperdrive for excessive periods of time with a relentless fervor
- Not being completely truthful—for example, deleting information in which they might look bad and not showing emotions that might tarnish their image in some way

These examples are actually symptoms or manifestations of identification that often hide or defend against the following deeper developmental issues for Threes:

- Deeply exploring their inner thoughts, feelings, and experiences in order to be more truthful with themselves and more forthcoming with others
- Going more with the flow of events and experiences rather than feeling so driven to make things happen
- Learning the difference between doing and being, and appreciating themselves for who they are rather than only for what they do

To work with the Three's defense mechanism of identification, developers can use either an indirect or a direct challenge. It is often better to start with the indirect challenge, because it elicits more responsiveness and less resistance. However, with Threes who have depth and are self-reflective, a direct challenge may have a bigger impact.

INDIRECT CHALLENGE TO IDENTIFICATION
"You often talk about your work and what you do. It would be helpful for me to know more about you aside from these things, which are really more about roles you fulfill than about who you are."

DIRECT CHALLENGE TO IDENTIFICATION
"You seem to identify fully with what you do rather than who you really are. Tell me about the real you behind these images of success."

Body Center Challenge: The "Why would you want to do that?" Question

When Three learners say they want to change something about themselves, asking them this question works effectively as a way of supportively challenging their desires. As a response to this technique, the Three learner either changes his or her course of action or becomes more deeply committed to the original plan. This technique is especially useful in two situations: (1) The Three learner articulates an intention to take action that sounds productive, or (2) the Three learner expresses an intention to take action that might be risky or could be counterproductive to his or her best interests.

Because Threes are so highly action-oriented, the "Why would you want to do that?" challenge can be extremely useful to them, helping them really think through what they want to do. At the same time, Threes may become impatient with the question, since they have likely already made the decision to take action and are merely informing the developer. As a result, developers should be prepared for some Three learners to become abrupt after being asked this question.

"Why would you want to do that?" Challenges for Threes

A Three's Productive Intention to Act

"I want to have more balance in my life; I work too hard."

Developer's challenge

"Why would you want to have more in your life than just work?"

Developer's follow-on response

- If the Three cannot think of an answer or gives an unconvincing answer, say: *"It doesn't sound like you really want to do this."* After the Three responds, say: *"What does having more in your life mean to you?"* Wait for the response.
- When the Three gives a convincing response, say: *"It sounds like this matters to you a great deal. Please tell me more about this and your current thinking about how you might proceed."*

A Three's Counterproductive Intention to Act

"I'm not going to tell this person that I am upset with him/her."

Developer's challenge

"Why would you not want to share your real feelings with this person?"

Developer's follow-on response

- If the Three gives you a reason that makes sense to you, say: *"It sounds like you've made a wise choice."*
- If the Three gives you a reason you believe is possibly unwise, say: *"I think there's more here than you are willing to look at. How often do you share real feelings with others?"*

Transformative Paradoxical Challenges

Most Threes like paradoxical challenges because they are intellectually demanding and stimulating, but some find them tedious and time consuming.

Since Threes who dislike paradoxical challenges are usually at the lower ranges of self-mastery, it is best not to use them with these individuals.

After the developer states the paradox for the Three, it is important for the developer to be silent but remain ready to address questions. Threes can have huge breakthroughs when challenged with a paradox that illuminates so accurately the internal dilemma they have experienced most of their lives.

THE THREE PARADOX

Allison was a very successful attorney, with high-profile cases and many satisfied clients. However, her peer relationships caused concerns among others at the firm, with many of her colleagues perceiving her as competitive, self-centered, and sharp-tongued. Although Allison would have preferred to have more cordial relationships with the other attorneys, she believed that their attitudes toward her were their problem, not hers.

Working with a coach was not Allison's idea; she did so at the request of the firm's managing partner. However, Allison came to like and respect her coach and began to share her deeper feelings: "I don't know why some of the other attorneys don't like me. My friends appreciate me, and I have great relationships with several of the firm's associates. And I know my clients love me. Sometimes I feel isolated in the office, so I either find reasons to be with my clients or come to the office, close my door, and just work as hard as I can."

Paradox Explanation

Threes want to be valued for who they are rather than just for what they do; however, because they try to create a positive image and share only what they achieve, no one really knows the person behind the persona.

Developer's Paradox Statement

"What you are describing is someone who is very successful—if success is defined as being a powerhouse attorney. You are also describing someone who is feeling perplexed and isolated with regard to peer relationships. Although we have a special relationship as coach and client, I want to tell you how I would react to you if I were your peer. If I worked with you, I would see a person who was driven, successful, competitive, and highly accomplished, but I would wonder, Who is the real Allison? How many people do you show who you really are, deep down inside?"

> NOTE Use the paradoxical challenge only with moderate to high self-mastery Threes; low self-mastery individuals may not be psychologically stable enough to handle the ambiguity inherent in paradoxes.

THREE COACHING CASE STUDY SUMMARY: MATT

Determine Coaching Goals and Learner Motivation

Make sure the goals can be accomplished in the time available and are linked to one or more of the learner's key motivators.

> Matt wants to have more balance in his life. He is aware that he spends most of his time working in a highly driven way, often at the expense of his family life. In addition, he has difficulty relaxing; when he does have discretionary time, he fills it with activities he has wanted to do for a long time—for example, jogging in preparation for a marathon or signing up to volunteer at the local art museum, which requires 40 hours of training. When asked why he wants more life balance, Matt states, "I think I'm out of balance and want to spend more time with my young son."

Assess the Learner's Level and Range of Self-Mastery, Then Use Level-Appropriate Coaching Approaches

Determine the learner's normal (average) level and range of self-mastery.

> Matt is slightly above the midpoint of moderate self-mastery. He is highly aware of his habits—for example, overworking on a consistent basis when the only real pressure on him is what he himself creates, and having a strong tendency to fill any available time with activity (and having difficulty stopping himself until he becomes exhausted). At the same time, Matt is usually aware of what he is feeling, although he may not share all his emotional reactions with others. His lowest self-mastery level is slightly below his average level (which is still moderate self-mastery), and he has moments of being in the high self-mastery level, primarily when he spends time with his son or takes an occasional day for himself to relax and reflect.

Select the development approach(es) from the chart on pages 88–89 that would be most effective with the learner, and experiment with these.

> Matt likes to structure his days; otherwise, he feels anxious. Encouraging him to slow down and do something he enjoys for an hour each day is something he would definitely respond to positively. Having him report on this at each coaching meeting would reinforce this behavior, because Matt would not want to admit he hadn't done his assignment. Gradually have him learn to relax and slow down without the structure, then reinforce him each time he does this. Explore who Matt really is outside of work by asking him to talk about his interests and hobbies, as well as his values and what he cares about most. This will ignite his passion about doing what he loves rather than doing what he feels he should do.

Use Coaching Techniques That Challenge Growth

Plan how you will use each of the four coaching techniques from this section, and use them at appropriate moments during the coaching process.

Head Center Challenge: "What if?"

What have you heard the learner say or imply that reflects a mental model or assumption you can challenge? How will you phrase this "What if?" challenge?

> All of the following challenges would be effective with Matt.
> *"What if you didn't have to schedule everything you do?"*
> *"What if you actually had time for your son?"*
> *"What if you could actually relax?"*

Heart Center Challenge: Recognizing and Leveraging Defense Mechanisms

When have you observed the learner use a particular defense mechanism? Would a direct or an indirect challenge be more effective? How would you phrase this defense mechanism challenge?

> Matt identifies with his work as well as with the roles he plays—for example, being a strongly contributing team member, a great employee, a good father, a good husband, and more.
>
> **INDIRECT CHALLENGE**
> *"If you had two days that were totally under your control and you could use these any way you desire to just be yourself, how would you spend that time?"*
>
> **DIRECT CHALLENGE**
> *"You seem to identify with what you do, talking about yourself in terms of the roles you fill, but not who you are aside from these. Who are you aside from these roles?"*

Body Center Challenge: "Why would you want to do that?"

What behavior has the learner stated that he or she plans to do? Do you think this is a wise course of action? How would you phrase this "Why would you want to do that?" challenge?

> *"Why would you want to have more balance in your life? Why would you want to 'smell the roses'?"*

Transformative Paradoxical Challenge

What paradoxes have you observed in the learner? Select the most significant one. How would you phrase this paradoxical challenge?

"You say you want more balance in your life, and I believe you want this, yet you structure every waking hour with work and activities."

NOTE Paradoxical challenges should be used only with moderate or high self-mastery learners. Low self-mastery learners are not in a psychological state to handle the complexity and ambiguity inherent in the resolution of this level of paradox, and deep-level or complex paradoxes can increase their anxiety. While less powerful paradoxes can be used with these learners, developers should do so with caution.

DEVELOPMENT ACTIVITIES FOR THREES

Developers can suggest the following activities to Three learners.

Core Issue: Take time each day to get to know yourself.

Make a commitment to spend at least 30 minutes each day just *being*. This means not working or doing any activities in which you focus on something external (such as watching a film or going shopping). If you don't quite understand the idea of *being,* ask three people who are very different from you what this concept means to them and how they go about simply being. Experiment with the ideas they suggest.

Expansion Through Wings and Arrows
WING TWO   Show more personal warmth and empathy.

When conversing with someone, ask yourself: *What are the various feelings this person might have?* When someone discusses a difficult or emotional situation with you, paraphrase what you hear, placing particular emphasis on the deeper feelings implicit in what the other person says. For example, if a person discusses an experience in which he or she was demeaned in public, say "That must have felt terrible. You must be hurt and angry."

WING FOUR   Tap your creativity.

Every artist begins with a blank page, so simply start doing something. Begin writing, drawing, or taking photographs. After you become more comfortable with a particular artistic medium, you can pick a theme such as flowers, beauty, challenge, suffering, irony, generations, and so on. Find some way to express that theme. Try alternative ways to express this idea. Remember that you are doing this for yourself, not for others to evaluate whether or not what you have done is good enough. Enjoy the process, and if the product also pleases you, that's merely a bonus!

ARROW LINE NINE   Learn genuine humility.

Notice when you begin to talk about what you have done or are about to do, and refocus the conversation on other people. When you begin to feel excited about what you have just accomplished or feel uncomfortable because some of your efforts are not yielding the success you desire, tell yourself this: *My worth as a human being is not based on what I do, and neither is anyone else's.* Finally, spend time in the company of people you would not normally perceive as successful. Get to know them as people and try to discover what is special or unique about them aside from anything they may have accomplished. Focus on them purely as human beings.

ARROW LINE SIX   Push yourself to be completely honest.

Although you believe you are honest, look at the notion of honesty in a new way. Honesty is more than simply saying what is on your mind. Honesty and truth-telling involve the capacity to be totally honest with yourself and the willingness to be completely forthcoming with others. The issue for you is your tendency to shape information about yourself or your circumstances in a way that removes or deemphasizes the negative and accentuates the positive. Tell the whole truth about yourself and your reactions to one new person each day.

Communication: Show your emotions.

Tell stories about yourself to others, but make these stories not so much about your achievements as about events that have really mattered to you. Convey not only events, but also the feelings you had about them. For example, where you might normally say, "I got a promotion yesterday," you could say, "I'm so happy today—I got a promotion I really wanted. I can hardly believe it!"

Conflict: Explore your deeper feelings when you become upset.

When you feel upset, examine some of these deeper issues that may be the cause: looking bad in front of others; feeling competitive with someone else; appearing less than fully competent; and disliking others who appear to be failures in some way, as if their work will reflect poorly on you. Questions to ask yourself include these: *What is it about appearing to be successful that is so important to me? If this were not my ongoing intention, how would I be different, and how would my thoughts, feelings, and behavior change? What would happen if I were not so focused on impressing others?*

Teams: Rather than becoming impatient with prolonged discussion, help teams deal with differences.

Remind yourself that effectively dealing with differences is fundamental to the team's ultimate success and that relationship issues are just as important as those related to the task; encourage people to communicate about such issues, and be willing to offer your own reactions as well.

Leadership: Honor your leadership gift of obtaining results and enhance your capacity to pay equal attention to people and work.

Your dual focus on goal achievement and efficiency can have the effect of minimizing the human side of work. Conduct a human-impact analysis each time you make a decision, and take the results very seriously.

· SIX ·

Coaching Enneagram Style Four

Fours desire deep connections both with their interior worlds and with other people, and they feel most alive when they authentically express their feelings and personal experiences.

Center of Intelligence · Heart Center

HOW TO IDENTIFY FOURS

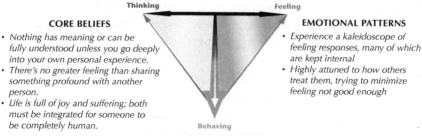

CORE BELIEFS

- *Nothing has meaning or can be fully understood unless you go deeply into your own personal experience.*
- *There's no greater feeling than sharing something profound with another person.*
- *Life is full of joy and suffering; both must be integrated for someone to be completely human.*

EMOTIONAL PATTERNS

- *Experience a kaleidoscope of feeling responses, many of which are kept internal*
- *Highly attuned to how others treat them, trying to minimize feeling not good enough*

WORKPLACE BEHAVIORS

Engage in extensive introspection · Want to be unique or special · Can appear moody · Use self-referencing language · Seek inspiration and want to be understood

The "Sensitive Heart"

Fours are among the most sensitive of all the Enneagram styles, although their sensitivity is first and foremost focused on their own internal reactions and feelings. Many Fours are also sensitive to the feelings of others, particularly when these involve deep emotions and profound experiences.

Emotional Patterns of Fours
*Experience a kaleidoscope of feeling responses, many of which
are kept internal*

Fours have rich, dynamic, and dramatic interior lives in which they review
and revisit past occurrences as well as future desires and scenarios. Many
Fours describe their interior world this way: "It's as if I'm watching multiple
movies simultaneously, in full color and with accompanying soundtracks."
Although many Fours go to great lengths to communicate their inner experiences to a variety of other people, others do so more selectively. Moreover,
because what is occurring within them is both complex and constantly shifting, it can be difficult for them to express all of their inner experiences in a
way that others can understand.

*Highly attuned to how others treat them, trying to minimize
feeling not good enough*

Fours feel that there is something within them that sets them apart from others. Although they often interpret this as a deficiency, they can also perceive
this difference as something that makes them unique or even better than others. Their sensitivity to feeling not good enough is connected to their tendency to absorb negative information about themselves as if this negative
data were true, but to reject positive information about themselves without
absorbing or integrating it into their sense of self. Internalizing so much negative data gives Fours an interior reservoir of painful feelings, which makes
them reactive to anything that might imply something negative about them.

Workplace Behaviors of Fours
Engage in extensive introspection

Fours seek to understand the true meaning of events through in-depth introspection and authentic interpersonal conversations. Fundamentally, Fours
trust their own inner experiences and feelings more than anything else, yet at
the same time they wonder whether their personal reactions are universal
enough.

Want to be unique or special

Fours want to be seen as different and special in some way. Sensitive to nu-
ance and subtlety, Fours view the world through the artist's sensitivity to symbolic meaning, and in fact many of them are artists—for example, in music,
visual arts, writing, filmmaking, and dance.

Can appear moody

While Fours relate intensely for extended periods of time when interactions
feel meaningful to them, they can also withdraw precipitously into their own

worlds, even becoming moody, dramatic, or emotionally unpredictable. This approach-withdrawal dynamic becomes most apparent in relationships and is referred to as "push-pull." Fours may first engage another person with great intensity, and then push the other person away due to fear and anxiety. When the other person then withdraws from the relationship, Fours try to pull him or her back into relating. This push-pull cycle can continue indefinitely.

Use self-referencing language

More often than any other Enneagram style, Fours tell personal stories and use words like *I, me, my,* and *mine* frequently. While the purpose of this communication style is to establish a connection between themselves and others, this behavior can also be interpreted as Fours redirecting the conversation to themselves.

Seek inspiration and want to be understood

More than anything, Fours like to feel inspired, creative, and understood by other people, and they enjoy helping others feel the same. However, when they feel the lack of these things—for example, when they have to do uninteresting, repetitive tasks or be involved in long conversations about mundane subjects—they become bored, frustrated, disenchanted, and disheartened.

FAMOUS FOURS

Johnny Depp	"There are four questions of value in life: What is sacred? Of what is the spirit made? What is worth living for, and what is worth dying for? The answer to each is the same. Only love."
	"As a teenager I was so insecure. I was the type of guy that never fitted in because he never dared to choose. I was convinced I had absolutely no talent at all. For nothing. And that thought took away all my ambition too."
Princess Diana	"I understand people's suffering, people's pain, more than you will ever know yourself."
	"I wear my heart on my sleeve."
Anthony Hopkins	"Why love if losing hurts so much? I have no answers anymore; only the life I have lived. The pain now is part of the happiness then."
	"I am able to play monsters well. I understand monsters. I understand madmen."

Subtypes: Three Variations of Four

All Fours desire a feeling of deep connection both with their own interior worlds and with other people as a way to avoid feeling deficient or not good enough. Because they believe there is something lacking within themselves—although they cannot define exactly what this is—Fours consciously and unconsciously compare themselves to others (referred to as envy) as a way to determine what is wrong, consequently feeling superior, deficient, or both. There are three distinct ways in which Fours manifest these characteristics, called subtypes.

Self-Preservation Subtype Fours try to bear their suffering in silence as a way to prove that they are good enough by virtue of enduring inner anguish. In addition, they engage in nonstop activity and/or reckless behavior as a way to feel excited and energized and to avoid not feeling as good as others. Of all three subtypes, self-preservation subtype Fours do not appear to be as envious or sensitive as the other two subtypes of Four.

Social Subtype Fours focus more on their deficiencies, as well as on earning the understanding and appreciation of the groups to which they belong. They want understanding and appreciation for their suffering and sorrows, and desire acknowledgment for their heartfelt contributions to groups, while at the same time feeling marginal to or not fully part of groups.

One-to-One Subtype Fours feel compelled to express their needs and feelings outwardly and can be highly competitive with others to gain attention, to be heard, and to be acknowledged for their perspectives and accomplishments. Winning is perceived as another venue for being understood, and coming out on top is seen as a way to resolve their continuous comparisons with others.

Wings and Arrow Lines for Fours

Because Fours feel such an intense desire to express their feelings, to experience deep connections with others, and to avoid feeling rejected, not good enough, or deficient, they can become intensely emotional and subjective. Fours are prone to moments of elation and despair, and they can have difficulty manifesting their desires and intentions. Access to their wings (styles Three and Five) and arrows (styles Two and One) can counterbalance these qualities in Fours.

Wings for Fours

THREE WING   When Fours have a Three wing, they are more action oriented, have higher and more consistent energy levels, exhibit more poise and confidence, and are more comfortable with being highly visible rather than shying away from visibility or feeling ambivalent about it.

FIVE WING   Fours with a Five wing are more objective and analytical, which provides a counterpoint to their more subjective emotional way of relating with others. In addition, they have an increased ability to perceive situations from a more considered and less reactive perspective and often demonstrate more self-restraint and self-containment.

Arrow Lines for Fours

ARROW LINE TO TWO   Because Fours normally focus on their own internal responses and personal experiences, a strong link to their arrow line Two greatly enhances their attunement to other people. This increased attention to others helps these Fours be more responsive and more consistent in their interactions.

ARROW LINE FROM ONE   When Fours have a strong connection to their arrow line One, they become more objective and discerning of people and events rather than making assessments based primarily on their emotional reactions. This provides them with greater balance, increased emotional and mental clarity, and enhanced attention to details.

Three Typing Questions for Fours

1. When you feel something very strongly, do you hold on to your emotions intensely for extremely long periods of time, constantly replaying your thoughts, feelings, and sensations?
2. Do you think of melancholy as a pleasurable experience?
3. Do you continually search for deep connections with others and feel distraught when these connections become severed?

HOW TO COACH FOURS

Areas of Strength	Areas for Development
• Inspiring	• Intense
• Creative	• Self-conscious
• Introspective	• Moody
• Expressive	• Guilt-ridden

COACHING OVERVIEW

Fours can vary in their reactions to feedback, but almost all Fours will be concerned that negative feedback will cause them to feel defective. Because they lack effective filters to help them determine whether a negative perception is accurate and also discount or downplay positive information about themselves, receiving feedback can be a challenge for them. They take negative feedback as a confirmation that something is wrong with them, and they may savor positive remarks momentarily, but then quickly reject the information without integrating any of it into their self-perception. As a result of this automatic "injection of the negative or rejection of the positive" pattern with receiving feedback, Fours often need the developer to help sort out the truth and accuracy of the information presented. While Fours may prefer developers who are sympathetic and understanding, developers who are warm, yet objective and direct, will help them the most.

Fours may not always like hearing it, but they do appreciate being told the truth. Deep inside, most Fours know that they can have an unbalanced perception of reality and may need to rely on someone else's input. A trustworthy developer is in an ideal position to offer this type of assistance, but the proper timing is essential. The optimal moment for discussing negative information is directly after Four learners have expressed their feelings and perceptions about the information; at this time, Fours are usually quite receptive to what the developer has to offer, as long as it is said with kindness and clarity.

First, Determine Coaching Goals and Learner Motivation
Goal Identification: What to Ask Fours

Some Fours like to talk at length, others tend to be quiet and more withdrawn, and some can be both talkative and withdrawn from moment to moment. Talkative Fours want the developer to listen closely to everything they say—and this can take some time—while quieter Fours need developers to do a great deal of probing to get a clear response from them about their coaching goals. However, because all Fours want to be understood and are driven by their personal values and a quest for deeper meaning, the following questions work well with them:

• *As you think about our forthcoming coaching experience, what would mean the most to you to achieve as a result of our time and effort?*
• *Please help me understand why these matter so much to you.*

When discussing the Four learner's goals, developers should help the Four clearly connect the key development motivators listed below to specific coaching goals. This link may be obvious to learners as they discuss why each coaching goal is important, but if it is not, developers can do one of two things: (1) Ask Four learners, *"What personal and professional benefits will you gain when you achieve this goal?"* or (2) explain the connection between the goal and the motivator directly by saying, *"This will help you be far more self-accepting and will enable you to manifest more of your dreams."*

Key Development Motivators for Fours

- To help them know more about themselves at the deepest levels and become more truly self-accepting
- To make lasting connections with others that can be sustained without having to constantly engage in deep, meaningful interactions
- To be less volatile, emotional, and reactive
- To feel more capable of making things happen and to manifest their dreams rather than feeling that things happen *to* them

Second, Assess the Learner's Level and Range of Self-Mastery, Then Use Level-Appropriate Coaching Approaches

The best way to determine the self-mastery level of the learner is to read the behavioral descriptions for all three levels in the chart below and answer these questions:

1. What is this person's normal (average) level of self-mastery?
   ☐ Low ☐ Moderate ☐ High
2. What do I know and what have I observed that leads me to this conclusion?
3. What is this person's range of self-mastery—that is, the individual's highest and lowest levels?
4. What do I know from my own observations or other data that leads me to this conclusion?

Fours: Self-Mastery Levels and Coaching Approaches to Enhance Development

High Self-Mastery · The Appreciator

Core understanding

Everything has meaning and significance, and everyone is connected at the deepest levels.

Enneagram Fours with high self-mastery emanate centeredness, tranquility, and calm. Their artistic expression is universal, because they are open to both the delight and the sadness that life brings. Grateful and graceful, they deeply appreciate what they have rather than lamenting what they lack. These Fours exhibit an inner wholeness and constancy, and their gentle empathy and genuine concern draws others to them. When facing a difficult challenge, they do not go into emotional turmoil, because they are able to reflect on their own experience, understand other people's points of view, and examine related contextual factors.

Coaching approaches to enhance the Four's self-mastery
Provide encouragement and additional methods for expansion.

- Positively reinforce the Four's strengths, true authenticity, real feelings (beyond excessive emotional expression), and emotional intuition.
- Verbally affirm their contributions, particularly at times when they neither expect nor demand it.
- Encourage Fours to honor and use their insights, full abilities, and creativity; help them learn to take action to make their ideas and dreams a reality.
- Teach them how to accept and internalize positive feedback that is true and how to filter out negative feedback that is untrue.
- Emphasize the importance of maintaining their emotional balance by using whatever methods work best for them on a daily basis—for example, artistic expression, exercise, meditation, or journal writing.

Moderate Self-Mastery · The Unique Individual

Core concern
Feeling significant, feeling special, and finding meaning

With a moderate degree of self-mastery, Fours can be either dramatic or reticent as they seek meaningful relationships and authentic conversations. They can also be quite imaginative, transforming their inner experience, anguish, and search for meaning into artistic expression. Their conversations are frequently self-referencing, with excessive use of words such as *I, me,* and *mine;* prolonged personal stories; and redirection of conversations to themselves. Constantly comparing themselves with others to determine whether they are superior or deficient, these Fours have difficulty being self-accepting. Yearning, moody, and sometimes melancholic, they can also be reflective, empathic, and gifted.

Coaching approaches to enhance the Four's self-mastery
Stimulate motivation and provide concrete development actions.

- Help them realize that neither they nor anyone else is the center of the universe— that is, not everything happens in relation to them.
- Focus on the positives in the Four, others, and the situation, and help them to also do this rather than focusing only on the negative and on what is missing.
- Validate their emotions and the importance of interpersonal connections, but emphasize putting emotions and connections with others in the service of productive action.
- When Fours become too self-focused or negative, lighten up the conversation with humor.
- Model accepting and valuing what is rather than what could be, and help Fours find meaning and pleasure in routine, everyday activities. This involves being consciously in the present rather than focusing on the past or the future.

Low Self-Mastery · The Invisibly Defective

Core fear
Being intrinsically defective and completely disconnected

Fours with low self-mastery are bitter, depressed, emotionally volatile, hypersensitive, and self-absorbed, and they feel deeply wounded by anything they perceive as a slight or a rejection. Unable to extricate themselves from their negative self-perception, they can become tormented, deeply ashamed, alienated, full of rage, withdrawn, or highly aggressive, accusing individuals in particular and life in general of intentionally harming them. While they may express themselves in a variety of artistic forms, their art has a tragic quality from which there seems to be no escape.

Coaching approaches to enhance the Four's self-mastery

Offer support, guidance, and boundaries.

- Validate their feelings, but help Fours take positive action.
- Provide positive feedback whenever possible; encourage Fours to internalize the positive and recognize that they overinternalize the negative.
- Don't accept their self-criticism or sense of low self-worth; encourage them to tell you what they have done well.
- When they are overinternalizing negative information by blaming themselves, help Fours make the issue more external by focusing on the context or on others who share responsibility. When Fours are overexternalizing by blaming others, help them to focus realistically on their self-responsibility.
- Be alert to Fours' tendency to become isolated; reach out to them and ask what they are thinking and feeling.

Once you have an initial assessment of the Four learner's self-mastery level, read the recommended approaches appropriate to that level and select those you believe will be most effective for the learner.

Third, Use Coaching Techniques That Challenge Growth

As you read the following four coaching techniques, it can be helpful to think about several Fours you know and how you might use the techniques with those individuals. Although all Fours have a similar interior architecture, their behavior varies depending on their Enneagram subtypes. For example, self-preservation subtype Fours can be alternately subdued and frenetic, social subtype Fours tend to be more withdrawn, and one-to-one subtype Fours tend to be the most dramatic and intense. Fours also exhibit some differences based on factors such as self-mastery level, empathy, use of wings and arrows, experience, age, gender, and culture.

Head Center Challenge: The "What if?" Question

"What if?" challenges work well in situations in which the learner makes assumptions that something is important and inviolate. These assumptions are part of the learner's unchallenged beliefs and paradigms. After hearing the Four learner say something involving an explicit or implicit assumption, the developer poses a relevant "What if?" question. The chart on the following page lists three common mental models for Fours, the question the developer should ask to challenge each assumption, and the ways in which the developer should respond once the Four has answered the developer's challenge.

"What if?" Challenges for Fours

Common Assumption No. 1

"It's not going to work out very well."

Developer's challenge
"What if it did work out well?"

Developer's follow-on response
- If the Four says, "It won't," ask: *"How do you know that to be true?"* and then be silent. If the Four responds with stories of despair in which things didn't work out well, ask: *"Can you think of a time when things did work out well and tell me about that?"*
- When the Four can say what would happen if it did work out well, say: *"Good. Now let's discuss what you can do to increase the chances of a positive outcome, but also what you can do if it doesn't work out as you desire."*

Common Assumption No. 2

"People just don't really understand what I'm experiencing."

Developer's challenge
"What if others really do understand you, mentally and emotionally?"

Developer's follow-on response
- If the Four can't think of such a situation, tell a relevant compelling story about a time when you felt misunderstood but when, in fact, someone else understood you even better than you understood yourself. Then say: *"Do you think this has ever happened to you?"*
- When the Four can articulate what would happen if others could understand him or her, ask: *"What can you do to increase the chances of this and what are you actually doing to hinder being understood?"*

Common Assumption No. 3

"Others just don't pursue life experiences as deeply and completely as I do."

Developer's challenge
"What if others actually do experience life deeply and completely, just not using the same process that you do?"

Developer's follow-on response
- If the Four doesn't think that this could possibly be true, ask: *"How do you know that, really?"*
- When the Four gives a concrete and positive response, say: *"Have you considered that in your deep consideration of your own experiences, you may actually be overemphasizing something or unintentionally eliminating something else?"*
  Hint: Many Fours use the expression of feelings as a mask or cover for deeper feelings that they don't want to consider.

Many Fours like "What if?" challenges, because this question makes them think and be self-reflective in a new way—that is, using their minds as well as their feelings. At the same time, other Fours do not like to have their assumptions challenged, taking such challenges as a dismissal or negation of their view of reality. Should this occur, the developer can say, *"What if your assumption isn't the only way to perceive the situation?"*

Heart Center Challenge: Explore the Learner's Defense Mechanism
The Four's Primary Defense Mechanism: Introjection

When used by Fours, *introjection* functions as a counterintuitive defense mechanism. Instead of repelling critical information and negative experiences that can cause them anxiety or pain, they introject the information—that is, Fours fully absorb, internalize, and incorporate these data into their sense of self. Fritz Perls, the father of Gestalt therapy, refers to this phenomenon as swallowing something whole without being able to differentiate information that is true from information that is untrue. Fours introject negative information—and repel positive data—about themselves as a way of coping with painful information and neutralizing external threats. They prefer to deal with self-inflicted damage rather than having to respond to criticism or rejection from others.

Fours engage in introjection on an ongoing basis, unconsciously seeking clues that someone is upset with them or that they are deficient in some way. The defense mechanism is triggered most strongly when they feel anxious about impending negative feedback or when they become close to others and then worry about being rejected. With a lack of clear boundaries to differentiate what to internalize and what to not take seriously, combined with their tendency to absorb negative data but reject positive information, most Fours continuously defend against not feeling good enough.

Ironically, Fours don't realize that the very defense mechanism they use to fend off negative information actually creates their reservoir of negative self-perception. Examples of the Four's defense mechanism of introjection include the following: being highly sensitive to the possible negative reactions of others; having an intense desire to be fully understood; needing to express themselves at length; feeling deeply hurt when they believe others do not grasp what they are saying or empathize with their feelings; over-identifying with what they feel and believing that they *are* their feelings,

INTROJECTION

Someone a Four knows and likes pays little attention to him at a business event; instead of ignoring this or wondering what may be occurring in this person's life separate from their relationship, the Four personalizes this lack of interaction, assumes the person is mad at or doesn't like him, and then agonizes over this for days.

rather than understanding that feelings are something they have; tending to blame other people rather than themselves when someone is upset with them or they feel anxious, thus transporting the hurt and responsibility to someone else. These examples are actually symptoms or manifestations of introjection that often hide or defend against the following deeper developmental issues for Fours:

- Integrating objectivity with emotionality to find an equilibrium of the heart and mind, rather than believing that truth lies only in the realm of feelings
- Feeling a deep and true sense of self-worth rather than absorbing negative data wholeheartedly, rejecting positive information without discernment, and continuously comparing themselves to others so that they feel either deficient or superior in some way
- Being able to focus simultaneously and equally on themselves and other people rather than focusing primarily on themselves and on their own feelings and inner experience

Working with the Four's defense mechanism of introjection can be complicated. When Fours are blatantly using this defensive strategy, they are usually in a state of heightened emotionality and are feeling hurt, angry, and/or anxious. At these times, Fours may become highly reactive to anything the developer says that in any way implies that the Four has done something wrong. When Fours are angry, their anger may be unleashed on the developer (whereas when Fours feel sad, they may become highly withdrawn). Although developers should proceed with caution and courage when working with the defense mechanism challenge of introjection, doing so can make an enormous positive difference in the growth trajectory of the Four learner. It is best to start with the indirect challenge, as it elicits more responsiveness and less resistance. However, if the Four learner already recognizes that he or she absorbs almost all negative data and if you have an excellent relationship with the learner, a direct challenge may have a bigger impact.

INDIRECT CHALLENGE TO INTROJECTION
"When you receive negative feedback, you seem to take it in so deeply, but when something positive happens, you appear to enjoy it at the moment but then discard it. Do you think that is true?"

DIRECT CHALLENGE TO INTROJECTION
"You seem to internalize everything that might possibly be negative, yet discount or only partially hear that which is positive. No wonder you often feel hurt or discounted so readily. You need to set up new, clear boundaries with filters so you can take in both positive and negative data, but only that which is accurate and useful."

Body Center Challenge: The "Why would you want to do that?" Question

When Four learners say they want to change something about themselves, asking them this question works effectively as a way of supportively challenging their desires. As a response to this technique, the Four learner either changes his or her course of action or becomes more deeply committed to the original plan. This technique is especially useful in two situations: (1) The Four learner articulates an intention to take action that sounds productive, or (2) the Four learner expresses an intention to take action that might be risky or could be counterproductive to his or her best interests.

Although Fours like this type of challenge, because they always like to think about why they want to do or not do something, it is important for them to elucidate the deepest and clearest reasons for their choices. Thus, the developer may need to ask them the reason behind their stated rationale, as demonstrated in the two examples in the chart below.

"Why would you want to do that?" Challenges for Fours

A Four's Productive Intention to Act

"I want to be less emotional."

Developer's challenge

"Why would you want to react with less intense feelings or have strong emotional reactions less frequently?"

Developer's follow-on response

- If the Four cannot think of an answer or gives an unconvincing answer, say: *"It doesn't sound like you really want to do this. Have you considered that you may like placing such an emphasis on feelings?"* Then wait for the response.
- When the Four gives a convincing response, say: *"You seem to understand how and why this would make a big difference in your life. Let's talk about how you can learn to do this."*

A Four's Counterproductive Intention to Act

"I expect too much from others, so I'm just going to be less involved with people."

Developer's challenge

"Why would you want to keep yourself away from others as a way of lowering your expectations?"

Developer's follow-on response

- If the Four gives you a reason that makes sense to you, say: *"You may have high expectations for people, get involved, and are then disappointed. Rather than not being involved, have you considered examining your expectations?"*
- If the Four gives a response indicating that he or she recognizes that the behavior is counterproductive, say: *"Now that you can see that this may not get you what you really want, what alternatives can you think of, and what might be the results of these?"*

Transformative Paradoxical Challenges

Fours often like paradoxes because these are complex and challenging. However, it is important that Fours actually integrate and absorb the paradoxical aspects of their own behavior, not just respond to the paradox as merely interesting information about themselves. If you believe this may be occurring, stop and ask the Four this question: *"I know this is intriguing, and you need to ask yourself this: Do you want to keep living in this paradoxical situation that is really of your own making?"*

THE FOUR PARADOX

Julie had just been hired as a production manager in the entertainment industry and was thrilled to be part of a high-performing team comprised of interesting and talented individuals. However, after a few months her excitement began to fade and resentment took over as she noticed a severe imbalance in the team members' workloads. While Julie was offering to help with new projects and was working herself to exhaustion, other team members rarely volunteered for additional assignments. Some of her teammates were annoying—one was too critical, another talked incessantly, and a third kept raising picky or irrelevant questions during team meetings.

Frustrated, Julie talked to her manager. "Why can't people do what they commit to doing?" Julie complained. "What's wrong? Is it me, or is it them? Why should I work so hard when others don't think they need to push themselves beyond their comfort zone? I used to like this team so much, but now I wonder if I can make it through the day without feeling agitated or sounding short-tempered." She paused, then added, "Maybe I should talk to one of my teammates and apologize for being edgy with him. I feel very removed from him and remote from a team that I used to think was exceptional."

Paradox Explanation

Fours want to have deep and lasting connections with others, but their behavior frequently reflects their desire to feel different, unique, and separate. Fours engage in push-pull behavior when others get too close, and they often pull away entirely when they feel disappointed or rejected. All of these behaviors then cause others to pull away from them.

Developer's Paradox Statement

"That is quite a swing—you want to be, and in fact are, very connected to this group, and then suddenly you're very distant from it. Separate out for a moment what the team did, and focus on the things you are doing. How do you pull away from this team, and what do you do that causes them to pull away from you?"

> NOTE Use the paradoxical challenge only with moderate to high self-mastery Fours; low self-mastery individuals may not be psychologically stable enough to handle the ambiguity inherent in paradoxes.

FOUR COACHING CASE STUDY SUMMARY: GARY

Determine Coaching Goals and Learner Motivation

Make sure the goals can be accomplished in the time available and are linked to one or more of the learner's key motivators.

> Although Gary earns his living as a computer technical support person, his real passion is computer graphics. As a result, he wants to figure out why he hasn't pursued a career in the field he cares about the most. When asked why this matters to him, Gary states, "Isn't everyone happiest when they do what they love?"

Assess the Learner's Level and Range of Self-Mastery, Then Use Level-Appropriate Coaching Approaches

Determine the learner's normal (average) level and range of self-mastery.

> Gary is normally at the midpoint of moderate self-mastery, although his range is large. He functions close to low self-mastery when he's deeply disappointed, but he moves to the higher range of moderate self-mastery when he is rested and engaged in doing computer graphics for friends. However, Gary's self-perception of his self-mastery level is distorted. During good times, he thinks he is at high self-mastery; when he feels troubled, he still believes he is in the midpoint area of moderate self-mastery. Gary also believes he is normally at the higher ranges of moderate self-mastery. Unfortunately, these distortions interfere with his growth, because he doesn't believe he has very much development work to do.

Select the development approach(es) from the chart on pages 107–109 that would be most effective with the learner, and experiment with these.

> The most important approach to use with Gary is to gently reveal his distorted perception of his self-mastery level—his average level and his range. This can be done in three ways: (1) showing him the self-mastery levels for Fours; (2) guiding him to more accurately assess his self-mastery level; and (3) helping him see that he does have ample room for growth. Resistance to this should be anticipated and mitigated by asking him what makes him perceive himself differently from the more realistic assessment. As a note, Gary may be doing this as a way to defend against feeling deficient. In addition, help Gary focus on elements of his life and work that are positive, including the enjoyable experiences he has doing computer graphics for friends and the feedback he receives on his work.

Use Coaching Techniques That Challenge Growth

Plan how you will use each of the four coaching techniques from this section, and use them at appropriate moments during the coaching process.

Head Center Challenge: "What if?"

What have you heard the learner say or imply that reflects a mental model or assumption you can challenge? How will you phrase this "What if?" challenge?

> All of the following challenges would be effective with Gary.
> *"What if you did commit yourself to computer graphics as a profession?"*
> *"What if you really like certain aspects of your technical support job more than you acknowledge?"*
> *"What if you had the courage and discipline to follow your passion?"*

Heart Center Challenge: Recognizing and Leveraging Defense Mechanisms

When have you observed the learner use a particular defense mechanism? Would a direct or an indirect challenge be more effective? How would you phrase this defense mechanism challenge?

> Gary has a very difficult time receiving positive feedback. He questions the information and then discounts it, or he allows the positive information to make him feel so extremely good—in fact, out of proportion to the feedback received—but then lets the good feeling dissipate entirely.
>
> **INDIRECT CHALLENGE**
> *"You tell me a lot about the negative things that happen to you, but far less about the positive ones. That's also true about what you say when describing yourself. What do you think about what I'm saying?"*
>
> **DIRECT CHALLENGE**
> *"I've noticed that whenever you hear or anticipate hearing something negative, you feel quite hurt by this and sometimes get angry, but you rarely absorb positive information. You hear it but don't internalize it. Have you considered that you have two switches—one that's always on for negative data, and another that's always off for positive information? I think you need new switches, and they should be dimmer switches so you can incrementally adjust them depending on the source and accuracy of the information."*

Body Center Challenge: "Why would you want to do that?"

What behavior has the learner stated he or she plans to do? Do you think this is a wise course of action? How would you phrase this "Why would you want to do that?" challenge?

> *"Why would you want to leave your technical support job and become a full-time computer graphic artist?"*

Transformative Paradoxical Challenge

What paradoxes have you observed in the learner? Select the most significant one. How would you phrase this paradoxical challenge?

The transformational challenge is not appropriate when Gary is in the lower ranges of moderate self-mastery, but it would be very useful when he is functioning at the high ranges of moderate self-mastery.

"You say you want to do work that gives you personal meaning and you have this unique talent in computer graphics, yet you don't move forward toward the thing you love the most."

NOTE Paradoxical challenges should be used only with moderate or high self-mastery learners. Low self-mastery learners are not in a psychological state to handle the complexity and ambiguity inherent in the resolution of this level of paradox, and deep-level or complex paradoxes can increase their anxiety. While less powerful paradoxes can be used with these learners, developers should do so with caution.

DEVELOPMENT ACTIVITIES FOR FOURS

Developers can suggest the following activities to Four learners.

Core Issue: Take pleasure in other people's positive qualities and accomplishments.

A counterintuitive way to do this is to first take genuine pleasure in your own positive attributes and accomplishments. Do not use any caveats or buts, such as "I'm smart, but he's smarter" or "I'm empathic, but I spend too much time thinking about myself." Simply enjoy who you are. Once you can do this, allow yourself to appreciate other people's qualities and achievements. Each day, think positively about yourself, then select another person to think positively about without making any comparisons to yourself.

Expansion Through Wings and Arrows
THREE WING   Stay in charge of yourself.

You can learn how to keep your feelings from interfering with the work you need to do by saying to yourself: *I am feeling very emotional, but I am not going to allow my feelings to take over. What tasks need my attention right now?* Each time you feel your emotions taking over, ask yourself the question again.

FIVE WING   Value your mental clarity.

Although you value your emotional reactions and experiences, you likely place less emphasis on your mind, even if you have highly developed analytical skills. There is, however, a unique wisdom in both your mind and your heart (as well as in your body). Use your mental agility for planning—for example, the next time you need to make a decision, develop a methodical process for how you will make the decision and design an implementation plan. Similarly, the next time you see a beautiful work of art, go to an excellent play, watch a good film, or listen to a fine piece of music, in addition to enjoying the experience, also analyze the component parts the artist used that contributed to the quality of what you saw or heard.

ARROW LINE TWO   **Focus on others.**

By focusing more on others than on yourself, you can move beyond your own framework into the worlds of other people. When you start to go inward and realize that you are likely to spend a great deal of time dwelling on your own responses, stop and ask yourself these questions: *What is someone else* [preferably someone directly involved in the event that has triggered your emotional reaction] *experiencing? What does he or she need?*

ARROW LINE ONE   **Take care of business.**

Although you follow your interests first, putting off tasks that you perceive as uninteresting or mundane in order to do tasks that you find creative and meaningful, you can overcome this tendency to let the smaller or less interesting things pile up by doing the following: (1) Create a plan for accomplishing tasks; (2) allot a specific time each day to handle routine tasks; (3) take care of routine tasks immediately so they don't pile up; and (4) regard mundane tasks as developmental opportunities—that is, find pleasure and satisfaction in ordinary work.

Communication: Reduce your self-referencing language.

Reduce the number of self-referencing words you use, such as *I, my, me, mine,* and *myself.* Use language that is less personalized and more objective. Tell fewer anecdotes about yourself, and make the ones you do tell much shorter.

Conflict: Explore how your anger relates to your self-development issues.

Growth does not come from the outside—for example, by getting another person to be less rejecting of you, reducing the immediate feeling of envy by increasing your credentials, changing your image, or encouraging other people to treat you as special in some way. While these tactics may reduce your anxiety momentarily, they do not support genuine long-term growth. Real growth occurs when you explore your anger and sensitivity to rejection, understand the role that envy (continuous comparison) plays in your life, and accept that everyone is special and no one is any more defective or flawless than anyone else.

Teams: Put your strength in working with team processes into perspective.

While it is important to honor and utilize your sensitivity to underlying team issues, it is equally important to remember that issues need only be discussed to the extent that they no longer impede the team's progress, not to the point at which every issue has been thoroughly examined. Practice your ability to facilitate issue identification and resolution using methods that are efficient as well as effective.

Leadership: Honor your leadership gift of pursuing your passion and enhance your capacity to be a fully balanced and consistent leader.

Employees need their leaders to be predictable, balanced, and consistent. Focus on the work and the organization as much as on the people, and more on both of these areas than on yourself. Find ways to balance your emotional life—for example, through daily walks, meditation, conversations with friends to whom you can speak openly, or coaching—so that your emotional life does not negatively impact those who work for you.

SEVEN

Coaching
Enneagram Style Five

Fives thirst for information and knowledge and use emotional detachment as a way of keeping involvement with others to a minimum.

Center of Intelligence · Head Center

HOW TO IDENTIFY FIVES

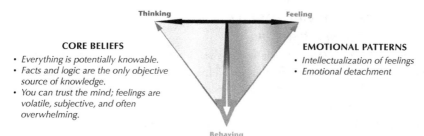

Thinking   Feeling

CORE BELIEFS
- *Everything is potentially knowable.*
- *Facts and logic are the only objective source of knowledge.*
- *You can trust the mind; feelings are volatile, subjective, and often overwhelming.*

EMOTIONAL PATTERNS
- *Intellectualization of feelings*
- *Emotional detachment*

Behaving

WORKPLACE BEHAVIORS
*Pursue information and wisdom • Cerebrally oriented •
Calm in a crisis • Easily drained • Self-reliant and private*

The "Compartmentalizing Mind"

Fives use their minds in a unique way called compartmentalizing, a process by which they take in and store information using mental categories as though these were file folders to access later. Fives also compartmentalize people, events, and experiences—for example, their friends may never meet one another. Fives often separate home from work to such an extent that they rarely discuss their personal lives at work or share their work lives at home.

Emotional Patterns of Fives
Intellectualization of feelings

Most Fives both experience and talk about their emotional responses in a cerebral way rather than expressing them directly, saying what they *think* about something rather than how they *feel*. If a Five who was passed over for a promotion is asked how he or she feels, the Five may say, "I think it was a political decision," rather than acknowledge feeling any anger or disappointment. Many Fives become confused when asked how they feel, having trouble distinguishing between a thought and an emotion.

Emotional detachment

Although many people may detach from their emotions to some degree, this is not the same as the emotional detachment of Fives. Fives disconnect from their emotions almost entirely at the moment these are occurring, then selectively review and re-experience some—but not all—of these emotions when they are alone and want to do so. Emotional detachment for Fives refers to their automatic, habitual, and almost complete disconnection from their feelings, a way of dealing with emotions that they have been using since childhood.

Workplace Behaviors of Fives
Pursue information and wisdom

Fives thirst for in-depth knowledge in their areas of interest, and their compartmentalization of the information helps them understand, store, and access it later. When it is needed, they retrieve the data and organize the information using a systems perspective, much like a flowchart in which the different parts affect each other in a sequential and logical process.

Cerebrally oriented

Fives appear highly cerebral, analytical, and logical, and some Fives can appear to not be fully in their bodies, as if they are observing themselves from the outside.

Calm in a crisis

Fives are extraordinarily stable, dispassionate, and clearheaded in a crisis as a result of their objectivity and ability to disconnect emotionally.

Easily drained

Fives experience most nonintellectual interactions as draining, even if they value and enjoy these interactions. They then need time alone to recharge their energy and replenish their inner resources.

Self-reliant and private

Fives are autonomous and independent to an extreme, and they place a high value on their personal privacy. There is, however, a wide variation among Fives in what they consider private information.

FAMOUS FIVES

Bill Gates	"I really had a lot of dreams when I was a kid, and I think a great deal of that grew out of the fact that I had a chance to read a lot."
	"I like my job because it involves learning. I like being around smart people who are trying to figure out new things."
Laura Bush	"When I was in my 20s, I was a bookworm—spent 12 hours of the day in the library. How I met George, I'll never know."
	"The power of a book lies in its power to turn a solitary act into a shared vision. As long as we have books, we are not alone."
Prince Charles	"What I want to know is: What is actually wrong with an elite?"
	"I just come and talk to the plants, really—very important to talk to them. They respond, I find."

Subtypes: Three Variations of Five

All Fives have an intense need to acquire knowledge and wisdom and a similarly strong desire to avoid intrusion and loss of energy, and they guard and preserve everything that they think they will need— for example, information, physical space, emotional privacy, personal energy, and resources. There are three distinct ways in which Fives manifest these characteristics, called subtypes.

Self-Preservation Subtype Fives are primarily concerned with being intruded upon and being overextended physically and energetically. In a sense, they hoard their involvement with others in the same way they guard their scarce resources.

Social Subtype Fives want to find and develop strong connections with individuals who share their super-ideals, but they become disengaged when forced to live in a way that is not aligned with these higher-order beliefs. They focus on the group in search of extraordinary individuals, then hoard these relationships and/or their shared ideas and, in the Five's view, superior values.

One-to-One Subtype Fives search for a strong, deep connection with one other person whom they can trust and share confidences with, then hoard themselves, the other person, and these special relationships.

Wings and Arrow Lines for Fives

Because Fives seek knowledge and wisdom, they can have limited emotional expression, resist work that does not give them a high degree of autonomy, strongly prefer low visibility within organizations, and take a long time to act, needing first to gather and analyze an abundance of information. Access to their wings (styles Four and Six) and arrows (styles Seven and Nine) can counterbalance these qualities in Fives.

Wings for Fives

FOUR WING   Fives with a Four wing are more emotionally sensitive and expressive and also have an aesthetic perspective, perhaps engaging in the arts themselves—for example, writing poetry, novels, or screenplays and/or being photographers or artists.

SIX WING   Fives with a Six wing emphasize and engage more readily with teams, tend to place greater value on loyalty, and may have enhanced intuitive insight. Although many other Fives can also be quite insightful, their insights come more from putting facts together and engaging in extensive analysis. When Fives have a Six wing, the insights come more quickly as the product of instantaneous processing.

Arrow Lines for Fives

ARROW LINE TO SEVEN   Fives with strong access to arrow line Seven can be playful and spontaneous, far more comfortable being in highly visible roles (as if they are actors playing a particular part) and more highly engaged during social interactions.

ARROW LINE FROM EIGHT   Fives with strong access to arrow line Eight display more depth of personal power, are less hesitant and more risk-taking and courageous, and move to action far more quickly.

Three Typing Questions for Fives

1. When a situation gets emotional, intense, or overwhelming, do you automatically disconnect from your feelings of the moment and then reconnect with some of these later, at a time and place of your choice?

2. Do you observe life rather than being fully engaged in it?
3. Do you create an invisible boundary between yourself and others so that other people understand they should not approach you unless invited to do so?

HOW TO COACH FIVES

Areas of Strength	Areas for Development
• Analytic	• Highly private
• Objective	• Detached
• Systematic	• Overly autonomous
• Expert	• Underemphasize relationships

COACHING OVERVIEW

Unless Fives have done a great deal of self-development work prior to coaching, they typically discuss highly sensitive coaching issues in a dispassionate way. This is particularly true when Fives are having a prolonged emotional conversation with the developer, discussing issues that are important to them, or feeling anxious about negative feedback they have received. This creates a challenge for developers, who need to help Fives learn to express their feelings while making sure they do not feel pressured to do so. Fives share their emotions sparingly, and they primarily do so only when they completely trust the other person—and it can take years to earn a Five's trust. In fact, most Fives resist any demands that they be more forthcoming.

To bypass this dilemma, developers can do the following when Fives appear to have no particular feeling about something. First, ask Fives what they think. Although many Fives balk at being asked what they feel, they will often answer questions about their thoughts by offering a statement that involves how they are feeling. Should Five learners say they don't have any feelings about the subject, developers can ask, using subtle humor: "Well, if you did have a feeling, what might that be?"

In addition, Fives compartmentalize the information they receive during coaching meetings. In effect, they hear one piece of data, place it in a category in their minds, and then move on to another piece of data without necessarily seeing the connection between the two pieces of information. The developer can help Five learners make these linkages by asking a simple question such as "Do you see the connection between this information and the earlier data?" or by making a statement that shows the direct relationship between the two sets of data. For example, the developer can say, "The reason people perceive your behavior in this way has to do with what we discussed in the earlier feedback. Do you understand the connection?"

First, Determine Coaching Goals and Learner Motivation
Goal Identification: What to Ask Fives

Because Fives do not like to be asked questions about their feelings unless they are very familiar with the developer, the developer can ask these simple questions at the beginning of the coaching relationship:

- *What do you think are the most important goals for the coaching?*
- *What makes each of these important?*

When discussing the Five learner's goals, developers should help the Five clearly connect the key development motivators listed below to specific coaching goals. This link may be obvious to learners as they discuss why each coaching goal is important, but if it is not, developers can do one of two things: (1) Ask Five learners, *"What personal and professional benefits will you gain when you achieve this goal?"* or (2) explain the connection between the goal and the motivator directly by saying, *"This will help you know how to interact with others with more comfort and predictability. Is that important to you?"*

Key Development Motivators for Fives
- To truly know themselves better using a systematic framework
- To better understand and anticipate the feelings of others
- To feel more comfortable and have more predictability when interacting with others
- To be better acknowledged in the organization for their talents and skills

Second, Assess the Learner's Level and Range of Self-Mastery, Then Use Level-Appropriate Coaching Approaches

The best way to determine the self-mastery level of the learner is to read the behavioral descriptions for all three levels in the chart on pages 127–128 and answer these questions:

1. What is this person's normal (average) level of self-mastery?
   ☐ Low ☐ Moderate ☐ High
2. What do I know and what have I observed that leads me to this conclusion?
3. What is this person's range of self-mastery—that is, the individual's highest and lowest levels?
4. What do I know from my own observations or other data that leads me to this conclusion?

Fives: Self-Mastery Levels and Coaching Approaches to Enhance Development

High Self-Mastery · The Integrated Wizard

Core understanding

True wisdom involves an integration of thoughts, feelings, and action and comes from direct experience.

When Fives have done the personal work of learning to fully experience their feelings in the moment and to completely engage in life rather than observing it from afar, they become lively, spontaneous, joyful, and imaginative. Their wisdom comes from the full integration of the head, heart, and body. These Fives have moved beyond a primarily cerebral way of existence into a state of contagious zest for ideas, feelings, and experiences.

Coaching approaches to enhance the Five's self-mastery

Provide encouragement and additional methods for expansion.

- Provide positive reinforcement every time Fives demonstrate personal sharing and full-hearted behavior; help them understand how they did this so they can recognize and repeat the behavior.
- Acknowledge and affirm them when they extend themselves to you or others in terms of time, information, and intellectual or emotional support.
- Encourage them to be fully integrated and real with you—head, heart, and body. This means sharing their ideas, expressing their true feelings, and being personally powerful and action oriented.
- Encourage Fives to be spontaneous. For example, suggest they take an improvisational acting or comedy class or go to a carnival with some friends and just be silly.
- Remember that your small gestures mean a lot to Fives—for example, a smile, being available when they need you, or a short statement that is entirely truthful without being harsh.

Moderate Self-Mastery · The Remote Expert

Core concern

Conserving inner resources and energy, maintaining privacy, and accumulating knowledge in order to feel competent

At the midlevel of self-mastery, Fives appear remote and private, guarding their time, energy, and autonomy and disliking surprises. They avoid situations in which they are likely to be the center of attention, as well as circumstances that require them to reveal personal information. Detached from their feelings of the moment, they are able to reconnect with their emotions later, when they are alone and feel comfortable. Hungering for knowledge about anything that interests them, these Fives keep their needs to a minimum and tend to be guarded and controlled, although they can be highly spontaneous with the few people they trust.

Coaching approaches to enhance the Five's self-mastery

Stimulate motivation and provide concrete development actions.

- Respect the Five's boundaries for space, time, and personal sharing, but gently push against these boundaries—through feedback, humor, or stories—to help Fives grow.

- Be aware that a trusting relationship with you and the Five builds over time; suggest ways Fives can increase their capacity to trust, and use your relationship to model how to do this.
- When giving them feedback, allow time for Fives to digest the data from one issue before you move on to another topic, including giving Fives time alone for processing if they desire.
- Provide positive reinforcement when they move beyond their comfort zones, particularly in the area of expressing emotions or sharing previously private information.
- Phrase requests as questions rather than demands; otherwise, Fives may withdraw.

Low Self-Mastery · **The Fearful Strategist**

Core fear
Being helpless, incapable, depleted, and overtaken

At the lowest level of self-mastery, Fives become frightened, withdrawn, and isolated. Hostile and haunted, they come to believe that others are planning to do them harm; as a consequence, they will plot and scheme to harm others as a way of circumventing what they imagine will be done to them. Secretive and implosive, they remove themselves from interaction with others and have extremely limited access to their feelings. Their minds become so overactive that their mental processes seem out of control, even to them.

Coaching approaches to enhance the Five's self-mastery
Offer support, guidance, and boundaries.

- Help Fives communicate regularly in a way that respects their boundaries for privacy and time but prevents them from withdrawing completely—for example, suggest a schedule of times when they can contact you for brief conversations, or create a two-minute period during meetings in which they talk about feelings.
- Reinforce the value of their strengths in analysis and objectivity as these relate to the quality of the Five's interactions with the boss, team, and customers.
- When Fives begin strategizing about how to defeat their foes, help them to recognize the potentially damaging effects of this and to consider more positive approaches.
- Model the sharing of moderate amounts of personal information; ask the Five to reciprocate.
- Invite conversations about what Fives are thinking and feeling without making demands that they do so.

Once you have an initial assessment of the Five learner's self-mastery level, read the recommended approaches appropriate to that level and select those you believe will be most effective for the learner.

Third, Use Coaching Techniques That Challenge Growth
As you read the following four coaching techniques, it can be helpful to think about several Fives you know and how you might use the techniques with those individuals. Although all Fives have striking similarities, they are also

very different based on factors such as self-mastery level, empathy, use of wings and arrows, subtype, experience, age, gender, and culture.

Head Center Challenge: The "What if?" Question

"What if?" challenges work well in situations in which the learner makes assumptions that something is important and inviolate—that is, a mental model. These assumptions are part of the learner's unchallenged beliefs and paradigms. After hearing the Five learner express an explicit or implicit assumption, the developer poses a relevant "What if?" question to the Five. Although Fives typically have a large number of beliefs and assumptions that they hold strongly and may initially balk at having these challenged, many also appreciate being asked to examine their thoughts from a different perspective.

The chart below lists three common mental models for Fives, the question the developer should ask to challenge each assumption, and the ways in which the developer should respond once the Five has answered the developer's challenge.

"What if?" Challenges for Fives

Common Assumption No. 1

"Logic is the only thing you can trust."

Developer's challenge

"What if you could trust something in addition to logic?"

Developer's follow-on response

- If the Five says, "Nothing," answer: *"Nothing?"* If no concrete answer is offered, ask: *"Is there anything in addition to logic that can be trusted, at least some of the time?"*
- When the Five names something, ask: *"And what would be the benefit to you of doing that?"* After the answer, ask: *"How would you learn to trust that as well as logic?"*

Common Assumption No. 2

"Emotions have no real relevance to the workplace."

Developer's challenge

"What if emotions—yours and others'—did have a big impact on the workplace?"

Developer's follow-on response

- If the Five cannot think of such a situation, tell a relevant compelling story, then ask: *"Have you ever seen or experienced something similar?"*
- When the Five articulates a situation in which emotions did matter in the workplace, ask questions to elicit more depth and insight.

Common Assumption No. 3

"You can't really count on other people to do anything except what serves their interests."

Developer's challenge

"What if you could count on people for reasons other than self-interest?"

Developer's follow-on response

- If the Five can't think of such a scenario, ask: *"When have you done something that impacted others and that was not done primarily from your own self-interest?"*
- When the Five gives a concrete and positive response, ask: *"How important are these things to you?"* Follow the answer with this: *"Let's talk about the ways you may not show this is important to you and about how you can let others know you want to be able to count on them."*

Heart Center Challenge: Explore the Learner's Defense Mechanism
The Five's Primary Defense Mechanism: Isolation

Isolation occurs in Fives as a way for them to avoid feeling overwhelmed and empty. Fives isolate themselves by retreating into their minds, cutting themselves off from their feelings, and compartmentalizing—that is, isolating each part of themselves from the whole or the related parts. For example, Fives separate their thoughts from their feelings and/or feelings from behaviors, as well as separating their personal and work lives. Fives may also isolate themselves from other people and separate their relationships so that their friends never meet one another; in fact, some Fives even have secret lives.

Fives demonstrate subtle and blatant forms of isolation on a regular basis, but it is best to wait until a clear case of isolation occurs in the context of the coaching so that the example is concrete rather than abstract. This is especially important because abstraction is another form of overintellectualization for the Five. Examples of a Five's isolation include the following: responding to either very negative or highly positive coaching data in a totally impassive manner; being neutral or emotionally vacant about something that would normally upset someone; refusing to discuss topics that they admit to having some feelings about; and seeming far more remote or removed than normal. These examples are actually symptoms or manifestations of isolation that often hide or defend against the following deeper developmental issues for Fives:

- Learning to engage emotionally in real time rather than automatically disengaging from their emotional responses
- Being willing to share more of themselves—including their thoughts, feelings, and personal experiences—with others

ISOLATION

Another person wants to discuss an important issue with a Five, and the issue involves emotional content. Instead of engaging in a discussion that requires her to feel anything, the Five becomes entirely intellectual, disconnecting from the feelings to such a degree that she is not only unaware of having any feelings but also experiences no real empathy for the other person. In other words, the Five completely cuts off from the other person, but more important, completely cuts off from herself.

- Becoming a central part of events, interpersonal interactions, and organizations rather than staying on the periphery

To work with the Five's defense mechanism of isolation, developers can use either an indirect or a direct challenge. It is often better to start with the indirect challenge, because it elicits more responsiveness and less resistance, but if the Five learner appears receptive or you have an excellent relationship with this person, a direct challenge may have a bigger impact.

INDIRECT CHALLENGE TO ISOLATION

"You've told me what you think about this, but it's not clear how you feel. Sometimes you separate thinking and feeling, but they are in fact interconnected. Let's talk more about what you think, about how you feel, and also about your behavior, looking at why these three things are really inseparable."

DIRECT CHALLENGE TO ISOLATION

"You're separating things that are connected and isolating yourself as a result. Just now, you've described how you isolate or separate yourself from other people by not going to meetings and not expending the effort to develop networks at work. What causes you to do this?"

Body Center Challenge: The "Why would you want to do that?" Question

When Five learners say they want to change something about themselves, asking them this question works effectively as a way of supportively challenging their desires. As a response to this technique, the Five learner either changes his or her course of action or becomes more deeply committed to the original plan. This technique is especially useful in two situations: (1) The

"Why would you want to do that?" Challenges for Fives

A Five's Productive Intention to Act

"I'm going to be more expressive with my coworkers."

Developer's challenge

"Why would you want to be more expressive?"

Developer's follow-on response

- If the Five cannot think of an answer or gives an unconvincing answer, say: *"It doesn't sound like you really want to do this."* Then wait for the response.
- When the Five gives a convincing response, say: *"It sounds like this matters to you. Please tell me more about this and your current thinking about how to do it."*

A Five's Counterproductive Intention to Act

"I don't plan to do anything about my poor relationship with a teammate."

Developer's challenge

"Why would you want to do nothing about this relationship?"

Developer's follow-on response

- If the Five gives you a reason that also makes sense to you, say: *"That sounds like a good decision for you."*
- If the Five gives you a reason you believe is possibly unwise, say: *"You may believe this is a wise thing to do, but before you proceed, let's talk about the possible negative impact before you put this into action and later regret the consequences."*

Five learner articulates an intention to take action that sounds productive, or (2) the Five learner expresses an intention to take action that might be risky or could be counterproductive to his or her best interests.

When working with Five learners, developers also need to pay attention to any unproductive inaction that Five learners may exhibit and to then use the "Why would you want to do that?" question. For example, a Five learner told her mentor that while she wanted a higher position in her department, she was reluctant to mention this to her manager. Her mentor said, "Why wouldn't you want to mention that to your manager?"

Transformative Paradoxical Challenges

Fives like paradoxical challenges, because these inherently contradictory dilemmas stimulate their thinking and provide them with a complex and insightful understanding of their situation. Although it is best to use the paradoxical challenge after Five learners have realized that they may be their own greatest obstacle, most Fives also respond well when developers pose the paradox based on the developer's observations of the Five's past behavior.

After the developer states the paradox, it is particularly important to allow the Five time to think about it in silence. Fives will ask questions if they have any, but they often find paradoxes to be intellectually challenging and will therefore try to resolve them internally. However, developers need to make certain that Five learners share their insights with the developer, who can then add more information, ask questions, or provide additional insights as relevant.

THE FIVE PARADOX

Justin, a health-care manager, looked downtrodden when he met with his mentor, Victor. He explained: "I just got passed over for a promotion. How could they pick Evan over me? I've been here longer and surpass him in every way—intellect, experience, skills, and most of all, integrity. He's a real rat and would sell his own mother down the river if it would do him some good."

Victor asked, "So what explanation did they give you?"

Justin answered, "They gave me some story about how Evan knows more people in the organization, particularly the vice presidents. When they invoke the vice presidents, you know this had to be a political decision."

Paradox Explanation

Fives want to experience life fully and to genuinely connect with other people; however, their stance of observing life from afar and their disconnection from their own feelings prevent them from fully engaging in life and developing deep connections with others.

Developer's Paradox Statement

"Organizational politics can be tough and ugly at times, yet politics play a key role in many organizational decisions. Politics can also be thought of as a series of reciprocal relationships through which people influence one another. Let's examine your organizational relationships, where you fit into the influence network, and what in your behavior has hindered you from developing the relationships you need in order to be considered for promotion."

NOTE Use the paradoxical challenge only with moderate to high self-mastery Fives; low self-mastery individuals may not be psychologically stable enough to handle the ambiguity inherent in paradoxes.

FIVE COACHING CASE STUDY SUMMARY: AMANDA

Determine Coaching Goals and Learner Motivation

Make sure the goals can be accomplished in the time available and are linked to one or more of the learner's key motivators.

> Amanda wants to perceive the emotional responses of her employees more accurately. When asked why this matters to her, she states, "As a manager, I have to understand emotions more effectively, and I know I don't do this very well." When asked why this is important to her as a person (not just in her leadership role), Amanda could not think of an answer.

Assess the Learner's Level and Range of Self-Mastery, Then Use Level-Appropriate Coaching Approaches

Determine the learner's normal (average) level and range of self-mastery.

> Amanda is normally at the midpoint of moderate self-mastery, and although she rarely responds much lower than this, she can also have responses that are almost at the high self-mastery level. She is warm to those she likes and trusts at work, but more often she is remote. During coaching sessions, Amanda can give emotional responses, but only when she has strong feelings; otherwise, she must be asked about her emotions multiple times before she can answer.

Select the development approach(es) from the chart on pages 127–128 that would be most effective with the learner, and experiment with these.

> Amanda responds best to humor in coaching, particularly irony. Although she is extroverted and talkative, she does need time alone to reflect, particularly after she has been given an important piece of feedback to consider or when she has had a significant insight. Use more positive reinforcement when she expresses feelings, but this should initially be done in small doses, because Amanda becomes easily embarrassed when receiving positive feedback and needs to become more comfortable in this area.

Use Coaching Techniques That Challenge Growth

Plan how you will use each of the four coaching techniques from this section, and use them at appropriate moments during the coaching process.

Head Center Challenge: "What if?"

What have you heard the learner say or imply that reflects a mental model or assumption you can challenge? How will you phrase this "What if?" challenge?

All of the following challenges would be effective with Amanda.

"What if learning to understand others' feelings had a personal benefit for you beyond your managerial role?"

"What if you could learn to understand and anticipate your own feelings better?"

"What if you are much better at reading other people's feelings than you think you are?"

Heart Center Challenge: Recognizing and Leveraging Defense Mechanisms

When have you observed the learner use a particular defense mechanism? Would a direct or an indirect challenge be more effective? How would you phrase this defense mechanism challenge?

> Amanda knows and is respected by many people in the organization, has a strong marriage, and is so talkative that she does not feel particularly isolated. Her use of isolation is most obvious in her separation of thinking from feeling. Because she is very stable and outgoing, and she and her coach have a strong relationship, either a direct or an indirect challenge will be effective.
>
> ### INDIRECT CHALLENGE
> *"Can you tell me about times in your life when you have had thoughts and feelings simultaneously?"*
>
> ### DIRECT CHALLENGE
> *"You separate or isolate your feelings from your thoughts, but you actually have both at the same time. You need to practice experiencing and acknowledging them simultaneously."*

Body Center Challenge: "Why would you want to do that?"

What behavior has the learner stated he or she plans to do? Do you think this is a wise course of action? How would you phrase this "Why would you want to do that?" challenge?

> *"Why would you want to understand and anticipate the emotional reactions of people who work for you?"*

Transformative Paradoxical Challenge

What paradoxes have you observed in the learner? Select the most significant one. How would you phrase this paradoxical challenge?

> *"You say you want to be more relational with people, particularly those who work for you, yet in many ways you are not fully relational with yourself—for example, in not knowing how you feel and not being willing to share your emotional responses with others. How can you relate to others better without starting with yourself first?"*

NOTE Paradoxical challenges should be used only with moderate or high self-mastery learners. Low self-mastery learners are not in a psychological state to handle the complexity and ambiguity inherent in the resolution of this level of paradox, and deep-level or complex paradoxes can increase their anxiety. While less powerful paradoxes can be used with these learners, developers should do so with caution.

DEVELOPMENT ACTIVITIES FOR FIVES

Developers can suggest the following activities to Five learners.

Core Issue: Connect with and express your feelings.

For three days, once every waking hour, ask yourself this question: *What am I feeling right now?* Don't settle for a one-word answer. Then ask yourself this: *And what else am I feeling?* After three days, continue asking yourself both questions, but do so at those times when you are aware that you are becoming extremely analytical. Continue the above process for six months.

Expansion Through Wings and Arrows
FOUR WING   Connect with others on a deep level.

Every time you observe someone you know looking happier, more concerned, or more upset than usual and you are able to have a private discussion with this person, say, "I noticed that you seem to be happy [or concerned or upset] about something." Normally, the person will tell you more. As the person is speaking, ask a few simple questions that show your interest, or share your reactions to what he or she is saying.

SIX WING   Focus on the group.

When you participate in a group, ask yourself: *How can I contribute more to this group? What is it that the group needs from me, and how can I contribute in this way? How can I demonstrate my loyalty and commitment to them?*

ARROW LINE SEVEN   Become more spontaneous.

Practice being more spontaneous with individuals you know well. Select one event or interaction each day and say to yourself: I will let my guard down and just do or say what comes to me at the time. At the end of the day, reflect on this experience and ask yourself these questions: *How did I do? Was I spontaneous? What happened because of this that was positive? Did anything negative occur as a result?* Once you feel comfortable being more spontaneous, do so in an increasingly wider circle of friends and colleagues. Continue the above activity daily until you do it naturally.

ARROW LINE EIGHT   Take up more space.

Take up more space than you do normally. That is, when you are in a meeting (or at a social gathering) and you are not the person speaking, keep breathing deeply and maintain your physical presence, giving your full attention to all conversations and interactions—just as you would if you were the speaker. This allows you to be more fully present at all times.

Communication: Communicate with more warmth.

When you communicate with others in person, on the phone, or even via e-mail, breathe into your chest as you speak or write. This will connect you with your feelings, and as a result you will come across as a warmer person.

Conflict: Say something as soon as you are aware of feeling upset.

Make a commitment to take the initiative and share your concerns, even small ones, soon after they arise. Rather than considering this an intrusion, other people are likely to appreciate knowing what you think and feel. The biggest issue is for you to actually say something, since this means you need to acknowledge that something bothers you and to stay connected to your feelings.

Teams: Increase your capacity to engage rather than to withdraw.

When you attend a social gathering, force yourself to stand or sit right in the middle of where people are interacting. When you do this, look at other people and smile, which will encourage them to approach you. When someone approaches you, engage the person in an interaction by asking a question or offering some information about yourself.

Leadership: Honor your leadership gift of objectivity and enhance your capacity to be a fully integrated leader.

Examine the ways you could use your leadership gift even more without over-using it, while developing your capacity to feel, communicate, and empathize with a variety of emotions. When you do these things, you can trust yourself to take wise action more quickly.

EIGHT

Coaching
Enneagram Style Six

Sixes have insightful minds, are prone to worry, and create anticipatory or worst-case scenarios to help themselves feel prepared in case something goes wrong.

Some Sixes are more overtly fearful (phobic) while others move toward the fear as a way to prove they have no fear (counterphobic); most Sixes do some of both.

Center of Intelligence · Head Center

HOW TO IDENTIFY SIXES

Thinking   Feeling

CORE BELIEFS

- *Hope for the best, but plan for the worst.*
- *Authority figures are supposed to take care of everything, but they cannot be trusted to do so.*
- *Dutiful and loyal people like me can be counted on, and this may prevent negative things from occurring.*

EMOTIONAL PATTERNS

- *Anxiety, doubt, and vexation*
- *Overt displays of courage and risk taking*

Behaving

WORKPLACE BEHAVIORS

*See selves as problem solvers • Seek and create like-minded and loyal teams •
Worry and procrastinate • Project own feelings, thoughts, and behaviors onto others •
Respond with skepticism*

The "Doubting Mind"

The Six's mind is called the doubting mind. When considering what to do, how to solve a problem, and what decisions to make, Sixes immediately conjecture: *What if this happened? What if that doesn't work?* and more. Needing to consider what could go wrong before they commit to a course of action, Sixes automatically explore these possibilities in an effort to do anticipatory, preventive planning.

Emotional Patterns of Sixes
Anxiety, doubt, and vexation

Most Sixes are familiar with feelings of fear ranging from mild but chronic anxiety and overall wariness to extreme fear, such as panic or terror. An emotionally reactive style, Sixes experience these feelings instantaneously, then replay them in their minds and hearts, which recreates and intensifies the original anxiety. This vexation—the continuous replaying of concerns—fuels the Six's self-doubt, doubt concerning the intentions and behaviors of others, and doubt about what might occur in the Six's environment. Vexation helps Sixes feel prepared in case something goes wrong, yet it also aggravates their feelings of fear and doubt. This cycle is most obvious in phobic or overtly fearful Sixes, but it also occurs—although less frequently—among counterphobic Sixes, who deal with their fear and doubt by going headlong into fearful situations as a way to prove they are not afraid.

Overt displays of courage and risk taking

Most Sixes exhibit overt displays of courage or risk taking as a way to prove to themselves and others that they are not afraid. These displays of nerve can be verbal—for example, confronting their managers in public—as well as physical, such as skydiving or bungee-jumping. When the physical risk taking is extreme in nature, Sixes tend to do these activities only once, as a one-time badge or proof of courage. With less extreme activities, such as race-car driving or black diamond skiing, Sixes may do these multiple times to experience the adrenaline rush of fear mixed with excitement. All of the behaviors described above are driven by the emotion of fear, which propels Sixes forward to take such actions. Counterphobic Sixes tend to exhibit this risk-taking behavior on a more regular basis than phobic Sixes, but almost all Sixes engage in some version of this risk-defying behavior at certain times.

Workplace Behaviors of Sixes
See selves as problem solvers

Because Sixes anticipate problems and develop ways to prevent problems before these occur if possible, they have highly developed environmental scanning antennae that move very rapidly. Although some solutions come to them instantaneously, other problems—usually those that are more complex or have no obvious optimal solution—take them longer to consider and resolve.

Seek and create like-minded and loyal teams

Sixes like to bring groups together who share a common purpose, can provide support to one another as kindred spirits, and will meet their commitments with sincerity and loyalty. These kinds of teams make Sixes feel more certain, because they believe there is more safety and protection with others who think in a similar fashion. Their loyalty to other people, teams, and organizations also helps Sixes feel more assured that less harm will come to them. Although highly counterphobic Sixes also value like-minded and loyal teams and may even be instrumental in creating them, they are more likely to observe these teams from the periphery rather than being fully engaged with them.

Worry and procrastinate

While Sixes are pleased when things go well, they worry intensely when this is not the case and procrastinate when they are not sure what to do.

Project own feelings, thoughts, and behaviors onto others

Sixes unconsciously project their thoughts, feelings, hopes, fears, motivations, and behaviors onto others, imagining that what is actually true about themselves is instead true of someone else. Sixes often assume they are correct without clarifying the accuracy of these projections. The projections may be positive, neutral, or negative in nature.

FAMOUS SIXES

Richard Branson (counterphobic Six)	"My interest in life comes from setting myself huge, apparently unachievable challenges and trying to rise above them."
	"As an adventurer ... I try to protect against the downside. I make sure I have covered as many eventualities as I can. In the end, you have to take calculated risks; otherwise, you're going to sit in mothballs all day and do nothing."
George H.W. Bush (phobic Six with some counterphobia)	"I have opinions of my own, strong opinions, but I don't always agree with them."
	"It's no exaggeration to say that the undecideds could go one way or another."
Woody Allen (phobic Six)	"It seemed the world was divided into good and bad people. The good ones slept better ... while the bad ones seemed to enjoy the waking hours much more."
	"Confidence is what you have before you understand the problem."

Respond with skepticism

Sixes are highly skeptical of those who act as if complex problems have simple solutions, and they challenge ideas and people when they feel concerned. For example, Sixes ask "What if?" questions when they believe a solution has been reached without a full consideration of the risks and potential obstacles involved. Similarly, Sixes will publicly and privately challenge leaders whom they believe are using their authority unjustly or unfairly, often perceiving leaders as either good or bad, with few variations in between.

Subtypes: Three Variations of Six

All Sixes seek support and certainty, hoping that the best is possible, yet simultaneously fearing that this will not happen, and they doubt that others are trustworthy and/or that they themselves are capable of meeting the challenges involved. There are three distinct ways in which Sixes manifest these characteristics, called subtypes.

Self-Preservation Subtype Sixes manifest fear as an intense need to feel protected from danger, often seeking the family or a surrogate family to provide this. Self-preservation Sixes also use warmth and friendliness as a way to attract and maintain these types of support groups for the purpose of making themselves feel safe.

Social Subtype Sixes deal with fear by focusing on the rules, regulations, and prescribed ways of behaving within their social environment and organization in an attempt to keep their own behavior in the acceptable range, trying to make sure they do nothing that will cause authority figures to chastise or punish them for going astray.

One-to-One Subtype Sixes are generally the most counterphobic. They express their fear primarily through the denial of their anxieties and vulnerabilities by pushing against the fear, appearing bold, confident, and sometimes fierce. They can also engage in physical or verbal behavior that makes them feel and appear highly courageous.

Wings and Arrow Lines for Sixes

Because Sixes seek meaning, certainty, and trust and try to prevent negative scenarios from occurring, they can be quite reactive when they feel fearful or anxious. They either spiral into distrust and doubt (phobic Sixes) or engage in high-risk actions to prove they are not afraid (counterphobic Sixes). Access to their wings (styles Five and Seven) and arrows (styles Three and Nine) can counterbalance these qualities in Sixes.

Wings for Sixes

FIVE WING   When Sixes have a Five wing, they are more internally than externally focused and are also more self-contained and restrained, thus tempering their tendency to be reactive. In addition, they have an increased passion for knowledge and use the pursuit of knowledge not only to gather information in order to feel prepared, but also for the pure enjoyment of learning.

SEVEN WING   It is sometimes said that Sixes see the glass as half empty and Sevens see it as half full. Thus, when Sixes have a Seven wing, they see the whole glass and therefore tend to be more cheerful, less worried, more optimistic, and more energetic.

Arrow Lines for Sixes

ARROW LINE TO THREE   Sixes with access to Three can bypass their uncertainty by focusing on concrete goals and approaching their work with palpable confidence.

ARROW LINE FROM NINE   Sixes use their connection to Nine to relax, something very helpful to the normally tightly wired Sixes. For example, taking time to walk or enjoy nature fills Sixes with a feeling of safety and calmness. They are more appreciative of different viewpoints and perspectives, a quality that can be invaluable in times of duress when Sixes start projecting and imagining their perspective is the only viable one.

Three Typing Questions for Sixes

1. Do you constantly anticipate multiple scenarios, thinking about what could go wrong and trying to plan so that this will not occur?
2. Do you have strong positive or negative reactions to authority figures and challenge them when you are concerned?
3. Do you project your thoughts and feelings onto others, having difficulty discerning whether something is really occurring or whether you are creating it in your mind?

HOW TO COACH SIXES

Areas of Strength	Areas for Development	
• Loyal	• Worrying	
• Collaborative	• Dislike ambiguity	
• Persevering	• "Analysis paralysis"	
• Anticipate problems	• Martyring	

COACHING OVERVIEW

Sixes often become anxious about various aspects of coaching, worrying before, during, and after each coaching meeting. They become especially anxious when they are about to receive feedback, whether from the developer, from data feedback from interviews, or from a 360° feedback process. They may also worry about whether they are worrying too much or too little, or worrying about the right things. Developers should not be concerned about this, because Six learners engage in this type of anticipatory scenario planning in most areas of their lives. At the same time, developers can help assuage these concerns by maintaining a calm, warm, and consistent demeanor and make reassuring comments at various times during coaching meetings. This enables Six learners to focus more on what is really being said than on what they think *might* be occurring. Statements like the following can be helpful: "You may feel apprehensive about the information we're discussing. Let me assure you that you have all the ability you need to work with anything negative, and that there is a great deal that is positive as well." Similarly, developers can suggest, "Any time you have any concerns whatsoever, please bring them up and I'll help you with them."

In addition, developers need to be watchful for the Six's tendency to project his or her own thoughts, feelings, motivations, and fears onto people and situations, including the developer and the coaching process. Although these projections can be either positive—for example, the Six believing that the developer is incredibly wise and that the coaching is going to be the most beneficial development experience of his or her career—or negative, the thoughts these projections contain may not be based on a full understanding of the situation. Most Sixes do not realize they are projecting or that their projections might not be entirely accurate, and developers can effectively help them differentiate between an accurate insight, a projection, and a perception that contains elements of both.

First, Determine Coaching Goals and Learner Motivation
Goal Identification: What to Ask Sixes

Sixes generally like to discuss their coaching goals, recognizing that doing so provides them and the developer with a common direction. Developers should expect that these initial goal conversations will likely be somewhat lengthier than is the case with most other Enneagram styles, because Six learners often think out loud and express themselves with a great deal of complexity. This is partly a result of the fact that Sixes may have considered many possible goals and scenarios prior to the coaching discussion and may be uncertain which goal or goals are the most important. In addition, Sixes may use this initial coaching conversation to calibrate the degree to which they can trust the developer, and the prolonged goal conversation may be a way to assess the developer. Further, because Sixes are prone to self-doubt and often second-guess themselves, they may agree to certain goals but revisit and revise these multiple times during the first few coaching meetings. The following questions can help Six learners gain greater clarity about their coaching goals:

- *What are your hopes, dreams, and goals for the coaching that would make you feel your time was extremely well spent?*
- *What makes each of these important?*
- *Can you prioritize your goals, telling me why you've put them in this order?*

When discussing the Six learner's goals, developers should help the Six clearly connect the key development motivators below to specific coaching goals. This link may be obvious to learners as they discuss why each coaching goal is important, but if it is not, developers can do one of two things: (1) Ask Six learners, *"What personal and professional benefits will you gain when you achieve this goal?"* or (2) explain the connection between the goal and the motivator directly by saying, *"This will help you feel less anxious and trust yourself more."*

Key Development Motivators for Sixes
- To feel more secure, certain, and confident
- To be less reactive and more in control of themselves
- To be able to truly trust themselves and others to make good decisions and take care of situations
- To not have to hide their anxieties, which includes not feeling anxious so frequently, thus having less of a need to hide their reactions

Second, Assess the Learner's Level and Range of Self-Mastery, Then Use Level-Appropriate Coaching Approaches

The best way to determine the self-mastery level of the learner is to read the behavioral descriptions for all three levels in the chart on pages 146–147 and answer these questions:

1. What is this person's normal (average) level of self-mastery?
   □ Low □ Moderate □ High
2. What do I know and what have I observed that leads me to this conclusion?
3. What is this person's range of self-mastery—that is, the individual's highest and lowest levels?
4. What do I know from my own observations or other data that leads me to this conclusion?

Sixes: Self-Mastery Levels and Coaching Approaches to Enhance Development

High Self-Mastery · The Courageous One

Core understanding

Meaning and support exist both inside and outside themselves.

Intellectual and insightful, Sixes with high self-mastery have learned to trust their own inner authority rather than look to other people to keep them safe. As a result, they are confident, calm, and resilient, and they connect with others in a deep, steady, and warmhearted way. Because they have learned to trust their own inner authority, Sixes with extreme self-mastery are clear and courageous. They know that they can look after themselves and that there is little in the world from which they truly need to be protected.

Coaching approaches to enhance the Six's self-mastery

Provide encouragement and additional methods for expansion.

- Provide positive reinforcement for the Sixes' real courage—not counterphobic behavior—as well as their strengths and insights.
- Directly acknowledge and affirm them when they are willing to trust themselves and others and are able to sustain that trust.
- Notice and acknowledge their hard work, diligence, and analytic ability, in addition to their lightheartedness and humor.
- Suggest ways they can use greater awareness of their physical sensations as a way to avoid constantly being in a thinking and analyzing mode.
- Reinforce Sixes for honoring and trusting their own inner authority and following their own advice rather than looking to outside authority for direction.

Moderate Self-Mastery · The Loyalist

Core concern

Safety, belonging, and being able to trust

Sixes with moderate self-mastery can be insightful, clever, overly busy, endearing, and approval seeking; they can also be antiauthority, wavering, short-tempered, and reactive. Alternating between being trusting and distrusting, they can be plagued by doubts and confusion. On the one hand, these Sixes desire the safety that cohesive groups can provide; on the other, they fear groups unless these groups are characterized by a strong sense of like-mindedness. They are thus loyal to friends, groups, and leaders whom they trust, but that trust is tenuous at best and is easily broken if others do not live up to the Six's hopes and expectations.

Coaching approaches to enhance the Six's self-mastery

Stimulate motivation and provide concrete development actions.

- Encourage them to look at all the data and not give more weight to negative information or thoughts; help them understand the difference between fact and inference.
- Work on building trust between yourself and the Six, including talking about potential areas of mistrust.
- Value the positive side of the Six's habit of imagining threats, while simultaneously and gently highlighting the downside of this way of thinking.

- Help the Six differentiate between intuitions that are accurate and projections that contain inaccuracies.
- Explicitly appreciate the Six's loyalty and preparedness.

Low Self-Mastery · The Coward

Core fear
Having no support or sense of meaning and being unable to survive

Sixes with low self-mastery display an extreme amount of anxiety and frenzy as they go about trying to make their frightening worlds less dangerous. They engage in continuous worst-case scenario development and projection, imagining all the bad things that could happen to them and believing that these creations of the imagination are completely true. With a tendency toward paranoia, these Sixes can become clingingly dependent, panicky, and punitive. Looking for solace, they find little, because they reject anyone who disagrees with their worldview or dares to offer an opinion contrary to theirs.

Coaching approaches to enhance the Six's self-mastery
Offer support, guidance, and boundaries.

- Without either challenging or validating their fears directly, provide evidence of positive outcomes to counter their fears and worst-case scenarios; make sure not to create an overly positive scenario, just a realistic one.
- Encourage Sixes not to rely so heavily on repeating and reanalyzing their thoughts, and encourage them to also value contributions from their feelings and their guts.
- Provide concrete evidence to help dislodge their projections; generate alternative possible scenarios, but present these as hypotheses rather than fact-based truths.
- Be alert to any opportunities to build trust.
- Listen attentively at length, even when Sixes repeat their ideas. Be careful to not imply agreement when this is not the case, but don't directly disagree either. Err on the side of empathic listening and try to understand how the Six perceives the situation.

Once you have an initial assessment of the Six learner's self-mastery level, read the recommended approaches appropriate to that level and select those you believe will be most effective for the learner.

Third, Use Coaching Techniques That Challenge Growth

As you read the following four coaching techniques, it can be helpful to think about several Sixes you know and how you might use the techniques with those individuals. Sixes can be very different from one another depending on their degree of phobia versus counterphobia, as well as such other factors as self-mastery level, empathy, use of wings and arrows, subtype, experience, age, gender, and culture.

Head Center Challenge: The "What if?" Question

"What if?" challenges work well in situations in which the learner makes assumptions that something is important and inviolate—that is, a mental model. These assumptions are part of the learner's unchallenged beliefs and paradigms. Although Sixes frequently ask themselves and others "What if" questions, they do so to illuminate potential problems, not to challenge their mental models. However, their familiarity with "What if?" thinking makes them ready recipients for this type of challenge from developers. After hear-

"What if?" Challenges for Sixes

Common Assumption No. 1

"You have to plan for the worst."

Developer's challenge

"What if you also planned for the best?"

Developer's follow-on response

- If the Six says, "I can't," answer: *"What if you could?"* If there is still no concrete answer, ask: *"If you only plan for the worst rather than the best and all the variations in between, what will you miss?"*
- When the Six gives a concrete example, ask: *"And how else would you benefit from this?"* After the answer, ask: *"How can you apply your problem-prevention skills to your opportunity-identification skills?"*

Common Assumption No. 2

"If I can anticipate issues in advance, then I can relax."

Developer's challenge

"What if you could relax without having to anticipate every issue?"

Developer's follow-on response

- If the Six cannot think of such a scenario, tell a relevant compelling story, then say: *"You must have a similar story. Can you tell me about it?"*
- When the Six offers some great benefits or tells a real story, ask: *"How can you expand this experience into other situations?"*

Common Assumption No. 3

"I must demonstrate dutifulness and loyalty; this prevents negative things from happening."

Developer's challenge

"What if you could prevent negative occurrences without having to be constantly dutiful and loyal?"

Developer's follow-on response

- If the Six cannot think of such a scenario, ask: *"Have you ever prevented something negative from happening using other skills and qualities? What were these?"*
- When the Six gives a concrete and positive response, say: *"Good. How can you use these qualities even more, so that you are not so reliant on duty and loyalty?"*
- To take this even deeper, another "What if?" question can be asked: *"What if some negative things can't be prevented and extensive anticipatory planning actually makes them worse? Do you have examples of that?"*

ing the Six learner express an obvious or implicit assumption, the developer poses a relevant "What if?" question to the Six. The chart on page 148 lists three common mental models for Sixes, the question the developer should ask to challenge each assumption, and the ways in which the developer should respond once the Six has answered the developer's challenge.

Heart Center Challenge: Explore the Learner's Defense Mechanism
The Six's Primary Defense Mechanism: Projection

Projection is a defense mechanism in which individuals unconsciously attribute their own unacceptable, unwanted, or disowned thoughts, emotions, motivations, attributes, and/or behaviors to others. While the projection may be positive, negative, or neutral, it occurs because the individuals who are projecting perceive the projected attributes as difficult to acknowledge or threatening to believe about themselves. Because Sixes make these attributions unconsciously, they imagine that they are true, although at a deeper level they are not entirely certain about this. Although Sixes use projection as a way to create some certainty and thus reduce their anxiety in ambiguous, uncertain, or potentially dangerous situations, these projections—particularly if they are negative in nature—ironically raise the Six's anxiety level. In addition, when Sixes project something negative or positive that is untrue, they create a false reality without knowing they are doing so.

Although Sixes project on an ongoing basis, they project most often and most intensely when they are anxious. The more anxiety they feel, the more difficult it becomes for Sixes to differentiate between a projection and an insight—that is, something that is true. Examples of a Six's negative projections include the following: blaming someone or something else for a failure, attributing malevolent motives to another individual, and assuming something negative is going to occur before an event takes place. Sixes also engage in positive projections that are manifestations of their hopes and desires—for example, imagining that a leader is extraordinarily benevolent or can perform Herculean feats, believing that someone they like has no flaws, and assuming

PROJECTION

A Six feels frightened by a coworker, although there is no concrete data to support this idea. The Six believes that this person wants to compete with him for a desired promotion and is planning ways to undermine the Six in order to gain the new job. The Six begins to plan and strategize how to undercut the coworker, justifying his actions by believing they are necessary in order to prevent the coworker from causing harm.

another person is highly intelligent while incorrectly criticizing their own intellect. These examples are actually symptoms or manifestations of projection that often hide or defend against the following deeper developmental issues for Sixes:

- Learning to differentiate between an insight (something that is accurate and based on clear-sighted intuition) and a projection (something based solely on imagination) rather than assuming that all their thoughts are true
- Trusting their own inner authority rather than looking to someone or something outside themselves for meaning and certainty
- Having faith in themselves and others to be able to handle whatever occurs rather than going into doubt or engaging in high-risk behavior to prove they are not afraid

To work with the Six's defense mechanism of projection, developers can use either an indirect or a direct challenge. It is often better to start with the indirect challenge, because it elicits more responsiveness and less resistance, and this is particularly true with Six learners when they are feeling anxious or highly vulnerable. At these times, Sixes can become highly reactive and engage in even more projection and/or highly counterphobic behavior, and they may direct this at the developer. However, if the learner is ready or you have an excellent relationship with the learner, a direct challenge may have a bigger impact.

INDIRECT CHALLENGE TO PROJECTION
"You've told me about this and what you believe to be the situation. Can you tell me more about how you know this is true? Then let's discuss alternative interpretations of the situation."

DIRECT CHALLENGE TO PROJECTION
"You probably know that you project your own qualities onto something else when you feel concerned or uncertain. Tell me first how what you just said may be true of you. That clarity will help us talk more realistically about what may or may not be true in this situation."

Body Center Challenge: The "Why would you want to do that?" Question

When Six learners say they want to change something about themselves, asking them this question works effectively as a way of supportively challenging their desires. As a response to this technique, the Six learner either changes his or her course of action or becomes more deeply committed to the original plan. This technique is especially useful in two situations: (1) The Six learner articulates an intention to take action that sounds productive, or (2) the Six

"Why would you want to do that?" Challenges for Sixes

A Six's Productive Intention to Act

"I want to worry less."

Developer's challenge

"Why would you want to worry less often?"

Developer's follow-on response

- If the Six cannot think of an answer or gives an unconvincing answer, say: *"It sounds like you may not want to do this."* After the Six responds, say: *"Have you considered that worrying serves a function for you that you don't want to give up?"* Then wait for the response.
- When the Six gives a convincing response, say: *"It sounds like this matters to you. Please tell me more about this and your current thinking about how to do it."*

A Six's Counterproductive Intention to Act

"I'm going to challenge my boss at our next meeting."

Developer's challenge

"Why would you want to confront your boss at that time?"

Developer's follow-on response

- If the Six gives you a reason that also makes sense to you, say: *"It sounds as though you've made a wise choice."*
- If the Six gives you a reason that is possibly unwise, say: *"You may want to do this, but before you proceed to do something that may be very risky, let's talk about the possible negative impact before you put this into action and later regret the consequences."*

learner expresses an intention to take action that might be risky or could be counterproductive to his or her best interests.

Because Sixes can be highly reactive and prone to counterphobic, high-risk behavior, the "Why would you want to do that?" challenge can be extremely useful to them, helping them consider more fully the consequences of alternative actions. At the same time, because Sixes may interpret this challenge as an accusation, developers need to make certain they deliver it in a supportive yet neutral way.

Transformative Paradoxical Challenges

Sixes like paradoxical challenges because they often think in paradoxes, although they don't always know how to resolve them. Because of this, it is especially important for developers to state the paradox as simply and clearly as possible. It is also best to use the paradoxical challenge when Six learners are in the throes of the paradoxical situation or when they are reviewing a past issue that is paradoxical and wanting the developer to help them understand it better.

After stating the paradox, it is particularly important for the developer to remain silent but alert to the ways the Six will respond to the paradox. For example, Six learners may actually exhibit the paradox in the very way they respond to it. They may immediately understand the paradox but then ask the developer questions about its meaning. Alternatively, they may challenge the developer, saying the developer is being unsupportive and critical by suggesting that the Six act paradoxically. Sixes almost always ask questions if they

THE SIX PARADOX

Anthony knew that he needed help to launch a new product for the consumer products division. He had considered asking some of his subordinates for assistance, but he wasn't certain they had the expertise. He had also contemplated requesting the services of a few employees in another department, but he concluded that he would not be able to count on their undivided attention to his work. Anthony did have some peers who had successfully launched products in the past; however, he had discounted the idea of enlisting these people, because he was worried they would either be too aggressive or would try to take the project over from him. In the end, he utilized the services of some of his subordinates, but by then the project had completely stalled.

Anxious and confused, Anthony shared his feelings with his mentor: "What can I do? I can't do it by myself, and I can't count on anyone else to help get this moving. This is such important work, and yet no one seems to care about it but me. My boss told me to get this done within six months and to find the resources to do it, but there's nothing available. I almost feel like this is a setup, but why would anyone want me to fail?"

Paradox Explanation

Sixes want to have faith in themselves and to trust other people; however, they continually second-guess themselves, project their own concerns and suspicions onto others, and then behave in guarded and accusatory ways. This causes Sixes to distrust themselves and others, and it also causes others to become suspicious and guarded with the Six in return.

Developer's Paradox Statement

"You say you want assistance, but you don't seem to trust anyone to provide it. You talk as if you also doubt your own ability to handle the situation, yet you've done so well in the past. What does it take for you to trust someone, including yourself?"

NOTE Use the paradoxical challenge only with moderate to high self-mastery Sixes; low self-mastery individuals may not be psychologically stable enough to handle the ambiguity inherent in paradoxes.

have them, but if the paradox works with them immediately and the timing is right, they will begin discussing what the paradox means in their lives and how best to resolve it.

SIX COACHING CASE STUDY SUMMARY: MARION

Determine Coaching Goals and Learner Motivation

Make sure the goals can be accomplished in the time available and are linked to one or more of the learner's key motivators.

> Marion, a well-respected journalist for a newspaper, wants to feel less anxious about deadlines, editors' comments about her work, her manager's responses to her, and more. When asked why this matters to her, she states, "I know I am an excellent journalist, but this constant agitation stresses me, disturbs my sleep, and interferes with my ability to work under pressure without making errors."

Assess the Learner's Level and Range of Self-Mastery, Then Use Level-Appropriate Coaching Approaches

Determine the learner's normal (average) level and range of self-mastery.

> Although Marion is slightly below the midpoint of moderate self-mastery most of the time, she slips into low self-mastery when she is stressed and does not perceive a clear solution to the issue she faces. She is extremely loyal, dutiful, and often insightful, except in regard to herself. In addition, she has a history of impulsive outbursts directed toward her bosses. Marion has moments of high self-mastery, and these come most often when she encounters extraordinarily difficult situations—for example, the death of a close friend. Thus, Marion has a wide range of self-mastery, which makes her unpredictable. At the same time, her high range offers her the capacity to increase her self-mastery at a rapid rate.

Select the development approach(es) from the chart on pages 146–147 that would be most effective with the learner, and experiment with these.

> Marion likes learning how to differentiate between projections and insights, because this gives her the ability to know which of her thoughts she can trust. However, she needs to fully explain her feelings and thoughts before she is willing to question the veracity of her perceptions. Continue working with her on this, affirming her each time she accurately differentiates between the two on her own. Reinforce her loyalty and preparedness, highlighting the value of these qualities. Once Marion feels sufficiently validated for her dutifulness, help her assess the liabilities and benefits involved. Encourage her to relax more and to not feel that everything she does is a test in which she must prove herself.

Use Coaching Techniques That Challenge Growth

Plan how you will use each of the four coaching techniques from this section, and use them at appropriate moments during the coaching process.

Head Center Challenge: "What if?"

What have you heard the learner say or imply that reflects a mental model or assumption you can challenge? How will you phrase this "What if?" challenge?

> All of the following challenges would be effective with Marion.
> *"What if you didn't have to worry constantly?"*
> *"What if your boss does believe in you and you can't accept this?"*
> *"What if your boss does have some issues with a specific piece of work you submit?"*

Heart Center Challenge: Recognizing and Leveraging Defense Mechanisms

When have you observed the learner use a particular defense mechanism? Would a direct or an indirect challenge be more effective? How would you phrase this defense mechanism challenge?

> Marion sometimes imagines her manager is angry with her when in fact it is she who is upset with the manager. She also imagines the developer is thinking something that he/she is not thinking. Because Marion has a wide range of self-mastery, the direct approach works best when she is at a moderate-to high-functioning self-mastery level. However, when she is distressed and functioning in the lower ranges of self-mastery, the indirect approach is better.
>
> **INDIRECT CHALLENGE**
> *"You've just said something, and I wondered if you could tell me how you know this is true?"*
>
> **DIRECT CHALLENGE**
> *"You've said you believe your boss may be angry or upset with you. While this may be true, it could actually be a projection on your part—really, your own feelings about the boss. Are you angry with your boss in any way?"*

Body Center Challenge: "Why would you want to do that?"

What behavior has the learner stated he or she plans to do? Do you think this is a wise course of action? How would you phrase this "Why would you want to do that?" challenge?

> *"Why would you want to worry less?"* followed by *"Maybe some worrying does you some good. What good do you think it does?"*

Transformative Paradoxical Challenge

What paradoxes have you observed in the learner? Select the most significant one. How would you phrase this paradoxical challenge?

> *"You say you want to worry less and trust yourself more, and I believe you. At the same time, you actually seem to use worrying and questioning yourself as something you believe enables you to trust your thoughts, feelings, and decisions more. However, it doesn't seem to have this result."*

NOTE   Paradoxical challenges should be used only with moderate or high self-mastery learners. Low self-mastery learners are not in a psychological state to handle the complexity and ambiguity inherent in the resolution of this level of paradox, and deep-level or complex paradoxes can increase their anxiety. While less powerful paradoxes can be used with these learners, developers should do so with caution.

DEVELOPMENT ACTIVITIES FOR SIXES

Developers can suggest the following activities to Six learners.

Core Issue: Differentiate between an insight and a pure projection.

Spend 15 minutes each morning making a list of your uncensored thoughts about what you believe will happen that day. At the end of the day, review your list. For each item on the list, answer these questions: *Was this an insight, a pure projection, or a mixture of the two? How can I tell the difference?* After you have practiced this activity for several weeks, the answers to the second question will give you useful information.

Expansion Through Wings and Arrows
FIVE WING   **Practice self-containment.**

It is always beneficial to have the choice of whether to be expressive or not to show precisely what you are thinking and feeling. The best way to do this is to learn to calm yourself at will. When you feel calm, you have more behavioral choices available. A simple statement that you repeat to yourself on a daily basis, breathing in while you say it, is very helpful. Select one from among these that appeals to you:

> *There is meaning and certainty in the world.*
> *I'm fine and everything will be okay.*
> *I'm able to handle whatever occurs.*
> *I can count on both myself and others.*

SEVEN WING   Give yourself permission to have fun.

Ask yourself what you do for fun. Most Sixes feel challenged in answering this question. Write down three things you really like to do, then make a firm commitment to yourself to do each of these at least once a week. Each time you do one of these things, tell yourself that it is okay to do it and that you deserve it.

ARROW LINE THREE   Focus on results.

Focus on a specific goal itself rather than focusing so strongly on how you will achieve this goal and on all the problems that could arise. Keep it simple, and ask yourself: *What is the most effective and efficient way to achieve this specific goal?* If you are unable to answer that question, you can "trick" yourself by asking this: *If it were someone other than me in this situation, what would I suggest that he or she do?* You are likely far better at giving concrete, clear, and focused advice to others than to yourself.

ARROW LINE NINE   Spend time going with the flow.

Allow yourself at least 30 minutes per day of unplanned and unstructured time alone. Be spontaneous and engage in any activity as the desire comes to you. Do something you truly want to do, solely because you would enjoy it and not because you *should* do it or because someone expects you to. If another enjoyable activity arises, go with it, engaging in it for as long as you truly want to. Continue the above process, allowing yourself to do only what you truly desire.

Communication: Focus on the positive probabilities before raising the negative possibilities.

When you communicate with others, start with what you most want to occur, discuss its value and how to best make this happen, then outline obstacles that might arise and present ways to overcome these. Although you would normally start with what might go wrong, it is important that you share your desires first, then raise the possible problem areas.

Conflict: When distressed, take a walk and calm your mind and emotions.

While it is usually productive to discuss issues related to conflict, before doing so spontaneously, first calm yourself by taking a walk and thinking about nothing except what you feel and see while walking. This calms your emotional reactions and mental processes so that you will be less reactive and more deliberate in your actions. Once you are calm, talk to the other person.

Teams: Keep a healthy level of interdependence within your teams.

Make sure you do not become overly enmeshed in a team, but do not keep yourself marginal, either. Find a healthy way of functioning within a team so that you make a strong, consistent contribution without giving up your freedom for the sake of support or feeling a need to avoid the team for the sake of your autonomy.

Leadership: Honor your leadership gift of insight and planning, and learn to become comfortable with your own authority.

Take a serious look at your history with bosses and authority figures, particularly in those cases where your reactivity to authority may have hurt your career and/or those with whom you work. Discuss this with three trusted friends. Learn from your past experiences.

NINE

Coaching
Enneagram Style Seven

Sevens crave the stimulation of new ideas, people, and experiences; avoid pain; and create elaborate future plans that will allow them to keep all of their options open.

Center of Intelligence · Head Center

HOW TO IDENTIFY SEVENS

Thinking   **Feeling**

CORE BELIEFS
- *Life is full of endless possibilities.*
- *Why worry when you can be happy?*
- *No one has the right to restrict or limit me.*

EMOTIONAL PATTERNS
- *Joyfulness and enthusiasm*
- *Avoidance of "negative" emotions, particularly sorrow and fear, through positive reframing*

Behaving

WORKPLACE BEHAVIORS
Adore idea generation • Like everything to be positive • Are in perpetual motion • Dislike restraints, needing to keep themselves constantly stimulated • Have difficulty focusing

The "Synthesizing Mind"

The Seven's mind, called the synthesizing mind, responds instantaneously to stimulation, moving faster than a nanosecond to a new idea connected to the original thought, then triggering another idea, and so forth. Because Sevens become fascinated with information from so many different disciplines and have an abundance of data upon which to draw, these fast and loose associations can be instantly transformed into highly creative, surprisingly original—although not always practical—new ways of doing things. As a result of their desire for constant mental stimulation and their rapid mental processing, Sevens may have a breadth, but not necessarily a depth, of knowledge.

Emotional Patterns of Sevens
Joyfulness and enthusiasm

When Sevens experience discomfort in any form (for example, emotional pain, anxiety, anticipation of something negative occurring, feeling limited by someone or something, or boredom), their initial response is to think about positive possibilities and future plans and to do so with creativity and zest. This keeps them adrenalized, stimulated, and upbeat, but it also distracts them from any feelings of discomfort and overrides these.

Avoidance of "negative" emotions, particularly sorrow and fear, through positive reframing

Reframing is a way in which Sevens avoid feelings they prefer not to have, such as sadness and fear. In this automatic or unconscious response to unwanted emotions, Sevens take a negative experience or thought and rename it so that it appears positive. For example, when receiving feedback that a work product was late, a Seven might say, "Yes, but I figured out two more sections we hadn't thought of earlier that will make the customer very happy."

Workplace Behaviors of Sevens
Adore idea generation

Sevens feel stimulated, valued, and close to others through the sharing of ideas. Not only does this keep them excited, but their life force feels activated. When others respond with agreement or new ideas, Sevens feel listened to and affirmed. In fact, they thrive on dialogue that goes back and forth in rapid fashion, preferring this "overlapping conversation"—where someone interjects thoughts and adds comments (but not criticism) while the other person is still in mid-sentence—to "sequential conversations," in which each person waits for the other to finish before speaking. Although Sevens are interested in what others say, they listen to the first part of an idea, believe they understand the crux of what is being said, and then respond immediately.

Like everything to be positive

Sevens are highly optimistic, fun loving, and enthusiastic, often telling stories as a way to communicate and infusing humor into difficult situations. In addition, they like others to respond with a similar positive, energetic tone.

Are in perpetual motion

Sevens' minds are in constant motion, as are their bodies. At a meeting, Sevens typically fidget in their chairs, shake their legs, tap their feet, stand up and pace around the room, and/or leave the room and return to the meeting multiple times.

Dislike restraints, needing to keep themselves constantly stimulated

Addicted to the adrenaline rush of excitement, Sevens like being overly busy and juggling plans, and multitask to an extreme. They have difficulty saying no to anything that stimulates them, even when they have more to do than can be realistically accomplished in the time available. In addition, Sevens crave having all options available to them, and they intensely dislike anything that puts restraints on their time and freedom.

Have difficulty focusing

Sevens feel challenged when they have to stay focused on one thing for any length of time, becoming easily distracted by new thoughts and external stimuli. Focusing can be excruciatingly painful for Sevens, because it makes them stay still, thus allowing their feelings of anxiety and sadness to more readily emerge.

FAMOUS SEVENS

Howard Stern (radio personality)	"My energy level is through the roof and I'm excited about it."
	"My mother was very involved with me. And we had a dialogue constantly. And it was like an umbilical cord. As long as the words were flowing back and forth, we were connected and feeding each other."
Bill Clinton	"I may not have been the greatest president, but I've had the most fun eight years."
	"A lot of presidential memoirs, they say, are dull and self-serving. I hope mine is interesting and self-serving."
John F. Kennedy	"We need men who can dream of things that never were."
	"Change is the law of life. And those who look only to the past or present are certain to miss the future."

Subtypes: Three Variations of Seven

All Sevens have an insatiable thirst for new stimulation of all kinds and distract themselves with interesting people, ideas, and pleasurable experiences, which allows them to avoid their fear of painful emotions and difficult situations. There are three distinct ways in which Sevens manifest these characteristics, called subtypes.

Self-Preservation Subtype Sevens try to create close networks of family, friends, and colleagues, not only to keep themselves feeling both stimulated and secure but also to generate new and interesting opportunities to pursue.

Social Subtype Sevens sacrifice some of their need for stimulation in the service of the group or of some ideal that is extremely important to them. Although they are aware of wanting to pursue their desire for excitement, they choose to postpone it.

One-to-One Subtype Sevens are dreamers, with a need to see the stark reality of the world through rose-colored glasses, and they are the most optimistic of the three subtypes of style Seven. Often, they become fascinated with one other person, become satiated with that person over time, then find someone new who intrigues and stimulates them.

Wings and Arrow Lines for Sevens

Because Sevens seek stimulation and pleasure while trying to avoid feeling pain and discomfort, they can be highly unfocused, unrealistically optimistic, exhausted from exerting so much physical and mental energy, and impulsive in their actions. Access to their wings (styles Six and Eight) and arrows (styles One and Five) can counterbalance these qualities in Sevens.

Wings for Sevens

SIX WING Sevens with a Six wing add the capacity to see the glass as being both half full and half empty. Because these Sevens have an increased perceptiveness and an ability to anticipate potential problems, their actions become more deliberate and less based on their instantaneous reactions.

EIGHT WING Sevens with an Eight wing tend to be more direct, assertive, and powerful. They have a more grounded presence and an increased desire to put their ideas into action.

Arrow Lines for Sevens

ARROW LINE TO ONE When Sevens have access to arrow line One, their sense of responsibility and ability to focus increase, as well as their precision and attention to detail. Although some Sevens use these qualities on an ongoing basis, many display these most often as work deadlines approach.

ARROW LINE FROM FIVE   Sevens expend vast amounts of energy, and they eventually become fatigued. Access to Five allows them to take time for themselves without engaging with others (although this may last only a few hours every few months). In addition, some Sevens who have an extremely strong link to Five enjoy quietude on a more regular basis, engage in self-reflection more often, and tend to be more self-contained.

Three Typing Questions for Sevens

1. Do you continuously seek new and stimulating people, ideas, or events to keep life exciting, adrenalized, and forward moving?
2. Do you avoid pain and discomfort whenever possible, using your mind to conjure up new possibilities and plans and to reframe negative situations so they can be seen as positive?
3. Do you have trouble sustaining your focus on work projects, people, and conversations without a considerable amount of effort on your part?

HOW TO COACH SEVENS

Areas of Strength	Areas for Development	
• Imaginative	• Impulsive	
• Enthusiastic	• Unfocused	
• Engaging	• Rebellious	
• Quick thinking	• Pain avoidant	

COACHING OVERVIEW

Initially, Seven learners may be excited about coaching, but they will avoid coaching meetings if they anticipate feeling uncomfortable, inadequate, or restricted—for example, if they imagine they will hear negative information or have to deal with troubling emotions. Sevens may cancel meetings, arrive late, or simply not show up. When Sevens do these things, they do not realize that they are avoiding the meetings; they rationalize their behavior by explaining that what they were doing prevented them from meeting with the developer. The developer's most important coaching challenge is to get Seven learners to make a full commitment to coaching and to obtain their agreement to attend all coaching meetings. Doing this involves patience, compassion, and clarity on the part of the developer. *Patience* is required because Sevens may be late or miss their appointments so often that developers feel frustrated and even disrespected. *Compassion* is needed so developers can understand that when Seven learners miss meetings, it is usually because they are feeling extremely anxious and don't know what else to do. *Clarity* is essential, because developers need to be absolutely clear with Seven learners that this repetitively avoidant behavior will not get them the results they say they want.

During the coaching meetings themselves, Sevens like to talk more than listen and to discuss as much information as possible in the shortest amount of time. This creates a dilemma, because Sevens process large amounts of information quickly but may not interpret it accurately. These inaccuracies are the result of multiple factors. First, Sevens reframe or rationalize negative information so that it appears positive, and they often believe these reframed storylines. Second, Sevens may listen only to the developer's first few statements, think they understand everything, and then begin thinking or talking about something else. Third, Sevens become easily distracted, particularly by external stimuli such as sounds and visual objects. Finally, Sevens are highly sensitive; when they feel hurt, it can be hard for them to listen fully. For all of these reasons, developers need to make sure that Seven learners are truly hearing what is said—for example, by asking them regularly what they are thinking and feeling about the topics being discussed—and that they are fully attentive during the coaching meetings.

First, Determine Coaching Goals and Learner Motivation
Goal Identification: What to Ask Sevens

Although Sevens like the idea of generating coaching goals, they may resist adhering to them. For example, they may create many more goals than are realistic to achieve in the time available, or they may agree to certain goals but then try to change them throughout the coaching process. They do this for three reasons: (1) Sevens often have many ideas about what to accomplish and are reluctant to give any of them up; (2) a commitment to a specific goal can feel like a limitation on the Seven's freedom; and (3) changing goals frequently means that Sevens cannot be easily held accountable for specific results. In addition to being aware of these tendencies in Seven learners, developers can ask questions about the Seven's goals in a way that excites them and makes them more likely to make commitments and to keep them. Here are three ways to help Seven learners define clear coaching goals (use only one of the three questions; otherwise, Sevens will become more unfocused):

- *I want you to think about the time when the coaching is complete and it has been highly successful. What do you imagine you have been able to accomplish?*
- *Would you take a little time to dream about what you most want for yourself from the coaching?*

- *Please give me three positive words or phrases that most reflect what would be said about you by yourself and others after the coaching is complete.*

Whichever question is chosen should be followed up with these questions (use all three questions in sequence):

- *What makes each of these really important to you?*
- *Which of your goals are the most important to you, and why?*
- *Tell me which goals you are absolutely sure matter so much that they can sustain your interest and energy throughout the coaching.*

When discussing the Seven learner's goals, developers should help the Seven clearly connect the key development motivators listed below to specific coaching goals. This link may be obvious to learners as they discuss why each coaching goal is important, but if it is not, developers can do one of two things: (1) Ask Seven learners, *"What personal and professional benefits will you gain when you achieve this goal?"* or (2) explain the connection between the goal and the motivator directly by saying, *"This will help you have the kind of influence and impact you really want."*

Key Development Motivators for Sevens
- To learn something exciting and personally beneficial
- To read others better and develop deeper and more consistent empathy
- To transform their ideas into reality
- To be taken more seriously by others
- To feel more complete as a person

Second, Assess the Learner's Level and Range of Self-Mastery, Then Use Level-Appropriate Coaching Approaches

The best way to determine the self-mastery level of the learner is to read the behavioral descriptions for all three levels in the chart on pages 166–167 and answer these questions:

1. What is this person's normal (average) level of self-mastery?
   ☐ Low ☐ Moderate ☐ High
2. What do I know and what have I observed that leads me to this conclusion?
3. What is this person's range of self-mastery—that is, the individual's highest and lowest levels?
4. What do I know from my own observations or other data that leads me to this conclusion?

Sevens: Self-Mastery Levels and Coaching Approaches to Enhance Development

High Self-Mastery · **The Focused Inspirer**

Core understanding

Genuine happiness and a feeling of wholeness come from integrating negative and positive experiences.

Enneagram Sevens who have chosen to do the challenging work of self-development have learned how to tame their highly active minds, which is not an easy task. In learning to do this, Sevens increase their capacity to focus—on people, tasks, and feelings, and on learning something in depth—rather than dispersing their energy. They complete their work effortlessly, listen well, and emanate happiness and peaceful joy. Spirited and deep, these Sevens have a true sense of wonder and inspire those around them, not by energizing others but through their calm, yet vital presence.

Coaching approaches to enhance the Seven's self-mastery

Provide encouragement and additional methods for expansion.

- Provide positive reinforcement when Sevens demonstrate the ability to sustain their focus and remain calm over long periods of time, especially when they are anxious or sad.
- Affirm their ability to inspire others through innovative ideas, and help them inspire others through their empathy, compassion, and ability to take effective action.
- Reinforce the Seven's "heartfulness" as well as his or her mental agility; encourage the Seven to speak from the heart as often as possible.
- Help Sevens make their implicit connections between ideas explicit and to organize these so others can better understand them.
- Encourage them to take extended periods of time to be completely alone and with minimal stimulation as a way to accelerate their growth.

Moderate Self-Mastery · **The Stimulator**

Core concern

Satisfaction, stimulation, and feeling good

At the midlevel of self-mastery, Sevens can be creative and engaging but also frenzied and impatient. Their minds work so fast that they often have a great many half-thought-through notions, most of which they express. They also tend to overestimate their competence and knowledge, considering themselves quick studies. Addicted to the adrenaline rush of new and stimulating experiences, they sometimes find it difficult to focus and to carry tasks through to completion. When the energetic and playful Seven is confronted about something he or she has done that is less than stellar, the Seven will reframe the event by portraying it in positive rather than negative terms.

Coaching approaches to enhance the Seven's self-mastery

Stimulate motivation and provide concrete development actions.

- Help them continuously expand their repertoire of emotional responses—particularly sadness—and to increase their capacity for deeply felt emotional empathy.

- Be enthusiastic about their projects and ideas, but gently caution them to set realistic limits on the number of projects that can be accomplished well and on time, and what to realistically expect of others.
- Help them slow down and focus on a continuous basis; give them ideas about what will best help them to do this—for example, breathing more deeply into their bodies, not double scheduling, and keeping their bodies still rather than pacing or fidgeting when they talk.
- Emphasize the rewards of having more focus and self-discipline; explain this by way of a personal story about you or someone you know well.
- Help Sevens understand that pain and discomfort are normal and temporary aspects of the human condition, and that these feelings will dissipate more quickly if they allow themselves to fully experience these emotions.

Low Self-Mastery · The Frenetic Escape Artist

Core fear

Pain, deprivation, and not feeling whole

At the lowest level of self-mastery, Sevens are so consumed by anxiety that they alternate between manic behavior (hyperactivity to an extreme) and depression. Joyless and prone to causing scenes, these Sevens are perpetually fleeing from self-reflection and looking around to see whom they can blame for their circumstances. Feeling cornered and trapped, they engage in self-destructive or self-defeating behaviors.

Coaching approaches to enhance the Seven's self-mastery

Offer support, guidance, and boundaries.

- Encourage Sevens to slow down slightly; too much slowing down would be impossible and make them highly anxious. Frame slowing down in positive terms—for example, as an inward journey full of new experiences.
- Initiate conversations about what Sevens think and feel, as well as about what is occurring in their lives. Do this using a lighthearted, compassionate tone; help them focus during conversations by providing gentle comments when they become distracted.
- Encourage them to discuss their anger and frustration, while cautioning them about the consequences of acting on these feelings, and particularly taking impulsive action.
- Empathize with their desire to do everything, but reinforce the need to set boundaries and limits in order to be effective and not become exhausted.
- Provide comfort by explaining that feeling pain, discomfort, and anxiety are normal.

Once you have an initial assessment of the Seven learner's self-mastery level, read the recommended approaches appropriate to that level and select those you believe will be most effective for the learner.

Third, Use Coaching Techniques That Challenge Growth

As you read the following four coaching techniques, it can be helpful to think about several Sevens you know and how you might use the techniques with those individuals. Although all Sevens have striking similarities, they are also very different based on factors such as self-mastery level, empathy, use of wings and arrows, subtype, experience, age, gender, and culture.

Head Center Challenge: The "What if?" Question

"What if?" challenges work well in situations in which the learner makes assumptions that something is important and inviolate—that is, a mental model. These assumptions are part of the learner's unchallenged beliefs and paradigms. After hearing the Seven learner express an explicit or implicit assumption, the developer poses a relevant "What if?" question to the Seven. The following chart lists three common mental models for Sevens, the question the developer should ask to challenge each assumption, and the ways in which the developer should respond once the Seven has answered the developer's challenge.

Developers should be aware that some Sevens may appear to like the "What if?" challenge but respond to it as if it is a game in which they can demonstrate their mental agility. A telltale sign of this is refusal to engage in a coaching conversation that pursues the implications of the mental model being discussed. Should this occur, developers need to redirect Sevens to refocus on the original mental model or assumption being challenged.

"What if?" Challenges for Sevens

Common Assumption No. 1

"This is a very big problem; it will all work out just fine."

Developer's challenge

"What if it doesn't work out just fine?"

Developer's follow-on response

• If the Seven says, "It will," respond by saying: *"So, everything in your life has always worked out with no problems whatsoever?"* If the Seven continues to say there have never been problems, say: *"You'd be the first person I've ever met who could realistically say this."* Then be silent.

• When the Seven can say what would happen if the problem doesn't work out fine, say: *"Good. Now let's discuss what you can do to increase the chances of a positive outcome, but also what you can do if it doesn't work out fine."*

Common Assumption No. 2

"It really wasn't my fault."

Developer's challenge

"What if it truly was your fault?"

Developer's follow-on response

• If the Seven cannot accept any fault or responsibility, tell a relevant compelling story, then say: *"Let's reexamine the situation to determine what was your responsibility."*

- When the Seven can articulate his or her responsibility, ask questions to elicit more depth and insight, as well as discussion of how this information can be useful going forward.

Common Assumption No. 3

"This person has no right to restrict me or tell me how to do my work."

Developer's challenge

"What if this person does have the right to tell you what to do?"

Developer's follow-on response

- If the Seven can't think of any reason why the person has the right to direct his or her work, ask: *"Do you ever have the right to direct someone else's work? Does anyone at work have the right to direct your work?"*
- When the Seven gives a concrete and positive response, say: *"Let's look at different ways to name this; you initially said 'restrict,' which implies 'limit.' What are some other words that would describe the same thing but be neutral or even positive?"*
  Hint: manage, oversee, guide, support, request

Heart Center Challenge: Explore the Learner's Defense Mechanism
The Seven's Primary Defense Mechanism: Rationalization

Rationalization is a defense mechanism by which individuals explain unacceptable thoughts, feelings, and behaviors in a way that entirely avoids or obscures their true motivations, intentions, or the effects of the behavior. When Sevens rationalize, they do so by positive reframing, justifying their behavior by explaining it in highly positive terms. Sevens use reframing to avoid pain, discomfort, sadness, guilt, and anxiety, as well as to avoid taking personal responsibility for what has occurred.

Sevens rationalize by reframing primarily when they feel or anticipate feeling distressed. They also reframe ideas as part of the way they think; this can be an asset when they generate new ways of doing things or engage in creative problem solving. In these positive instances, Sevens may take an issue such as an impending reorganization about which people are anxious and say, "Yes, but the reorganization also provides us with the opportunity to reexamine how we do things and to create enormous improvements." However, when Sevens rationalize their own unacceptable behavior, it becomes a problem both for them and for the organization. Examples of this include excusing their lateness in delivering quality work on time—for example, by stating that there were three new ideas in the work that would not have been there had it been delivered on time—or by explaining a verbal outburst at a meeting by saying, "Yes, but I saved others who felt the same way from having to say anything." These two examples are actually symptoms or manifestations

RATIONALIZATION

When Sevens receive negative feedback, they create an explanation about why what they did had real value to the other person, the team, or the organization. For example, when walking into a meeting a half hour late, a Seven might say, "I know I'm late to the meeting, but I created a new product idea on the way."

of rationalization that often hide or defend against the following deeper developmental issues for Sevens:

- Being able to focus mentally, emotionally, and physically at will rather than being unfocused as a way to avoid pain, discomfort, and feeling restricted
- Accepting and integrating the reality of pain and discomfort along with pleasure rather than seeking only positive, pleasurable, and highly stimulating experiences
- Feeling genuine and consistent empathy for others rather than speculating about the emotions of others as a result of their own limited emotional repertoire

To work with the Seven's defense mechanism of rationalization, developers can use either an indirect or a direct challenge. It is often better to start with the indirect challenge, because it elicits more responsiveness and less resistance, but if the learner appears receptive or you have an excellent relationship with this person, a direct challenge may have a bigger impact.

Some Sevens need the indirect challenge because they are so sensitive when it comes to their own feelings, but other Sevens say they need to be challenged directly or they do not absorb what is being said. The best way to indirectly challenge a Seven's reframing is to reframe the exact same situation in a different way that also requires the Seven to take more responsibility for his or her behavior. The best way to directly challenge Seven learners is to be as simple and direct as possible.

INDIRECT CHALLENGE TO RATIONALIZATION

"What you've just described—that you've received feedback that you don't listen as effectively as you could, but your explanation is that you understand everything by just listening to a few words—can be understood in a different way. Effective listening actually involves both parties listening fully to everything the other says. In this way of listening, others would also completely listen to all the ideas you have."

DIRECT CHALLENGE TO RATIONALIZATION

"Although there is some truth in what you say, it is also a rationalization for your behavior. Tell me what you don't want to really acknowledge about yourself in this situation."

Body Center Challenge: The "Why would you want to do that?" Question

When Seven learners say they want to change something about themselves, asking them this question works effectively as a way of supportively challenging their desires. As a response to this technique, the Seven learner either changes his or her course of action or becomes more deeply committed to the original plan. This technique is especially useful in two situations: (1) The

---

"Why would you want to do that?" Challenges for Sevens

A Seven's Productive Intention to Act

"I want to be more focused."

Developer's challenge

"Why would you want to be more focused?"

Developer's follow-on response

• If the Seven cannot think of an answer or gives an unconvincing answer, say: *"It doesn't sound like you really want to do this. Have you considered that you may like being unfocused?"* Wait for the response.
• When the Seven gives a convincing response, say: *"It sounds as though this is important to you. If you could focus at will, what would you be able to do that you can't do now?"* Follow the Seven's answer with this statement: *"Let's talk about how you can learn to focus at will so you have the choice."*

A Seven's Counterproductive Intention to Act

"I'm going to ask my staff what they think about this issue, even though my boss told me not to do that."

Developer's challenge

"Why would you not want to follow your boss's request?"

Developer's follow-on response

• If the Seven gives you a reason that makes some sense to you, it is more than likely that the Seven is using reframing to rationalize the behavior and they are good enough at it to almost convince you! Say: *"That sounds convincing, and you may want to do this, but it may be very risky for you personally. Before you put this into action and later regret the consequences, let's talk about the possible negative impact."*
• When the Seven gives a response showing that he or she recognizes the behavior as counterproductive, say: *"Good. Now what is it you really want in this situation, and what are some productive ways to achieve this?"*

Seven learner articulates an intention to take action that sounds productive, or (2) the Seven learner expresses an intention to take action that might be risky or could be counterproductive to his or her best interests.

This technique is especially useful for Sevens. First, Sevens usually have a great number of things they want to do, but these may be mere ideas about what to do rather than commitments to take action. Thus, a challenge to a productive intention to act draws this to their attention and supports them in making a clear decision to act. Second, the technique also challenges their potential counterproductive behavior. Because almost all Sevens are spontaneous, this can lead to impulsivity when they are highly excited or extremely anxious. The "Why would you want to do that?" challenge helps them reflect more on what they are about to do and whether it is really going to lead to a positive result.

Transformative Paradoxical Challenges

Sevens have agile minds, and they like paradoxical challenges because these make them think. However, enjoying the complexity of paradox thinking doesn't necessarily mean either that they understand its meaning or that understanding it will change their behavior. It is therefore especially important for developers to state the paradox in very clear language and to let Sevens talk about their responses out loud. The developer can then hear whether or not the Seven is absorbing the information or is merely rationalizing and reframing the paradox. If Sevens begin to reframe, developers can use the defense mechanism challenge for Sevens; in doing so, it is best to use the more direct version of this challenge in order to get the Seven's complete attention.

THE SEVEN PARADOX

Marcy's meeting with her manager was more serious than any of the others that had preceded it. Fretful and downhearted, Marcy explained: "I so much want to be thought of as a future leader in this bank. No one ever considered me for the management position that's available. I suppose I could just apply and see what they do with that. Shouldn't everyone have that opportunity? Perhaps there's something I've said and done. Maybe it's my style. This firm is old-fashioned anyway. I try to lighten the atmosphere with my jokes. Oh, well, I can look for another job. I have a few opportunities now. Maybe upper management has heard that I'm looking."

Paradox Explanation

Sevens want to feel whole, complete, and totally okay about themselves; however, they avoid the behaviors that would ultimately make them feel settled, fully satisfied, and completely self-accepting—for example, staying

---

focused on a task until it is complete, delving into feelings and thoughts in greater depth, and accepting pain as well as pleasure.

Developer's Paradox Statement

"Let me give you some feedback—my own personal reaction. What you say you want is for the company to consider you a person of substance and a strong candidate for a management position. However, your own behavior is undermining your ability to reach those goals. For example, when people make jokes during serious conversations or present a number of ideas rapidly, particularly ideas that seem polar opposites—as you just did with me—others often stop listening, and they may even feel annoyed. If you want to have a greater personal impact and be taken more seriously in the organization, there are two areas you need to examine: (1) your ability to stay focused on one thought, one feeling, and one task at a time and in far greater depth, and (2) your use of humor to avoid difficult situations."

> NOTE Use the paradoxical challenge only with moderate to high self-mastery Sevens; low self-mastery individuals may not be psychologically stable enough to handle the ambiguity inherent in paradoxes.

SEVEN COACHING CASE STUDY SUMMARY: RANDALL

Determine Coaching Goals and Learner Motivation

Make sure the goals can be accomplished in the time available and are linked to one or more of the learner's key motivators.

> Randall wants to be considered for his manager's job when this person retires in six months. However, Randall believes that others in the organization do not perceive him as a serious contender for this position, based, he thinks, on their view that Randall does not have the depth of knowledge or organizational respect required. When asked why this matters to him, he states, "I've always wanted this since I began working in this group. I want to be taken seriously. In fact, I'm not really sure how I'm perceived or why others think I would not be a candidate for this job."

Assess the Learner's Level and Range of Self-Mastery, Then Use Level-Appropriate Coaching Approaches

Determine the learner's normal (average) level and range of self-mastery.

> Although Randall is a successful lawyer—he is intelligent and has an engaging interpersonal style—his normal self-mastery level is at the lowest end of the moderate range. Although he is normally quite energetic and enthusiastic,

he is rarely self-reflective, has difficulty sustaining his focus in most instances, and avoids negative feedback as much as possible—for example, he reframes constantly, brings up extraneous topics as distractions, and continually makes jokes in meetings. Although the content of the jokes is not objectionable, the timing of his delivery is inappropriate. For example, he makes jokes at moments when everyone else is trying to solve serious problems. His range of self-mastery is limited; his highest point is only slightly above his average level, but when he becomes distressed, he functions in the low self-mastery level.

Select the development approach(es) from the chart on pages 166–167 that would be most effective with the learner, and experiment with these.

During coaching meetings, help Randall learn to focus for longer and longer periods of time during conversations, calling it to his attention when he distracts himself by moving around and jumping from topic to topic. Emphasize that it is important for him to learn to focus, so that he can do this in meetings with others at work, and explain that this is likely one reason that others may not take him as seriously as he desires. Tell stories of others who have reaped rewards from being able to focus and from showing self-discipline. However, base these stories on other successful professionals rather than yourself, because Randall does not listen fully to personal stories about the developer. Be prepared to use approaches from the low self-mastery level when Randall is under duress; in particular, empathize with his desire to do everything, but also be clear that he needs to set boundaries for himself.

Use Coaching Techniques That Challenge Growth

Plan how you will use each of the four coaching techniques from this section, and use them at appropriate moments during the coaching process.

Head Center Challenge: "What if?"

What have you heard the learner say or imply that reflects a mental model or assumption you can challenge? How will you phrase this "What if?" challenge?

All of the following challenges would be effective with Randall.
"What if you were taken seriously at work?"
"What if you took yourself more seriously at work?"
"What if you could be taken seriously at work without having to receive a promotion to prove this to yourself?"

Heart Center Challenge: Recognizing and Leveraging Defense Mechanisms

When have you observed the learner use a particular defense mechanism? Would a direct or an indirect challenge be more effective? How would you phrase this defense mechanism challenge?

When Randall discusses the possibility of not receiving the promotion, he rationalizes this by explaining that people who receive promotions are not happy, that being promoted is merely an example of the political game that he finds tedious, and that his jokes are useful because they make people laugh. These are only a few of his many rationalizations. His excessive use of reframing suggests that giving a direct challenge to his defense mechanism would be the most effective approach.

INDIRECT CHALLENGE
"You say repeatedly how much being considered as a serious contender for the manager position would mean to you, yet you have many more reasons why this either is not desirable or why you aren't being considered that have nothing to do with your qualifications. Can you explain this to me?"

DIRECT CHALLENGE
"I know you want this position very much, but you rationalize why you may not get it, making the organization the villain in the process."

Body Center Challenge: "Why would you want to do that?"
What behavior has the learner stated that he or she plans to do? Do you think this is a wise course of action? How would you phrase this "Why would you want to do that?" challenge?

> *"Why would you want to be a manager?"*

Transformative Paradoxical Challenge
What paradoxes have you observed in the learner? Select the most significant one. How would you phrase this paradoxical challenge?

> The transformational challenge is not appropriate for Randall. Although he functions at the moderate level, he is in the lower ranges and functions at the low self-mastery level under duress. As a result, a paradoxical challenge could make him highly anxious. It is better to help him reach the middle of moderate self-mastery before using paradoxes with him.

NOTE See the Seven paradox story for an example of how to express the paradox to a Seven. Paradoxical challenges should be used only with moderate or high self-mastery learners. Low self-mastery learners are not in a psychological state to handle the complexity and ambiguity inherent in the resolution of this level of paradox, and deep-level or complex paradoxes can increase their anxiety. While less powerful paradoxes can be used with these learners, developers should do so with caution.

DEVELOPMENT ACTIVITIES FOR SEVENS
Developers can suggest the following activities to Seven learners.

Core Issue: Stay focused by learning to go inward.

The biggest challenge for you will be to focus on your physical sensations and emotional reactions. For an hour each day, practice bringing your focus to both your emotions and your physical sensations. Once you have developed the ability to do this, practice this inner focusing on a regular basis, particularly at times when you feel either highly stimulated or anxious.

Expansion Through Wings and Arrows
SIX WING   Face your fears.

When you feel at all uncomfortable, nervous, or unsettled or when your attention becomes diverted from what you were doing, thinking, feeling, or saying because you felt uncomfortable, ask yourself this question: *What am I feeling fearful about?* Be vigilant in your response by not taking the answer at face value. Ask yourself probing questions such as this: *Underneath that fear, what am I feeling most fearful or worried about?*

EIGHT WING   Talk less so you will influence others more.

Because you probably talk frequently, saying whatever you are thinking about various topics in rapid succession, others may not know which ideas are the most significant ones or when it's the right time to comment on an idea. Instead, consider what you want to say in advance, determine when you will say it, and consider the best timing for your comments. When you learn to do this, you will increase your ability to influence others.

ARROW LINE ONE   Complete your tasks early.

Begin tasks far sooner than you normally would. For example, if you think a task should take one week, and your tendency is to start it just two days before the deadline, then begin the task four days before the deadline. Another alternative is to start and continue the least interesting tasks first, because you might otherwise choose to do the interesting tasks first and delay the more boring work until later. Reversing this can help you get both the interesting and monotonous tasks accomplished.

ARROW LINE FIVE   Spend time alone.

Once a week, spend three full hours by yourself doing something relaxing while reflecting and paying attention to your feelings and thought processes. The discipline of doing this will allow you to access far more of your interior world.

Communication: Slow your rate of speech.

Although you have a lot to say and a great deal of energy, your fast rate of speech can make it difficult for others to listen to everything you say. To be better understood by others, slow your pace to 50 percent of its normal rate. The easiest way to do this is to take a deep breath every ten seconds and take more time exhaling.

Conflict: Don't be afraid of negative feedback.

Although you may appear to others to want only positive feedback, you may actually pay more attention to negative feedback. Pay equal attention to both, making sure that you neither dismiss positive feedback nor reframe or over-explain negative feedback. It is important for you to just listen, asking questions for clarification when necessary.

Teams: Help teams develop clear structures and systematic processes.

When you help organize teams effectively, more people can participate and more ideas are both created and implemented. Put your creativity and attention toward developing coherent team infrastructures that are just slightly underorganized, so that creativity can abound with clear processes that everyone can follow.

Leadership: Honor your leadership gift of innovation and flexibility and enhance your ability to be solid and steadfast.

Explore rather than avoid the things that make you feel the most uncomfortable. When you become as fluid with pain and fear as you are with joy and pleasure, you will both feel and be perceived as someone who is personally powerful and truly confident.

TEN

Coaching
Enneagram Style Eight

Eights pursue the truth, like to keep situations under control, want to make important things happen, and try to hide their vulnerability.

Center of Intelligence · Body Center

HOW TO IDENTIFY EIGHTS

Thinking   Feeling

CORE BELIEFS

- The world is divided into two kinds of people: the strong and the weak.
- Bigger is better; almost any action is better than no action at all.
- You can never get enough of a good thing.

EMOTIONAL PATTERNS

- Deep, quick anger shows readily and propels them to take immediate action
- Feel, but rarely show, fear and sadness

Behaving

WORKPLACE BEHAVIORS

Like everything big, bold, and strategic • Macromanage and micromanage •
Are intense and direct • Protect certain people and groups in pursuit of justice • Can intimidate others

The "Take-Charge Body"

As a Body Center style, Eights like action and assert control by taking charge of situations with great speed and intensity. Because they are highly attuned to a situation's being out of control, their need to step in and take charge has an urgency and immediacy that is palpable and dramatic. Eights do this under most circumstances (unless they don't care about the situation), but they are particularly driven to take control when they feel vulnerable and anxious.

Emotional Patterns of Eights
Deep, quick anger shows readily and propels them to take immediate action

Eights are quick to anger and even quicker to respond, and they experience anger as energy that can overtake them unless it can be released immediately. In most cases, when the anger has been fully expressed, Eights are ready to move on. In addition to expressing anger verbally, the Eights' anger also propels them forward to take action. However, underneath their anger and quick action are often feelings of vulnerability, sadness, and/or anxiety.

Feel, but rarely show, fear and sadness

Above all, Eights protect themselves from feeling vulnerable or demonstrating any sign of weakness to others. Because of this, they rarely show such emotions, although some Eights may be aware of having these feelings when they are occurring.

Workplace Behaviors of Eights
Like everything big, bold, and strategic

Eights act bold, assertive, and authoritative, moving projects forward and preferring strategic challenges that have the largest possible impact.

Macromanage and micromanage

Eights enjoy macromanaging the big picture, charting the direction of the work and providing oversight so that it goes well. They intensely dislike micromanaging and being involved in the details of the work, often perceiving this as a waste of time. However, when things feel out of control, when they feel pressured by someone for information, or when they distrust someone else to do the work effectively and responsibly, Eights do dive into the daily details. While this describes many Eights in leadership roles, these tendencies are also displayed in Eights who are not in management positions.

Are intense and direct

Eights engage others directly and intensely through simple, concise word choice, sentence structure, speaking style, and body language. In most cases, they use few extra words such as adjectives and adverbs, preferring simple declarative statements instead. In addition, Eights expect honesty from other people; when others have opinions but convey these indirectly or remain silent, Eights may view this as a form of dishonesty.

Protect certain people and groups in pursuit of justice

Eights are highly protective of those for whom they feel responsible and will also protect individuals and groups they believe are being exploited or treated unjustly. Interestingly, while they defend others whom they believe need protection, Eights also have an antipathy toward individuals and groups they perceive as weak or as behaving like victims. Eights protect others not only as a way to show their greater strength, but also as a means of seeking justice, which they perceive as righting the wrongs of unjust behavior. Eights also become deeply disappointed when another person does not perform to his or her level of capability. Eights take this personally, particularly if they have defended, protected, or believed in these individuals.

Can intimidate others

Many Eights perceive themselves as tough on the outside but soft on the inside, and most are aware that others do not usually perceive them this way. Eights can also intimidate others—whether intentionally or not—as a result of their certainty, candor, style of speaking, physical presence, and energy. They may suppress their forward-moving, commanding energy in order to lessen this reaction, only to find that they are not being themselves and/or that others still feel intimidated. Eights can also purposely intimidate others, particularly when they are seeking some sort of revenge for what they perceive as unacceptable behavior.

FAMOUS EIGHTS

Arnold Schwarzenegger	"Strength does not come from winning. Your struggles develop your strengths. When you go through hardships and decide not to surrender, that is strength."
	"My relationship to power and authority is that I'm all for it. People need somebody to watch over them. Ninety-five percent of the people in the world need to be told what to do and how to behave."
Donald Trump	"I like thinking big. If you're going to be thinking anything, you might as well think big."
	"I'm not running for office. I don't have to be politically correct. I don't have to be a nice person. Like I watch some of these weak-kneed politicians—it's disgusting. I don't have to be that way."
Rosie O'Donnell	"I always think: Go big or go home."
	"When you're silent, it's as good as lying."

Subtypes: Three Variations of Eight

As a way to pursue control and justice and to avoid and deny their anxiety and sadness or feelings of vulnerability, Eights engage in a variety of self-satisfying behaviors and do this in an excessive way (for example, taking big and immediate action, working superhuman hours, eating too much food, and exercising for three hours a day for a week and then not exercising for two months). There are three distinct ways in which Eights manifest these characteristics, called subtypes.

Self-Preservation Subtype Eights focus their excessiveness and energy on getting what they need for survival, and they become highly frustrated, intolerant, and angry when the fulfillment of these needs is thwarted. Of the three Eight subtypes, the self-preservation subtype Eights tend to speak the least and to approach situations—particularly those they deem important to their survival—in a highly strategic way that allows them to get the upper hand.

Social Subtype Eights vigorously protect others from unjust and unfair authorities and systems and challenge social norms. At the same time, they seek power, influence, and pleasure. Wanting loyalty from others and being highly loyal themselves, they derive a feeling of power from challenging others as well as from defending those under their protection, which makes them feel less vulnerable.

One-to-One Subtype Eights are the most intense, rebellious, and emotional of the three Eight subtypes. Provocative and passionate in a way that draws others toward them, these Eights derive their power and influence from being at the center of things, from the strong and energetic connections they develop, and from the fervent way in which they express their positions and values.

Wings and Arrow Lines for Eights

Because Eights seek control and justice and avoid feeling vulnerable or appearing weak in any way, they can become aggressive, dogged, and relentless workaholics who drive themselves to the point of chronic exhaustion or illness. At these times, they are unable to gain support for themselves and become impenetrable even to those who care about them most. Access to their wings (styles Seven and Nine) and arrows (styles Five and Two) can counterbalance these qualities in Eights.

Wings for Eights

SEVEN WING   Eights with a Seven wing add a lightheartedness to the usually more serious Eight outlook, are more high-spirited and independent, and tend to be far more adventurous, willing to try new things in their personal and professional lives for the sake of experimentation and enjoyment.

NINE WING   Eights with a Nine wing are interpersonally warmer, calmer, and less reactive, and they solicit and listen to others' opinions because they are more consensually oriented.

Arrow Lines for Eights

ARROW LINE TO FIVE   Eights with a link to Five often use the solitary qualities of Five as a way to recharge themselves after particularly stressful or painful events or after expending their excessive mental, emotional, and physical energy to make big things happen. Eights with an extremely strong connection to Five are often more highly self-reflective than other Eights, and they may engage in intellectual pursuits solely for the pleasure of learning.

ARROW LINE FROM TWO   Eights with a strong connection to Two are very warm, generous, and openhearted. They are gentler than Eights without this link, and they show a deeper level of empathy for others.

Three Typing Questions for Eights

1. Do you have an extraordinarily strong and bold exterior, one that is sometimes intimidating to others (intentionally or unintentionally) but that hides a less visible but highly vulnerable interior?
2. Do you tend to be excessive in what you do—for example, exercising two to three hours a day for a week but then not exercising for a month, or deciding that if one piece of chocolate cake is good, then eating the whole cake is even better?
3. Do you have immediate impulses to take strong and forceful action, particularly when you are feeling anxious or vulnerable?

HOW TO COACH EIGHTS

Areas of Strength	Areas for Development
• Direct	• Controlling
• Strategic	• Demanding
• Protective	• Disdain weakness
• Action oriented	• Intimidating

COACHING OVERVIEW

Although Eight learners typically look big, strong, and confident, they usually feel just as concerned and vulnerable beneath their bold exteriors as individuals of the other Enneagram styles who come for coaching. Eights tend not to show this interior side initially, even in situations where they respect and trust the developer. However, they will eventually open up. For example, if the developer says, "You really are a warm and sensitive person and go out of your way to help others succeed," this can unnerve an Eight, but in a good way. While knowing the information to be true, the Eight may have believed that this was not obvious to others. Being perceived in a highly positive way can make many Eights feel vulnerable, and they may even get misty-eyed. A follow-up question from the developer—such as "Are you aware that others appreciate you in this way?"—can elicit a wide range of unexpected and productive emotional responses from the Eight.

Eights can also become highly emotional and angry when they receive negative feedback, even when the information is truthful and accurate. In these situations, the most helpful way for developers to react is to let Eights fully express their feelings. Once Eights have purged themselves of these intense reactions, they are usually ready to talk; often, the Eight's post-anger period provides a valuable development opportunity. The developer can help the Eight explore a wide range of thoughts, feelings, and behaviors by using supportive and direct questions or comments, such as the following:

- What about this caused your strong reaction?
- Tell me more about how you typically react in these situations.
- When you have these reactions, what else is going on inside you?

Eights usually want coaching to focus on the biggest picture possible, with details used as supporting information. They prefer this approach because they seek to understand the core issues and the overall patterns before they focus on smaller items. In addition, Eights do not like to waste time; going over what they consider to be minutiae can be highly annoying. An Eight learner often says, "Just tell me your main point!"

Eights are also prone to taking immediate action. For example, Eights create large action plans, but these plans may be too far-reaching to be achieved in a reasonable period of time. On other occasions, Eights may not know what to do. At these times, they may say to a developer they respect, "Tell me what to do!" In either case, the developer can help the Eight slow down, consider the data from many perspectives, then develop a manageable action plan after taking sufficient time to reflect on the meaning of the development conversation and all of the viable options for action.

First, Determine Coaching Goals and Learner Motivation
Goal Identification: What to Ask Eights

Because Eights are straightforward and do not like to be asked indirect questions, perceiving these as time wasting or manipulative, the developer can and should ask succinct, candid questions at the beginning of the coaching relationship:

- *What are your coaching goals?*
- *Why?*

When discussing the Eight learner's goals, developers should help the Eight clearly connect the key development motivators listed below to specific coaching goals. This link may be obvious to learners as they discuss why each coaching goal is important, but if it is not, developers can do one of two things: (1) Ask Eight learners, *"What personal and professional benefits will you gain when you achieve this goal?"* or (2) explain the connection between the goal and the motivator directly by saying, *"This will help you understand how to manage your vast energy and forward direction in the most productive ways."*

Key Development Motivators for Eights
- To know the truth from the widest perspective possible
- To understand others psychologically
- To feel less guilty for their own behavior and less responsible for other people
- To feel strong even when feeling vulnerable or weak
- To manage their abundant energy without imploding or exploding

Second, Assess the Learner's Level and Range of Self-Mastery, Then Use Level-Appropriate Coaching Approaches

The best way to determine the self-mastery level of the learner is to read the behavioral descriptions for all three levels in the chart on pages 186–187 and answer these questions:

1. What is this person's normal (average) level of self-mastery?
   ☐ Low ☐ Moderate ☐ High
2. What do I know and what have I observed that leads me to this conclusion?
3. What is this person's range of self-mastery—that is, the individual's highest and lowest levels?
4. What do I know from my own observations or other data that leads me to this conclusion?

Eights: Self-Mastery Levels and Coaching Approaches to Enhance Development

High Self-Mastery · The Truth Seeker

Core understanding

Vulnerability and weakness are part of being human, and multiple truths must be assimilated in order to reach the real truth.

The challenge for Eights who seek high self-mastery is to learn to manage their large, dynamic energy and reservoir of anger by fully acknowledging their long-hidden vulnerability. When they have accomplished this, Eights are generous, strong, openhearted, and open-minded. Although still direct and honest, they speak from the heart and the head as well as from the gut, and they solicit and embrace differing opinions. Their protectiveness of others is gentle rather than controlling, and they are grounded, warm, and deeply confident.

Coaching approaches to enhance the Eight's self-mastery

Provide encouragement and additional methods for expansion.

- Provide positive reinforcement and appreciation for all demonstrations of vulnerability, reminding them that true strength includes showing one's humanness.
- Recognize and acknowledge them for their warmth, caring, deep personal power, and hard work.
- Appreciate the energy and drive that they bring to tasks and projects; at the same time, ask them how well they are taking care of themselves, helping them make a commitment to doing so on a regular basis.
- Help them savor the moments of success and pleasure at work as well as the contributions they make to others before they move on to bigger tasks, projects, and challenges.
- Be available to them on request, and affirm them for asking for support and assistance.

Moderate Self-Mastery · The Immovable Rock

Core concern

Self-protection and showing weakness

Eights who possess moderate self-mastery try hard to manage their frustration and anger. Although they can be sensitive and generous, they can also be controlling, dominating, and aggressive. Quick to respond, they are also quick to take action, and they expect immediate responses from others. They have strong opinions, and their presence is almost always felt, even when they are quiet. As a result, others often look to them for decisions and clarity of direction. Although these Eights can be humble regarding their accomplishments and often become embarrassed when complimented in public, they also like to be appreciated and respected. If given a large challenge, they rise to the occasion. If anyone tries to constrain these Eights or force them to contain their vast energy, they become angry, blaming, and/or sick.

Coaching approaches to enhance the Eight's self-mastery

Stimulate motivation and provide concrete development actions.

- Address issues directly; do not feel intimidated and tell the complete truth. Otherwise, Eights will not trust you.

- Acknowledge and reinforce manifestations of their vulnerability and generosity.
- Communicate regularly to create clarity and alignment regarding vision, direction, and ways to move forward with coaching without making the Eight feel controlled.
- When Eights dominate excessively or get angry, help them recognize that these behaviors are masks or covers for their feelings of vulnerability. Explore these underlying issues.
- Provide feedback to help Eights understand their strong impact on others; offer concrete examples when doing so, even using situations that have occurred during coaching.

Low Self-Mastery · The Bully

Core fear

Being harmed, controlled, or extremely vulnerable

Eights with low self-mastery can be direct to the point of cruelty, unleashing a flood of anger and destructive punitive behavior. Believing that they must overcome their enemies by whatever means necessary, they justify their actions by blaming the other person for what is, in fact, their inability to acknowledge their own intense vulnerability. At worst, they can deteriorate into antisocial and/or violent behavior, because they cannot contain or control their explosive anger.

Coaching approaches to enhance the Eight's self-mastery

Offer support, guidance, and boundaries.

- Confront problematic behavior directly and tell the truth, matching the Eight's intense energy.
- If you think grudges or revenge may be fueling the Eight's reactions and behavior, inquire about this in a neutral way.
- Remember that when they feel vulnerable, they often don't admit it to themselves or they show it by becoming angry or trying to take control; respond to them in a calm and clear way, trying to help them understand what may be fueling their reactivity.
- Initiate conversations about what they are thinking and feeling in order to build the relationship.
- Don't be afraid of an Eight; create mutual respect by addressing issues directly.

Once you have an initial assessment of the Eight learner's self-mastery level, read the recommended approaches appropriate to that level and select those you believe will be most effective for the learner. A note for assessing the self-mastery level of Eights: It is important to spend enough time and have sufficient data to make an accurate assessment. Although some Eights are self-aware and can self-report accurately and reliably, others may not have a clear and realistic view of themselves. In addition, an Eight may appear far more trusting, relational, and vulnerable with the developer than they are with others at work, depending on how much they trust the developer. Consequently, it can be extremely helpful to have other data sources beyond the developer's direct experience with the Eight learner, and also to observe the Eight within his or her real work context, if possible.

Third, Use Coaching Techniques That Challenge Growth

As you read the following four coaching techniques, it can be helpful to think about several Eights you know and how you might use the techniques with those individuals. Although Eights have strong similarities, they are also very different based on factors such as self-mastery level, empathy, use of wings and arrows, subtype, experience, age, gender, and culture. In addition, Eights who are more introverted take charge or assert themselves in more subtle ways then do extroverted Eights, who tend to use commanding language and a loud voice more frequently.

Head Center Challenge: The "What if?" Question

"What if?" challenges work well in situations in which the learner makes assumptions that something is important and inviolate—that is, a mental model. These assumptions are part of the learner's unchallenged beliefs and paradigms. After hearing the Eight learner express an explicit or implicit assumption, the developer poses a relevant "What if?" question. Eights usually have a few core assumptions that they believe to be absolutely true, and they adhere to these with great tenacity. For this reason, they may strongly resist "What if?" challenges in these particular areas. When challenging Eights, developers have to ask "What if?" questions in a neutral manner and at the same time hold their ground and not appear weak or tentative. The dilemma for the developer is that while Eights do not like being challenged, they also respect the strength and courage of those who do confront them.

The chart below lists three common mental models for Eights, the question the developer should ask to challenge each assumption, and the ways in which the developer should respond once the Eight has answered the developer's challenge.

"What if?" Challenges for Eights

Common Assumption No. 1
"Working on small projects is a total waste of time."

Developer's challenge
"What if a small project has a big impact and is an excellent use of time?"

Developer's follow-on response
- If the Eight says, "It never does," answer: *"Never?"* If there is still no concrete answer, ask: *"Are you saying you've never seen a small project have a large impact?"*
- When the Eight gives an example, ask: *"What if you could have a big impact by choosing some smaller projects in addition to bigger ones?"* After the answer, ask: *"How would you and the organization benefit from that?"*

Common Assumption No. 2

"I can't share my weaknesses with others or they'll take advantage of me."

Developer's challenge

"What if you could share your weaknesses and vulnerabilities and people didn't take advantage of you?"

Developer's follow-on response

- If the Eight can't think of such a scenario, tell a relevant compelling story, then ask: *"Have you ever seen or experienced something similar?"*
- When the Eight gives an affirmative answer, ask questions to elicit more depth and insight.

Common Assumption No. 3

"I can't control my anger."

Developer's challenge

"What if you could control your anger?"

Developer's follow-on response

- If the Eight can't think of such a scenario, ask: *"Can you remember a time when you were able to manage your anger and this had a positive result?"*
- When the Eight gives a concrete and positive response, ask: *"How important are these results to you?"* Follow the answer with this: *"Let's talk about the ways you can do this more."*

Heart Center Challenge: Explore the Learner's Defense Mechanism
The Eight's Primary Defense Mechanism: Denial

Denial is a defense mechanism by which individuals unconsciously negate something that makes them feel anxious by disavowing its very existence. These can include thoughts, feelings, wishes, sensations, needs, and other external factors that are unacceptable to the Eight for some reason. Denial comes in a variety of forms. A person may deny the reality of the unpleasant information altogether, admit that something is true but deny or minimize its seriousness, or admit that both the information and its severity are true but deny any personal responsibility for it.

Eights exhibit denial on a regular basis, but they do so most blatantly when they feel anxious, vulnerable, sad, or intensely angry for long periods of time. Some examples of denial include the following: agreeing to do projects that they have no intention of doing well, violating or ignoring rules or directives regardless of the consequences, and engaging in such behavior as overindulging in food or drink while acting as though no harm will come to them. More blatant examples include an Eight's being quite sick but not telling anyone and going to work anyway, at great detriment to his or her own wellbeing; Eights' spending far more money than they have on the assumption that more money will be available; and their feeling highly vulnerable but not admitting this to themselves or anyone else and becoming furious about something else instead. These examples are actually symptoms or manifestations of denial that often hide or defend against the following deeper developmental issues for Eights:

- Being forthcoming about their own deeper vulnerabilities and need for support rather than acting tough and strong, as if they are invulnerable and don't need others
- Allowing others to exercise autonomy and control rather than constantly taking charge and making others dependent on their leadership and strength
- Being receptive and responsive to input from others rather than believing they understand the truth and moving to immediate, unilateral action

To work with the Eight's defense mechanism of denial, developers can use either an indirect or a direct challenge. It is often better to start with the indirect challenge, because it elicits more responsiveness and less resistance, but if the Eight is ready or you have an excellent relationship with this person, a direct challenge may have a bigger impact. Eights generally prefer directness, but when they are feeling vulnerable, an indirect challenge may be more effective; otherwise, Eights may become highly confrontational in response.

INDIRECT CHALLENGE TO DENIAL
"Tell me more about all of the consequences of this behavior."

DIRECT CHALLENGE TO DENIAL
"You look like you are making yourself ill from overwork, lack of sleep and exercise, and food that would make a healthy person incapacitated, yet you act as though there is no problem with any of this. I think you are in denial about it."

DENIAL

Eights may work 70 hours a week for four months in a row, eating highly unhealthy food and getting no physical exercise while driving themselves to complete exhaustion, yet be unaware of their physical state until they are ready to collapse. Needing to believe in their own invincibility, Eights do not acknowledge—even to themselves—their personal, physical, and emotional limitations.

Body Center Challenge: The "Why would you want to do that?" Question

When Eight learners say they intend to do something, they have likely already begun taking action, and they can be immovable objects when questioned about it. As a result, the developer can expect a strong reaction to the "Why would you want to do that?" question, but this is exactly why this type of challenge is so important when coaching Eights. They often move to action as soon as they have thought about what action to take, and they do this with great immediacy and a sense of urgency, particularly when they are stressed, anxious, or feeling vulnerable. The "Why would you want to do that?" challenge is especially useful in two situations: (1) The Eight learner articulates an intention to take action that sounds productive, or (2) the Eight learner expresses an intention to take action that might be risky or that could be counterproductive to his or her best interests. As a note, many Eights can make bad ideas sound like good ones using the sheer force of their personality. Developers need to be alert to this possibility, more discerning about the

---

"Why would you want to do that?" Challenges for Eights

An Eight's Productive Intention to Act

"I want to slow down my urge to take such quick action."

Developer's challenge

"Why would you want to gain more control of your urge to take action?"

Developer's follow-on response

- If the Eight cannot think of an answer or gives an unconvincing answer, say: *"It doesn't sound like you really want to do this."* Then wait for the response.
- When the Eight gives a convincing response, say: *"It sounds like this is really important to you. Please tell me more about this, why it matters so much, and your current ideas about how to do it."*

An Eight's Counterproductive Intention to Act

"I want to leave this company."

Developer's challenge

"Why would you want to leave the organization?"

Developer's follow-on response

- If the Eight gives you a reason that also makes sense to you, say: *"This sounds very good."*
- If the Eight gives you a reason you believe is possibly unwise, say: *"You may want to do this, but before you go further with it, you need to consider the potentially negative impact of this on you, on others at work, and on your family. You don't want to regret this later because your action was solely instinctual."*

value of a particular course of action, and willing to challenge Eight learners multiple times.

Transformative Paradoxical Challenges

Most Eights like paradoxical challenges because they understand complexity, systems, and root cause analyses. Because they are highly instinctual and understand something best when they experience it directly, it is especially important to use the paradoxical challenge only after Eight learners have realized that they may be their own greatest obstacle to success.

After the developer states the paradox, it is essential to allow Eights time to think it through in silence. They may ask questions or make comments, but Eights are most likely to say something simple and direct, such as asking, "So what should I do about this?" The best answer is to say, *"Acknowledging it is the first step."*

THE EIGHT PARADOX

After reviewing his data feedback, Ryan, a supervisor in a pharmaceutical lab, told his manager, "This is very upsetting. I'm not aggressive! Why would anyone say that about me?"

The manager was surprised by Ryan's reaction and asked, "You really don't see yourself as assertive?"

Ryan became quiet and then responded, "But there are so many things I don't say—if people only knew how much I hold back about what I'm thinking."

Paradox Explanation

Eights want to be accepted and supported completely for who they are, including their vulnerabilities. However, they act so strong, independent, and in charge that very few people ever see their softer, more vulnerable sides or their need for nurturance and affirmation.

Developer's Paradox Statement

"You're obviously frustrated and hurt by this. Here's the dilemma. You try so hard to not come on too strong, but you are strong. Do you let others see your gentler side very often? Do you think others know that even you need their support? Can you see how, when you lead with strength and boldness, others would not understand that you also want and need their help?"

NOTE Use the paradoxical challenge only with moderate to high self-mastery Eights; low self-mastery individuals may not be psychologically stable enough to handle the ambiguity inherent in paradoxes.

EIGHT COACHING CASE STUDY SUMMARY: CHRIS

Determine Coaching Goals and Learner Motivation

Make sure the goals can be accomplished in the time available and are linked to one or more of the learner's key motivators.

> Chris wants to manage her anger and intensity in more constructive ways, but what she really wants is to have a long-term personal relationship and a family. Given her position as a senior vice president in her company and the number of hours she works, it is difficult to imagine her making the time that a personal life requires. When asked why managing her anger and intensity and having a personal life matter to her, Chris states, "I think the two goals are related, though I'm not sure how. I think I become intense and passionate to keep myself from feeling vulnerable, but I know I have to show more vulnerabilities or I will never have a deep relationship."

Assess the Learner's Level and Range of Self-Mastery, Then Use Level-Appropriate Coaching Approaches

Determine the learner's normal (average) level and range of self-mastery.

> Chris is normally at the high end of moderate self-mastery, but she rarely goes much higher than that; when she is deeply discouraged and frustrated, she occasionally functions at the lower range of moderate self-mastery.

Select the development approach(es) from the chart on pages 186–187 that would be most effective with the learner, and experiment with these.

> Chris needs to create a vision for her life, one that includes working and having a satisfying relationship and family life. Once she has a tangible vision, she can determine what action she needs to take. Encourage her to be increasingly vulnerable during the coaching meetings, and reinforce this behavior in sincere ways. After this, encourage her to be more vulnerable with others at work whom she already trusts, then get her to be more vulnerable with others she does not know as well. Chris has a tendency to confide very personal information when she trusts someone, and she needs to temper this when she decides to share more of herself at work. She needs to learn how to be selectively vulnerable—that is, to share differing amounts of herself with others depending on the nature of the relationship.

Use Coaching Techniques That Challenge Growth

Plan how you will use each of the four coaching techniques from this section, and use them at appropriate moments during the coaching process.

Head Center Challenge: "What if?"

What have you heard the learner say or imply that reflects a mental model or assumption you can challenge? How will you phrase this "What if?" challenge?

> All of the following challenges would be effective with Chris.
> *"What if you really could have it all?"*
> *"What if you could learn to manage your intensity and anger and develop a wonderful relationship within a year's time?"*
> *"What if you have all the skills and qualities to do it already, but you just don't realize that?"*

Heart Center Challenge: Recognizing and Leveraging Defense Mechanisms

When have you observed the learner use a particular defense mechanism? Would a direct or an indirect challenge be more effective? How would you phrase this defense mechanism challenge?

> Chris had been in denial that having a personal relationship really mattered to her, but this has changed. She may currently be in denial about how hard she works and the impact of this on her.
>
> **INDIRECT CHALLENGE**
> *"You seem to have been working very hard these last two months. How many hours a day do you think you are working at the office or at home, and what kind of a toll is this taking on you? How much rest are you getting?"*
>
> **DIRECT CHALLENGE**
> *"I don't think you let yourself know how much pressure you are under. I'll bet you're even in denial about how much you're working per week and how exhausted you really are."*

Body Center Challenge: "Why would you want to do that?"

What behavior has the learner stated he or she plans to do? Do you think this is a wise course of action? How would you phrase this "Why would you want to do that?" challenge?

> *"Why would you want to manage your anger and intensity?"*
> *"Why would you want to have a relationship and family?"*

Transformative Paradoxical Challenge

What paradoxes have you observed in the learner? Select the most significant one. How would you phrase this paradoxical challenge?

> *"You say you want a great ongoing relationship, yet you work to excess and drive yourself so relentlessly that there's no time for yourself, much less for a relationship."*

NOTE Paradoxical challenges should be used only with moderate or high self-mastery learners. Low self-mastery learners are not in a psychological state to handle the complexity and ambiguity inherent in the resolution of this level of paradox, and deep-level or complex paradoxes can increase their anxiety. While less powerful paradoxes can be used with these learners, developers should do so with caution.

DEVELOPMENT ACTIVITIES FOR EIGHTS

Developers can suggest the following activities to Eight learners.

Core Issue: Slow down your impulse to take action.

Each time you feel the impulse to take action—for example, giving an opinion, suggesting or demanding that someone else do something, or in any way mobilizing forward action—stop yourself and think: *What is going on inside me that makes me want to move forward so quickly? What will happen if I don't take action right now?*

Expansion Through Wings and Arrows
SEVEN WING Lighten up.

More often than not, Eights approach their work and life with great intensity as they try to transform ideas into action and make things work. Eights can learn to lighten up by pausing intermittently during times when they would otherwise be driving toward action. During these intervals, you should ask yourself these two questions: *What is occurring in this situation that is positive or engaging? What can I notice that is interesting or amusing?*

NINE WING Learn to be receptive.

Eights often make nearly instantaneous assessments and then respond immediately. To become more receptive, you will first need to go inside yourself and examine your reactions. Once you have done this, you can then say this to yourself: *Just because I have a certain reaction doesn't mean I know all I need to know. Let me put my reactions aside, not act on them yet, and then fully listen to what the other person is trying to tell me.*

ARROW LINE FIVE Take time out on a regular basis to recharge your energy.

Once a week, without fail, take three hours for yourself. Put this on your schedule and hold to it, no matter what may arise at work to demand your attention. During these three hours, do something that you truly enjoy that relaxes you—for example, a short golf game, a walk in the woods, or reading a good book. You will find that this time-out recharges your batteries and reduces your tendency to go into overdrive.

ARROW LINE TWO   **Acknowledge the best in others.**

Whenever you interact with someone, think of at least two positive attributes that the person possesses, then keep these qualities in mind as you interact with this individual. With people you don't particularly like or respect, force yourself to think of three positive qualities. After doing this activity for two weeks, practice giving one sincere compliment to at least two people each day.

Communication: Modulate your commanding language.

Change any thoughts or statements that convey ways to organize, structure, and control events to statements that are less directive and more contingent. Acknowledge and invite responses from others. In addition, include more variation in your sentence structure—for example, instead of using primarily declarative sentences with only nouns and verbs, use more adjectives and adverbs.

Conflict: Use your anger as a clue to deeper issues for your self-development.

A long, hard look at what lies beneath your anger will give you a tremendous amount of useful information. This will almost invariably lead to the territory that is most uncomfortable for you—your deep, often hidden vulnerabilities. Issues such as the need to control, the insistence on justice, and the desire to tackle the largest challenges and move things forward in significant ways almost always lead to an underlying issue of vulnerability.

Teams: Use your influence, not your control, to develop and support collaborative teams.

Rather than helping direct the team early on or pulling back in a wait-and-see stance, work collaboratively with other team members to clarify the team's direction, making a special effort to help members get to know one another.

Leadership: Honor your leadership gift of making important things happen and enhance your ability to make all employees feel safe and respected.

When something for which you are responsible does not succeed as planned, take care that your tone of voice, line of questioning, and general approach do not make others feel blamed. The perception of being blamed shuts down candid conversation and effective problem solving. In addition, ask yourself every day: *Whom and what am I not listening to?*

ELEVEN

Coaching
Enneagram Style Nine

Nines seek peace, harmony, and positive mutual regard and dislike conflict, tension, and ill will.

Center of Intelligence · Body Center

HOW TO IDENTIFY NINES

Thinking ← → Feeling

Behaving

CORE BELIEFS
- If we could all just get along, life would be peaceful.
- What's important is for people to listen to one another, treat each other with respect, and live and let live.
- Before making a decision, it's best to consider all perspectives and get everyone's input.

EMOTIONAL PATTERNS
- Experience a range of low- to medium-intensity feelings, but present a steady, even-tempered demeanor
- Keep anger at such a subliminal level that they are often not aware of feeling it

WORKPLACE BEHAVIORS
Are affirming, approachable, and facilitative • Like clear, structured processes and details • Can be passive-aggressive when pressured • Avoid conflict with others • Blend and merge energetically

The "Impassive Body"

Nines use their Body Center to deal with control in a counterintuitive way: they control by not letting others control them. They do this by being non-assertive, impassive, or inert. Although Nines ultimately do what they want according to their own preferred time frames, they also want to avoid creating conflict with others. As a result, Nines exercise control in several ways: not acknowledging to themselves or others what they really think or want; implicitly agreeing to do something, then not doing it; expressing themselves indirectly; and/or being affable and agreeable. When asked their thoughts about a controversial issue, instead of offering an opinion or stating that they don't want to discuss the topic, Nines might say the following, with a pleasant tone of voice, a laugh, and a smile: "Oh, I haven't really thought about this."

Emotional Patterns of Nines

Experience a range of low- to medium-intensity feelings,
but present a steady, even-tempered demeanor

Easygoing and affable, Nines keep most strong feelings to themselves, even controlling the extent to which they allow themselves to feel them. As a result, most Nines experience feelings in the low- to medium-intensity range even when they are actually feeling them more strongly. Keeping their body language pleasant and neutral and using only slight variations in facial expressions and tone of voice, Nines appear consistent, mellow, and positive. Because Nines often look agreeable and display few variations in emotional reactions, others perceive them as highly approachable, thus allowing Nines to develop an easy rapport with a variety of people.

Keep anger at such a subliminal level that they are often
not aware of feeling it

Although Nines like to mediate and resolve conflict between others, they do not like feeling angry themselves. As a result, Nines keep themselves from both experiencing anger and expressing it directly. In fact, it often takes Nines two to three times longer than most people to become aware of feeling upset.

Workplace Behaviors of Nines

Are affirming, approachable, and facilitative

Nines appear easygoing, nonjudgmental, and diplomatic, and they also act supportive of others through affirming comments, head nodding, and saying "Uh-huh"—which do not always mean they agree, just that they heard what the other person was saying. Nines may not always be as relaxed and nonjudgmental as they appear, because their internal tension and critical thoughts are not usually obvious to others. In addition, Nines are inclusive, collaborative, and facilitative, wanting everyone to be heard so that all perspectives are considered and every person feels he or she has been heard.

Like clear, structured processes and details

Nines enjoy familiar rhythms in their lives, and routines that help them feel oriented, and they like to create processes for doing activities at work and at home. In addition, Nines like detail, because they assimilate the big picture through understanding and organizing the operational details involved in tasks and projects.

Can be passive-aggressive when pressured

Nines dislike feeling controlled or pressured, but at the same time they have difficulty saying no when someone asks them to do something, even if they don't want to do it. For example, they may not like the task, may be too busy to do it, or may dislike the way in which they have been asked. However, they rarely say no or assert themselves directly; instead, they may either say "yes" and mean "no" or say "yes" but procrastinate, delaying the task for an indefinite amount of time.

Avoid conflict with others

Although Nines dislike having others feel angry with them, they can behave in ways that may cause other people to be upset—for example, by not stating their opinions directly or by not saying what they want. Nines also minimize their own feelings by not allowing themselves to feel anger very often or very deeply. They do, however, enjoy helping others resolve tensions, and they are usually quite skilled at listening empathically and helping others in conflict find common ground.

Blend and merge energetically

Nines like to feel connected to or in strong rapport with people and things that they like. They most often blend or merge their energy in harmonious situations and with people who have a positive and interesting manner. They become internally distressed when they are around chronically negative, complaining people or when disharmony between individuals or in groups cannot be resolved.

FAMOUS NINES

Walter Cronkite	"In seeking truth, you have to get both sides of a story."
	"And that's the way it is."
Dalai Lama	"Be kind whenever possible. It is always possible."
	"The purpose of our lives is to be happy."
Dwight D. Eisenhower	"I despise people who go to the gutter on either the right or the left and hurl rocks at those in the center."
	"Always take the job, but never yourself, seriously."

Subtypes: Three Variations of Nine

In order to maintain harmony and comfort and to avoid conflict, Nines numb themselves to their own reactions by becoming lethargic or by not paying attention to their own deeper feelings, needs, and impulses, thus disabling them from knowing what they think and want and which action is the right one to take. There are three distinct ways in which Nines manifest these characteristics, called subtypes.

Self-Preservation Subtype Nines use the comfort of routine, rhythmic, and pleasant activities as a way of not paying attention to themselves. Using these repetitive activities to distract themselves from more important issues, many self-preservation subtype Nines also acquire collections, and their desire for these objects increases the more they obtain.

Social Subtype Nines work extremely hard on behalf of a group, organization, or cause that they support or belong to as a way of not focusing on themselves. Social subtype Nines are usually very friendly, and their need to feel a part of things is rooted in their underlying feeling of not fitting in. Thus, Nines sacrifice themselves in the service of others, rarely showing the pain, stress, and overwork they experience as a result.

One-to-One Subtype Nines join or merge with others who are important to them as a way of not paying attention to their own thoughts, feelings, and needs. This fusion with others results in one-to-one subtype Nines becoming disconnected from their own deep desires and confusing their own intentions and fulfillment with those of these important others.

Wings and Arrow Lines for Nines

Because Nines seek harmony and comfort so fervently and avoid conflict to such a high degree, they can be highly acquiescent, have difficulty accessing their personal power and organizational influence, be reluctant to state their opinions directly in most circumstances, and ultimately lose touch with what they want and need, thereby becoming passive and inert. Access to their wings (styles Eight and One) and arrows (styles Six and Three) can provide a counterbalance to these qualities in Nines.

Wings for Nines

EIGHT WING   Nines with an Eight wing have a more take-charge orientation, exhibiting a solidity and forcefulness while still maintaining a desire to hear others' opinions. With a very strong Eight wing, Nines assert their own points of view more readily and make fast and clear decisions, even in the face of strong opposition.

ONE WING   When Nines have a One wing, they are more attentive—for example, they pay more attention to details and are more punctual and precise. Although Nines often diffuse their attention, a One wing increases their overall focus, acuity, clarity, and discernment.

Arrow Lines for Nines

ARROW LINE TO SIX   When Nines have a strong link to Six, their level of insight about self, others, and situations increases, and they tend to be more deliberative and verbally expressive.

ARROW LINE FROM THREE   Nines with a strong connection to Three have a stronger goal focus and results orientation, qualities that help them shift from the distractions of seeking comforting and comfortable activities to a more forward-moving, action-oriented approach to life and work.

Three Typing Questions for Nine

1. Do you automatically blend or merge with other people's positive energy but get distressed when you are around negativity, anger, and conflict that can't be resolved?
2. Do people find you easy to approach and nonjudgmental in almost all circumstances?
3. Do you have great difficulty expressing your opinions, particularly if they may be controversial in some way?

HOW TO COACH NINES

Areas of Strength	Areas for Development	
• Diplomatic	• Conflict avoidant	
• Easygoing	• Unassertive	
• Accepting	• Procrastinating	
• Affable	• Indecisive	

COACHING OVERVIEW

Even under normal circumstances, Nine learners need to feel a strong sense of connection with developers before they fully engage in the coaching experience. This need for rapport is even more crucial when they are about to hear constructive (negative) feedback and feel stressed. Developers can take extra steps to lessen the Nine learner's anxiety by doing the following: Take extra time at the start of the meeting to have a comfortable conversation about a topic of mutual interest; make sure your body language and tone of voice convey respect; pace the delivery of the feedback so the Nine learner doesn't become overwhelmed; and ask the Nine learner how he or she is responding at regular intervals during meetings.

Nines usually prefer that coaching discussions and feedback include specific details as well as multiple interpretations of the key issues, particularly if the information they receive is negative or controversial. This mirrors the way Nines process information and also makes it less likely that they will feel unfairly criticized. In addition, Nines generally do not like being told what to do, and they may perceive feedback or suggestions as demands to take specific action. At these times, Nine learners may become passive-aggressive, saying or implying to the developer that they will take action when they have no intention of doing so.

When Nine learners are ready to take action, developers can provide valuable assistance by helping them define and prioritize the most important items and then determine the action to be taken. Prioritization is a key challenge for most Nines as a result of their tendency to procrastinate, switching from working on one project to working on another or to shift from doing one task to doing a secondary or less important one. For this reason, developers can support Nine learners not only by helping them prioritize the key issues and desired action, but also by highlighting the particular way Nine learners diffuse their attention, confuse their priorities, and become inactive rather than assertive.

First, Determine Coaching Goals and Learner Motivation
Goal Identification: What to Ask Nines

It is especially important for Nines to define their coaching goals in clear and actionable terms, as this provides them with concrete guideposts throughout the coaching process. At first, Nines may have difficulty being highly specific about what they really want, and the developer's helping them do so is a major step in the growth and change process. Normally, Nines don't focus on themselves very much, and while they may enjoy the developer's focus and attention, Nines really need to learn to focus on their needs, desires, and intentions themselves. These questions from the developer help Nine learners define what they most want from the coaching experience:

- *Tell me about yourself and your desires and goals for the coaching we will do together.*
- *I can hear that these matter to you. Can you share more with me about why this is so?*

The questions above are phrased in a nonintrusive, inviting way and communicate to Nine learners that they and the developer will be working collaboratively during the coaching process—for example, the use of words such as *we* and *together*. In addition, the word *you* is also used frequently as an implicit way to say that the focus of the coaching is on the Nine, not the developer. This serves two purposes: First, it signals to Nines that they need to become clear about what they want from the coaching experience. Second, it communicates that the Nine learner will determine both the direction of the coaching and the actions that will result from the process. This is very important, because Nines can become resistant when they believe that someone is trying to take charge of or control their behavior in any way.

When discussing the Nine learner's goals, developers should help the Nine clearly connect the key development motivators listed below to specific coaching goals. This link may be obvious to learners as they discuss why each coaching goal is important, but if it is not, developers can do one of two things: (1) Ask Nine learners, *"What personal and professional benefits will you gain when you achieve this goal?"* or (2) explain the connection between the goal and the motivator directly by saying, *"This will help you become more comfortable asserting who you are and what you think in highly productive ways."*

Key Development Motivators for Nines

- To express themselves clearly and directly and to have greater influence and more authority than they might normally
- To have a strong, deeply held sense of personal power so that they feel empowered to take effective action
- To transform conflict into deeper and more connected relationships instead of avoiding it
- To work with other people from a sense of fully understanding both themselves and others

Second, Assess the Learner's Level and Range of Self-Mastery, Then Use Level-Appropriate Coaching Approaches

The best way to determine the self-mastery level of the learner is to read the behavioral descriptions for all three levels in the chart on pages 204–205 and answer these questions:

1. What is this person's normal (average) level of self-mastery?
   ☐ Low ☐ Moderate ☐ High
2. What do I know and what have I observed that leads me to this conclusion?

Nines: Self-Mastery Levels and Coaching Approaches to Enhance Development

High Self-Mastery · The Fully Conscious Individual

Core understanding

Unconditional regard connects everyone and everything.

Nines who have reached the level of high self-mastery no longer have difficulty taking a stand. In fact, they approach life in an active and purposeful way, knowing that they have the right to voice their opinions. They are involved, engaged, and extremely vital. Solid, substantial, and alert, they are also serene, deeply content, and "in flow," all of which come from a firm inner core.

Coaching approaches to enhance the Nine's self-mastery

Provide encouragement and additional methods for expansion.

- Help Nines create a clear vision for what they most want, then guide them in developing a concrete action plan; review the plan's progress on a regular basis.
- Review their successes regularly, having them explain how they accomplished what they did; offer additional insights when helpful.
- Each time Nines offer candid and clear statements about their feelings and opinions, offer a positive statement about the impact of this on you.
- Give strong, positive reinforcement each time Nines engage in conflict directly; provide additional strategies for conflict resolution when needed.
- Acknowledge Nines each time they take clear, purposeful action.

Moderate Self-Mastery · The Harmonizer

Core concern

Stability, harmony, and being heard

Nines at the moderate level of self-mastery want everyone to get along, desiring peace and harmony above all else. Because of this, they become adept at mediating differences but become highly anxious when conflict is directed at them. These Nines lose focus, pursuing activities that distract them rather than attending to the challenges in front of them. Nines at this level have trouble asking for what they want, prefer the predictable pace of routine activities, and act so agreeably that they often have many friends or at least many people who like being around them. They will rarely take a stand on something they believe in, opting instead to go along with what others want.

Coaching approaches to enhance the Nine's self-mastery

Stimulate motivation and provide concrete development actions.

- Help Nines learn different approaches to priority setting so they can find methods that work well for them.
- Appreciate their ability to see all sides, but encourage them to also state their own positions in a clear and unequivocal way.
- Provide positive reinforcement for all direct expressions of opinion or feeling they offer without your having prompted them to do so.
- Help them see that avoiding conflict creates more conflict, using concrete examples from your life as well as theirs.
- Ask them what they think and feel on a regular basis to help them become more comfortable expressing themselves.

Low Self-Mastery · The Sleeper

Core fear

Separation from others, being controlled, and discord

Nines with a low degree of self-mastery do not pay attention to themselves, and they have no energy to pay attention to anyone else. They ignore even the most life-threatening problems, refusing to face the most obvious consequences of their desire to pretend that everything is okay. Consistently neglectful and forgetful, Nines with low self-mastery become chronically sluggish and immovable. However, if they feel pressured to do something they don't want to do, they either become passive-aggressive—saying "yes" but meaning "no"—or burst forth with unleashed and seemingly bottomless fury.

Coaching approaches to enhance the Nine's self-mastery

Offer support, guidance, and boundaries.

- Provide concrete ideas for strategies that will make sure the work gets done; make sure Nines feel they are in control of this, or they will react negatively and not follow through.
- Gently but firmly address their passive-aggressive behavior; invite them to express frustration or anger directly, but don't push, as this creates more inertia.
- Validate their perspectives, then ask them about other ways they could perceive the situation. Help them assess what is the most realistic scenario.
- Ask about their preferences, opinions, and feelings several times during coaching meetings, but do so without any pressure. If they don't know, give them time to think and then respond.
- Avoid implicit and explicit power struggles related to the Nine's need to not feel controlled; repeatedly ask them for their ideas about how to proceed.

3. What is this person's range of self-mastery—that is, the individual's highest and lowest levels?
4. What do I know from my own observations or other data that leads me to this conclusion?

Once you have an initial assessment of the Nine learner's self-mastery level, read the recommended approaches appropriate to that level and select those you believe will be most effective for the learner.

Third, Use Coaching Techniques That Challenge Growth

As you read the following four coaching techniques, it can be helpful to think about several Nines you know and how you might use the techniques with those individuals. Nines are normally very similar to one another, although Nines who have a strong link to arrow lines Three or Six or a strong Eight wing may not initially appear as mellow and easygoing as other Nines. Nines can also appear different from one another, depending on factors such as their self-mastery level, empathy, how they use their wings and arrows, subtype, experience, age, gender, and culture.

Head Center Challenge: The "What if?" Question

"What if?" challenges work well in situations in which the learner makes assumptions that something is important and inviolate—that is, a mental model. These assumptions are part of the learner's unchallenged beliefs and paradigms. After hearing the Nine learner express an explicit or implicit assumption, the developer poses a relevant "What if?" question. The following chart lists three common mental models for Nines, the question the developer should ask to challenge each assumption, and the ways in which the developer should respond once the Nine has answered the developer's challenge.

"What if?" Challenges for Nines

Common Assumption No. 1

"Everyone needs to be heard, and all perspectives need to be acknowledged."

Developer's challenge

"What if everyone were not heard and all perspectives were not equally valid?"

Developer's follow-on response

- If the Nine says, "They have to be heard. All perspectives are valid," answer: *"What if not everyone wants to be heard, there is truly no time for everyone to be heard, or some perspectives are more informed and useful than others?"*
- When the Nine indicates an understanding that hearing everyone is not always possible or desirable and/or that nothing disastrous will occur as a result, respond: *"How would you be different or more free if you didn't feel compelled to make sure that everyone is always heard?"*

Common Assumption No. 2

"I really can't tell this person I disagree with what he's about to do."

Developer's challenge

"What if you could freely share your perspective on this?"

Developer's follow-on response

- If the Nine cannot think of such a scenario, tell a relevant compelling story of when you shared a different point of view with someone and it made a big difference to that person. Then say: *"You must have a similar story. Can you tell me about it?"*
- When the Nine suggests some great benefits to sharing his or her perspective or tells a relevant story, ask: *"How can you expand this insight and experience into other situations?"*

Common Assumption No. 3

"I need to wait until the end of a meeting to share my views."

Developer's challenge

"What if you didn't wait until the end, but instead shared your ideas early on or in the middle of the meeting?"

Developer's follow-on response

- If the Nine can't think of such a situation, ask: *"Have you ever shared your ideas and opinions at any time other than the end of a meeting? If so, what happened?"*
- When the Nine gives a concrete and positive response, say: *"See, you can do it. What would you and the team gain if you did this more often? What would you personally gain if you had the real choice to share your ideas at any time during the meeting? Then tell me about the lost opportunities."*

Heart Center Challenge: Explore the Learner's Defense Mechanism
The Nine's Primary Defense Mechanism: Narcotization

Narcotization is a defense mechanism in which individuals unconsciously numb themselves to avoid something that feels too large, complex, difficult, or uncomfortable to handle. Nines narcotize and distract themselves by engaging in prolonged rhythmic activities that are familiar, require very little attention, and provide comfort—for example, washing the dishes, working in the garden, continuous pleasure reading of books by the same author or within the same genre, going for a walk or a bike ride, engaging in frequent or extended casual conversations, and continuously changing channels on the TV. Nines also use daily routines such as morning or evening rituals to immunize themselves from being fully aware, and they feel agitated, irritated, or disoriented when these repetitive activities become disrupted.

Most Nines engage in narcotizing activities on a regular basis, but they do this most often when they feel pressured, uncertain, angry, anxious about their capabilities to do something, or discounted or overlooked. It can be difficult to determine what is upsetting Nines, because even they may not know for certain. However, when they engage in narcotizing behavior—especially when there is something else they should be doing or something they need to say—it is a clear indication that they have deadened themselves with something distracting and soothing. Additional examples of narcotization at work include the following: diffusing their attention by forgetting what they were discussing or not remembering something that was clearly stated; talking about nonessential topics for prolonged periods of time with people they feel

NARCOTIZATION

A Nine has an urgent and complex work assignment that needs to be completed today, but instead of focusing on this priority assignment, the Nine cleans up the office, files old expense reports, makes nonurgent phone calls, and works on lower priority work that is unrelated to the project at hand and has no looming deadline.

comfortable with and like; displaying various forms of procrastination, such as chronic lateness for appointments, meetings, and task-related commitments; not completing required paperwork on a timely basis; and bringing the same work home night after night without ever completing it. These examples are actually symptoms or manifestations of narcotization that often hide or defend against the following deeper developmental issues for Nines:

- Expressing their real thoughts, needs, opinions, and preferences in a clear and direct way on a regular basis, especially when these oppose the wishes of others
- Being active, assertive, and taking clear action rather than being deenergized, passive, or acquiescent
- Learning to embrace conflict when they are directly involved in it, rather than avoiding it out of fear that harmony and connectivity will be severed, and learning to deal with conflict constructively

Working with the Nine's defense mechanism of narcotization can be challenging for developers. An indirect challenge may go unnoticed because of the Nine's avoidance, but a direct challenge may be met with passive resistance or outright hostility. In addition, when they narcotize, Nines are almost always doing something. As a result, Nines often excuse their lack of follow-through about a priority task by explaining what they were doing instead.

INDIRECT CHALLENGE TO NARCOTIZATION
"Let's talk about the things you do that soothe you in times of duress and the activities you pursue that give you comfort."

DIRECT CHALLENGE TO NARCOTIZATION
"Even though you can be a highly aware person, you seem to numb yourself to what you really want and to what's most important in your environment. You need to look at how you do that and then, even more importantly, why you do that."

Body Center Challenge: The "Why would you want to do that?" Question

When Nine learners say they want to change something about themselves, asking them this question works effectively as a way of supportively challenging their desires. As a response to this technique, the Nine learner either changes his or her course of action or becomes more deeply committed to the original plan. This technique is especially useful in two situations: (1) The Nine learner articulates an intention to take action that sounds productive, or (2) the Nine learner expresses an intention to take action that might be risky or could be counterproductive to his or her best interests.

"Why would you want to do that?" Challenges for Nines

A Nine's Productive Intention to Act

"I'm going to be more assertive."

Developer's challenge
"Why would you want to assert yourself more?"

Developer's follow-on response
- If the Nine cannot think of an answer or gives an unconvincing answer, say: *"It doesn't sound like you really want to do this."* After the Nine responds, say: *"You might want to consider that for some reason, you gain more from being passive than you think you would gain from being more assertive."*
- When the Nine gives a convincing response, say: *"It sounds as though this matters to you. Please tell me more about this and about your current thinking on how to do it."*

A Nine's Counterproductive Intention to Act

"That person is chronically negative, so I'm just going to avoid him."

Developer's challenge
"Why would you want to avoid this person rather than speaking to him in a truthful way?"

Developer's follow-on response
- If the Nine gives you a reason that also makes sense to you, say: *"It sounds as though you've made a wise choice."*
- If the Nine gives you a reason you believe is possibly unwise, say: *"You may want to avoid him, but before you proceed to not say anything, let me ask you a question: Are you really making the choice not to speak to him or are you simply avoiding him as you typically do in these situations? True choice means you are capable of taking either action, but you choose one option."*

Because Nines have serious issues with taking action in a timely and assertive way, the "Why would you want to do that?" question is very important for them. Nines sometimes talk about doing something but don't seem to get around to executing it. For this reason, their response to the "Why would you want to do that?" question can be an important motivator for them to take action. Because Nines can be passive, using this same challenge about their inaction can illuminate the fact that nonaction can be a serious problem—that is, "Why would you *not* want to take this action?"

Transformative Paradoxical Challenges

Nines usually like paradoxical challenges because they find them amusing and intellectually stimulating, akin to a complex puzzle that fits together in unexpected ways. Paradoxes are actually ironically comical descriptions of human behavior in action, and the Nines' attunement to irony about the human condition makes them receptive to the paradoxical challenge. Nines may need help, however, in determining what action to take in order to resolve the two conflicting ideas held within the paradoxical statement. When asked for help, the developer needs only to say, "I think you already know what to do. The question is whether or not you have the courage and conviction to do it."

THE NINE PARADOX

Nicole, a senior engineer at a high-tech company, looked nervous as she entered the room for a meeting with her coach. The coach noticed this and asked, "Nicole, you usually come in here so relaxed. What's on your mind?"

Nicole blurted out, "I'm not sure what to do. Two of my colleagues, Shawn and Amy, are competing for the same promotion. Both of them have asked me to speak to my boss on their behalf, because my manager is making the ultimate decision. Both Shawn and Amy have their strong points, but I believe that Shawn has more experience. Amy and I are closer, and her interpersonal skills are stronger than Shawn's. On top of that, my manager called me and wants to schedule an appointment to find out what I think about both candidates and which of them I would recommend. I'm honored that he values my opinion, but not at the price of being caught in the middle."

Paradox Explanation

Nines want to be acknowledged and taken seriously; however, they act so easygoing and accede so readily to what others want that they don't assert themselves, and others then discount what they have to say.

Developer's Paradox Statement

"You say you want some help with how to remove yourself from the middle of this situation and keep everyone happy. That is not, I believe, the central issue. The bigger issue is that your boss is acknowledging you by soliciting your opinion, and this recognition is something that you say you want. However, instead of asserting yourself, you seem more concerned with making sure no one is angry with you."

NOTE Use the paradoxical challenge only with moderate to high self-mastery Nines; low self-mastery individuals may not be psychologically stable enough to handle the ambiguity inherent in paradoxes.

NINE COACHING CASE STUDY SUMMARY: JOE

Determine Coaching Goals and Learner Motivation

Make sure the goals can be accomplished in the time available and are linked to one or more of the learner's key motivators.

> Joe, a director in his company, wants to be more assertive. He is well respected for both his intellect and his ability to work with others, but he feels his affable manner and his difficulty being direct and assertive are hindering him professionally. When asked why this matters to him, he states, "I know I can do more for the company, and I would just like the satisfaction of knowing that I can speak my mind and that I'm listened to. I do feel others listen, but I just don't have as much impact or influence as I would like."

Assess the Learner's Level and Range of Self-Mastery, Then Use Level-Appropriate Coaching Approaches

Determine the learner's normal (average) level and range of self-mastery.

> Joe is almost always at the higher end of moderate self-mastery and rarely even goes below the moderate self-mastery midpoint. On occasion, he is in the high self-mastery range. He possesses a great deal of wisdom that he conveys in a folksy way—even though he has a Ph.D. in engineering from a prestigious university—and when he expresses his insights in a timely way, he has a big impact on those around him. These experiences seem to reinforce his ability to function at the high self-mastery level. In addition, his expressed motivations are completely aligned with the key development motivators for Nines, which means he is likely to take great advantage of the coaching experience.

Select the development approach(es) from the chart on pages 204–205 that would be most effective with the learner, and experiment with these.

> Because Joe's self-mastery level is consistent and so close to high self-mastery, he will be most stimulated to grow by the coaching approaches for high self-mastery Nines. Provide positive reinforcement each time Joe expresses himself quickly and clearly, especially when he does so in a context that contains some opposition to his thoughts. Be sure to reinforce him every time he does this during coaching conversations—for example, when he disagrees with the coach—and about examples he brings from work. Explore the positive impact of this behavior on others, but also how he felt about himself. This will provide additional reinforcement. Focus on action he takes in addition to the self-assertion described above. Encourage him to act, and acknowledge him each time he does so or reports having done so.

Use Coaching Techniques That Challenge Growth

Plan how you will use each of the four coaching techniques from this section, and use them at appropriate moments during the coaching process.

Head Center Challenge: "What if?"

What have you heard the learner say or imply that reflects a mental model or assumption you can challenge? How will you phrase this "What if?" challenge?

> All of the following challenges would be effective with Joe.
> *"What if you already know how to be assertive and just need to do it more?"*
> *"What if you were already highly respected and you just don't realize it?"*
> *"What if the respect you really desire most is self-respect?"*

Heart Center Challenge: Recognizing and Leveraging Defense Mechanisms

When have you observed the learner using a particular defense mechanism? Would a direct or an indirect challenge be more effective? How would you phrase this defense mechanism challenge?

> Joe already recognizes that he narcotizes when distressed; his primary method is eating. Because he is intellectually oriented, he also narcotizes by reading fiction when he should be working and is particularly drawn to mystery novels set in a historical context. For example, he has three favorite authors in this genre, has read every book by them, and keeps these books so he can reread them when he feels the need to relax. Because Joe is so high functioning and has an excellent sense of humor, either a direct or an indirect challenge to his narcotization will be effective. Using humor to do so will be helpful, but don't mention his eating habits, as he is sensitive about being somewhat overweight.
>
> **INDIRECT CHALLENGE**
> *"Have you been reading and rereading any of your mystery novels lately? If so, what have you been thinking, feeling, or wanting to do that you are avoiding?"*
>
> **DIRECT CHALLENGE**
> *"You seem to be dulling your senses now and clouding your insights about the issue we're discussing by forgetting or neglecting to mention some of the information involved. What makes this difficult for you to discuss?"*

Body Center Challenge: "Why would you want to do that?"

What behavior has the learner stated he or she plans to do? Do you think this is a wise course of action? How would you phrase this "Why would you want to do that?" challenge?

"Why would you want to assert yourself more?"

"Why would you not want to assert yourself in this particular situation?"

Transformative Paradoxical Challenge

What paradoxes have you observed in the learner? Select the most significant one. How would you phrase this paradoxical challenge?

"You say you want to have a bigger impact and more influence on those around you, yet you still seem focused more on making sure that no one is angry with you and that everyone is happy than you do on speaking candidly and helping others pursue action based on the truth."

NOTE Paradoxical challenges should be used only with moderate or high self-mastery learners. Low self-mastery learners are not in a psychological state to handle the complexity and ambiguity inherent in the resolution of this level of paradox, and deep-level or complex paradoxes can increase their anxiety. While less powerful paradoxes can be used with these learners, developers should do so with caution.

DEVELOPMENT ACTIVITIES FOR NINES

Developers can suggest the following activities to Nine learners.

Core Issue: Take a position.

Each morning, think about one opinion that you hold strongly; during the day, share that opinion with two people. Every day, select a new opinion or idea and discuss it with two new people. Continue this activity for two weeks, then reflect on the experience by asking yourself these questions: *Has it become easier to say what I really think? Are some topics easier to discuss than others? Are some people easier to share with?* After you've answered these questions, continue the activity for one month, selecting new topics and new individuals each day.

Expansion Through Wings and Arrows
EIGHT WING   **Step into your personal power.**

Every time you interact with others, keep your attention completely focused on yourself, the other person or persons, and the issues that are being discussed. This will help you feel and become more personally powerful. Your personal power is directly connected to your ability to maintain your full attention rather than diffusing your focus.

ONE WING   **Stay on top of your tasks.**

Make realistic to-do lists every day, prioritize the items, and check each one off as it is completed. Reward yourself with something you enjoy after you have completed the list and have followed your order of priority in doing so.

ARROW LINE SIX   **Be courageous and assert yourself.**

Summon your courage even when you feel afraid by saying the following words to yourself: *Although I feel afraid, I have the courage to assert myself more and to take action.* Use this idea to bolster your courage, letting yourself experience the exhilaration of taking action.

ARROW LINE THREE   **Focus on results.**

For every task or project you have, develop a clear goal or goals. Write the goals on a piece of paper that you then attach to a highly visible place—for example, your computer or a mirror at home. Refer to these goals each time you do any activity related to the task or project, and ask yourself this question: *Will what I am about to do take me further toward this goal?*

Communication: Be more direct and directive.

Because you probably have a good sense of what direction another person or a team should take, simply make the suggestion early in the conversation or meeting instead of waiting until the end. Practice making no apologies for your suggestion, such as explaining why the person doesn't have to do what you've suggested or explaining why your idea may not be the best course of action. Simply make the suggestion, doing so in as few words as possible, then wait until others respond.

Conflict: Make friends with your anger.

Have a written dialogue with your anger. Ask your anger: *Anger, tell me about yourself—what you are like, why you function the way you do, and what you want from me.* Write down whatever comes to mind. Keep this dialogue going until the conversation feels finished. Continue this written dialogue over the next several weeks while you reach increasing clarity.

Teams: Create a little conflict.

Be willing to disagree with other team members, trusting yourself enough to know that your ideas are good ones. When others disagree with you, either ask for clarification if you don't understand their viewpoints or hold your ground if you believe you are correct. Remember that disagreement is not personal; it is simply the sharing of ideas.

Leadership: Honor your leadership gift of inclusion and consensus and enhance your ability to lead by setting priorities and direction.

Instead of talking in paragraphs and using abundant detail, practice communicating with others by highlighting the key points you want to make, as if you were making a PowerPoint presentation.

TWELVE

Transformation

Organizations cannot succeed in the long run unless their employees—leaders and individual contributors alike—are highly talented, engaged, and committed to their own personal and professional development. Organizations are growing and changing at an unprecedented rate, and employees at all levels in the organization must keep up with this pace or be left behind. This chapter shows developers how to take their coaching to a deeper level, providing them with three transformative coaching activities to use with learners and a compelling development plan.

Seeking and Avoiding is a transformative activity that addresses the core motivational drives of each style. When learners constantly seek or avoid something, it defines and limits them, controls their behavior, and impedes their growth.

The Power of Words is a simple and elegant transformative activity that allows the learner to embody the qualities he or she most truly desires.

Hold It in a Bigger Space is an unusual physical transformative activity that works in magical ways for many people.

Extreme Growth: The Development Journey provides a holistic and integrative transformative development process that can be used repeatedly.

While the three activities and the development planning process can be used in short-term, crisis, and long-term coaching, the second and third activities—The Power of Words and Hold It in a Bigger Space—are ideally suited to provide hope and relief to learners engaged in crisis coaching.

ACTIVITY 1 · SEEKING AND AVOIDING

The following activity is very powerful, simple to do, and counterintuitive, which makes it stimulating and productive for the learner. Seeking and Avoiding focuses on the learner's chronic thought processes, feeling patterns, and automatic behaviors that are directly related to what the learner most fervently seeks and avoids. Rather than judging these motivations by suggesting there is something wrong with these deep-seated drives and that they should therefore be eliminated, the Seeking and Avoiding activity examines the benefits and liabilities of these motivations, then asks the learner to respond to this question: "What if you could *relax* this particular search and avoidance?" The word *relax* brings relief to the learner; rather than feeling pressured to give up something they believe is part of who they are, learners realize it is possible to lessen its influence so that it no longer controls them. This allows them more freedom and choice in their lives. Finally, the learner imagines relaxing the drive and is able to articulate the benefits of doing so, then addresses the question "How will you do this?" This enables learners to take concrete action.

In the chart on the following page, the exact phrasing of these questions is provided, followed by the *search for* and *avoidance of* words to insert into the blanks for individuals of each Enneagram style. An example for an Enneagram style Three follows on page 220.

Seeking and Avoiding Activity

Questions to Ask Learners

1. How does your *search for* _____ contribute to your well-being and success, as well as the success of the organization and those who work for or with you?

2. How does your *search for* _____ cause problems for you, the organization, and those who work for or with you?

3. How does your *avoidance of* _____ contribute to your well-being and success, as well as the success of the organization and those who work for or with you?

4. How does your *avoidance of* _____ cause problems for you, the organization, and those who work for or with you?

Summary Questions

1. What if you could relax your *search for* _____ and your *avoidance of* _____ ?

2. How will you do this?*

*If the learner cannot imagine relaxing the drive or has difficulty articulating the benefits of doing so, he or she is not ready for transformational growth. In that case, the developer can say, *"It sounds like you want to maintain this drive more than you want to change it,"* and then wait for the response.

Search for and *Avoidance of* by Enneagram Style

ENNEAGRAM STYLE	SEARCH FOR	AVOIDANCE OF
One	Perfection	Making mistakes
Two	Appreciation and being needed	Feeling unworthy
Three	Respect and admiration	Failure
Four	The expression of deep feelings and connections with others	Rejection and not feeling good enough
Five	Knowledge and wisdom	Intrusion by others and loss of energy
Six	Meaning, certainty, and trust	Prevention of negative scenarios
Seven	Stimulation and pleasure	Pain and discomfort
Eight	Control and justice	Feeling vulnerable and weak
Nine	Harmony and comfort	Direct conflict and ill will

Example of the Seeking and Avoiding Activity: A Three

Search for Respect and Admiration

Positive impact

As I seek to be respected and admired, I behave in respectable and admirable ways. These behaviors typically make me feel good about myself, both in and of themselves, and because they work; that is, they really do bring me the respect and admiration of others. The better I feel about myself in the world, the more effective I tend to be in my work and in my relationships. This translates to success all around. When I find myself, my clients, and those around me being effective and successful, I want to continue the behaviors that contribute to that. It's a reinforcing loop. Also, I become more willing to take risks and to trust in the outcome.

Negative impact

Pursuing success based on outside perspectives is terribly limiting. I'm only ever as good as my last success, and my memory of that is very short indeed. Needing external validation of internal worth limits my ability to be authentic, to take risks, and to be successful and effective. When I don't feel respected and admired (which is tantamount to being effective and successful – they're really the same thing), I become less willing to take risks and to trust in the outcome. I play it safer and become less effective as a result. It's the same loop backward.

Avoidance of Failure

Positive impact

It seems glib, but I really don't fail. Never mind that I got arrested as a teenager for youthful transgressions, flunked out of college, drank too much, got divorced— all these experiences have contributed to who I've become. Failure is not possible in my work—I will prepare, design, sweat until I'm absolutely certain that whatever the work is, I'm prepared for it and it will go marvelously and be a great success for all concerned. Interestingly, while all this preparation is in the service of eliminating even the slimmest chance of failure, once in front of the client I will often throw it all out and do what seems necessary and appropriate at the time. All the avoidance-of-failure prep work frees me up to be effective and successful in that way.

Negative impact

It's a lot of work. It's exhausting. I can turn into a real jerk when I'm scared. If you're good enough to help me with something that's going to be successful, great: I need you to work at my pace and on my timeline. If you're not, I need you to leave me alone while I figure out how to build something that's going to work, and believe me, you'll get the message about my displeasure loudly and clearly. Nice, huh?

Summary

What if you could relax your search for respect and admiration and your avoidance of failure?

Everything would be so much easier, calmer, less stressful, less dramatic, and more fun.

How will you do this?

Well, I'm learning. I've surrounded myself with good people I can trust, which is more of a work-around than actually dealing with it directly. The trick for me is trusting in what I already know about myself: I'm good, resilient, effective, successful—and I don't need external validation about that, I already know that. I need to trust my opinion as much as I trust yours. Taking tasks, work—and life—less seriously will help immensely. What's the worst that can happen, really?

ACTIVITY 2 · THE POWER OF WORDS

Because words are symbolic, they have the power to evoke strong reactions, unconsciously affecting thought patterns, feelings, and behaviors. Because words function in this manner, they can be used to modify and transform a learner's customary reactions in positive ways by having the learner first think about and reflect on them, and then embody them. When a learner embodies an evocative word by allowing the word to completely fill his or her body, he or she literally experiences this new and preferred way of being.

There are specific evocative words for individuals of each Enneagram style that serve as antidotes to each style's customary mental patterns, and other words that counterbalance each style's emotional habits. When learners embody the words that work best for their style, several things occur. First, the learner is transported into the experience of that word, including the thoughts, feelings, and behaviors the word implies. This deeply calms them. Second, being able to embody a word demonstrates to learners that they already know how to be in this state of being; it is nearly impossible to embody something you have never experienced at least once. This is highly reassuring to learners, because it gives them the faith and courage that they can do this more often. Third, when learners embody the state of being they most desire and do so on a regular basis, they begin to change in fundamental ways, shifting and transforming their ongoing patterns of thinking and feeling and, in turn, transforming their ongoing behavior.

The transformative words that impact the head and heart of each Enneagram style are listed in the chart on pages 222–224. A description of the basic activity and an advanced, more powerful variation is given in the chart on page 225.

Transformative Words

ENNEAGRAM STYLE	TRANSFORMATIONS TO CALM THE MIND	TRANSFORMATIONS TO CALM THE EMOTIONS
One	**Peacefulness · Faultlessness · Acceptance** Transform *resentment* (paying attention to flaws so that nothing ever seems good enough) into *perfection* (the insight that everything is as it should be, and that even imperfection is perfect)	**Compassion · Opening · Understanding** Transform *anger* (the feeling of chronic dissatisfaction with how things are) into *serenity* (an openhearted acceptance of all that occurs)
Two	**Self-care · Freedom · Liberation** Transform *flattery* (the gaining of acceptance through giving compliments or other forms of attention to others) into *free will* (the insight that acknowledging yourself and your own needs leads to autonomy and freedom)	**Humbleness · Release · Surrender** Transform *pride* (the inflated self-esteem and self-importance derived from doing for and being needed by others) into *humility* (the feeling of self-acceptance and appreciation without either self-inflation or deference to the opinions of others)
Three	**Trueness · Depth · Being** Transform *vanity* (the strategic thinking about how to create an idealized image based on being or appearing to be successful) into *hope* (the faith that you can be valued and appreciated for who you are rather than what you do and accomplish)	**Unfolding · Non-doing · Flow** Transform *deceit* (the feeling that you must do everything possible to appear successful, hiding parts of yourself that do not conform to that image, and believing that your image is the real you) into *truthfulness* (finding true self-acceptance through acknowledging both your successes and your failures, and realizing that your image is not your essence or true self)
Four	**Connectivity · Inseparability · Humanity** Transform *melancholy* (thinking continuously about what is missing, with accompanying thoughts of being separated from others) into *original source* (the insight that nothing is missing and everything is ultimately deeply connected, because we all emanate from the same source)	**Calmness · Centeredness · Constancy** Transform *envy* (consciously or unconsciously comparing yourself repeatedly to others in large and small ways, with accompanying feelings of deficiency or superiority) into *balance* (experiencing emotions in such a clear and centered way that thought, feeling, and action emanate from your inner self)

ENNEAGRAM STYLE	TRANSFORMATIONS TO CALM THE MIND	TRANSFORMATIONS TO CALM THE EMOTIONS
Five	**Interconnectedness · Wholeness · Oneness** Transform *stinginess* (a scarcity paradigm that leads to an insatiable thirst for knowing, a reluctance to share—knowledge, time, space, and personal information—and to strategizing about how to control your environment) into *omniscience* (the insight that only through direct personal experience and complete engagement can you know all things)	**Visibility · Abundance · integration** Transform *avarice* (the intense desire to guard everything about yourself combined with automatic detachment from feelings) into *non-attachment* (the firsthand experience that detachment is not the same as non-attachment, and that you must fully engage and become attached to something before you can learn to be truly non-attached)
Six	**Steadiness · Certainty · Confidence** Transform *cowardice* (the thoughts of doubt and worry that cause you to continuously create worst-case scenarios) into *faith* (the belief that both you and others can capably meet life's challenges, and that there is some certainty and meaning in the world)	**Strength · Bravery · Potency** Transform *fear* (feelings of anxiety, deep concern, and panic that the worst will occur, that others cannot be trusted, and that you are not up to life's challenges) into *courage* (the feeling of being able to overcome fear through fully conscious action, rather than turning to inaction or to action designed to prove that you have no fear)
Seven	**Attention · Focus · Presence** Transform *planning* (the mental process by which the mind goes into "hyper gear," moving in rapid succession from one thing to another) into *work* (the ability to direct and control the focus of your mental attention to one thing only, and to sustain that focus)	**Attunement · Fullness · Completeness** Transform *gluttony* (the insatiable, unrelenting thirst for new stimulation of all kinds—people, things, ideas, and experiences) into *sobriety* (the feeling of being a full and complete person, which comes from pursuing and integrating painful and uncomfortable experiences as well as pleasurable and stimulating ones)

ENNEAGRAM STYLE	TRANSFORMATIONS TO CALM THE MIND	TRANSFORMATIONS TO CALM THE EMOTIONS
Eight	**Multidimensionality · Reality · Unity** Transform *vengeance* (the process of rebalancing wrongs through thoughts related to anger, blame, and intimidation) into *truth* (the ability to seek and integrate multiple points of view in search of a higher or bigger truth)	**Freshness · Purity · Receptivity** Transform *lust* (excessiveness in a variety of forms—for example, work, food, or pleasure—as a way of avoiding and denying feelings and vulnerabilities) into *innocence* (the childlike feeling of vulnerability and openness, such that the need to control situations or to protect yourself or others is no longer present)
Nine	**Caring · Delight · Awareness** Transform *indolence* (the process of mentally diffusing your attention so that you forget what is important to you and refrain from stating your opinions, thereby minimizing conflict with others) into *love* (the belief that there is an underlying universal harmony based on our unconditional regard and appreciation for one another)	**Awakening · Clarity · Movement** Transform *laziness* (lethargy in paying attention to your own feelings and needs, thus disabling you from taking the action you most desire) into *right action* (the state of feeling fully present to yourself and others so that you know exactly what action you must take)

Power of Words Activities

Power of Words Basic Activity

Introduction

Explain that words have the power to shift and transform thinking and feeling patterns, and that there are specific words that work best for each Enneagram style. These words are the antidotes that calm and relax a person's normal patterns. Select one word from among the three mental transformation words or the three emotional transformation words for the learner's Enneagram style. Ideally, the learner selects the particular word, but if the individual is under extreme duress, the developer can select the word. If the learner seems mentally agitated, choose a mental transformation word; if the person's emotions need calming, select a word from the emotional transformation list.

Activity

Ask the learner to sit in a relaxed position, then to think of the chosen word and only this word, to reflect on it, and then to allow this word to completely fill and penetrate his or her whole body, allowing it to move and expand throughout the body. Suggest that once the person has completely embodied the word—that is, allowed it to completely fill the body—he or she allow the word to remain throughout the body while continuing to breathe. Allow this word embodiment to continue without interruption, for as little as three minutes or as long as five minutes if the learner seems to be enjoying the activity or is in crisis. When the learner is finished, ask him or her to discuss the experience.

Discussion

Different words can be used at different times, depending on the learner's needs. After learners have learned how to do this activity, they can also use words from other Enneagram styles, but it is best to begin with the words for their own style.

Power of Words Advanced Activity

The advanced activity involves embodying the word while walking around. The activity is identical to the basic activity except that learners embody the word while standing rather than sitting down; when they feel the word throughout the body, they begin walking in silence while maintaining the embodiment of the word.

The walking embodiment technique is more difficult because the individual must focus on both maintaining the embodiment and walking, but it is also more powerful as a catalyst for transformation. Most people can do this after they have learned the basic technique. Learners can do this easily on their own as they take daily walks or go from their car or train to the office.

ACTIVITY 3 · HOLD IT IN A BIGGER SPACE

Learners can use this activity any time they feel agitated or distressed or simply want to work on their type-based reactions to a specific person or event. The basic concept underpinning this activity is that holding on to emotional reactions does not get rid of them; it only makes them fester and grow stronger, precipitates behavior that is not in the learner's best interests, and can even make the learner sick.

The following activity helps people acknowledge and release their feelings. Because it works well with almost everyone, it can be invaluable when learners are in a crisis and nothing else seems to provide them relief.

Hold It in a Bigger Space Activity

The following instructions are worded as if the developer is guiding the learner through the process. Once the learner has demonstrated the ability to do this during a coaching meeting, the learner can use this activity on his or her own.

Explain that when people are distressed and/or in the midst of an Enneagram style–based reactive behavior, they tend to go into a contracted mode of functioning, tighten their muscles, become more fixed in their thought processes, and recycle their emotional responses. However, when people expand rather than contract, they not only receive relief, they literally experience and perceive the situation differently. This happens when they "hold something in a bigger space."

Introduction
Explain that you are going to do a guided imagery activity with the learner and that he or she needs to be seated comfortably and relaxed.

Activity
"Close your eyes, focus internally, and find the place in your body where the intensity of your reaction resides. That area will be your focus right now. Put all of your attention and energy into this area until you feel this intensity completely. Holding this place of high-intensity energy, allow—but do not force—slightly more space around it—say, an inch or so of white or clear space—then hold this bigger space with whatever is inside it for a few moments. Now, allow slightly more space around this. Allow it, don't force it, and experience what happens naturally. Continue to allow more space around it, allowing the white space to grow as much as it wants to, and allow what occurs to happen naturally, without forcing anything. Continue to allow more and more space until what is inside the space does what it wants; you are not forcing anything. Continue allowing more and more space around this until you feel finished. When you are done, gradually open your eyes."

Discussion
After learners open their eyes, developers should allow several minutes of silence. This allows learners to feel more present and to integrate more from the activity. Then, ask the learner to share what he or she experienced as completely as possible. Next, ask what insights or questions emerged. Remind learners that they can do this activity on their own whenever they wish to give themselves relief as well as a larger perspective on the situation.

DEVELOPMENT PROCESS: EXTREME GROWTH

When learners are ready to take action on their development, they need to create a plan that helps them both achieve and sustain the results they most desire. A development plan should be a stimulating, enjoyable, and intriguing journey that is also informative, practical, efficient, and effective—that is, it should help learners achieve their development goals. At the same time, it should also help learners be honest with themselves about their true commitment to growth. They need to honestly assess which of these they most desire:

No growth: They don't want to change anything, or the time is not right for them to do so.
Moderate growth: They want to make incremental improvements.
Extreme growth: They are ready to make fundamental shifts in their patterns of thinking, feeling, and behaving.

The planning tool Extreme Growth: The Development Journey takes learners through a sequenced journey that elicits knowledge and insight from their three Centers of Intelligence—the Head, Heart, and Body Centers. To accomplish this, learners complete the following six-step process:

Extreme Growth: The Development Journey

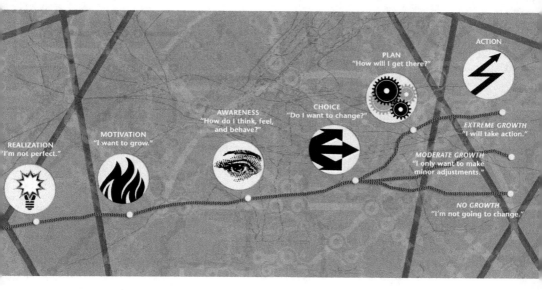

Step 1 · Realization—the knowledge that you aren't perfect (and that none of us ever will be)

Learners use their Head Center to consider possible directions for growth, their Heart Center to determine the support they need from themselves and others in order to grow, and their Body Center to acknowledge past related behavior; using all three Centers, they define their development goal.

Step 2 · Motivation—the impetus and inspiration for your development

Learners use their Head Center to assess whether they believe they can grow, their Heart Center to determine how deeply they desire this, and their Body Center to sense and imagine themselves acting in a dramatically different way; using all three Centers, they assess the strength of and reasons for their motivation.

Step 3 · Awareness—the objective understanding of your own reactions related to your development area

Learners use their Head Center to identify their thinking patterns related to the development area, their Heart Center to determine their relevant emotional response patterns, and their Body Center to honestly acknowledge their behavioral response patterns and consequences; using all three Centers, they assess their current awareness level.

Step 4 · Choice—the decision to take responsibility for yourself and to commit to your own growth and development

Learners use their Head Center to decide when and how to intercept old habitual responses and what to substitute in their place, their Heart Center to reassess their passion to change, and their Body Center to be honest and clear about their true commitment to change; using all three Centers, they make the choice of no growth, moderate growth, or extreme growth.

Step 5 · Plan—the creation of a development plan

Learners use the information from Steps 1 through 4 to develop an integrated development plan.

Development Plan

Development goal (completion date)
Write your goal from Step 1. State it in positive terms. Give yourself a realistic yet ambitious completion date.

Goal   **Date**

Development activities   **Success criteria**
Select one to three development   How will you know when you have
activities that will work well and   achieved success?
that you want to do.

1.   1.

2.   2.

3.   3.

Support needed
What support do you need from your coworkers, boss, organizations, and family, as well as from yourself?

Coworkers

Boss

Organization

Family

Self

Step 6 · Action—the ability to take constructive, sustained action (complete this step one month after the plan has been implemented) and to adjust the plan as needed along the way

Learners use their Head Center to assess their degree of success in intercepting and changing their thought patterns, their Heart Center to determine their degree of success in changing their emotional responses, and their Body Center to honestly assess their degree of success in changing their behavior and the areas for continued growth; using all three Centers, they adjust their development plan as needed.

SOME FINAL THOUGHTS

When coaching is successful, developers say that they have gained as much as, if not more than, the learner from the experience. Not only do developers feel deeply satisfied with the time they have spent and the results that have been accomplished, they have also learned to do the following: become more aware themselves; challenge their own assumptions; perceive their emotional reactions in a new way; feel more responsible for the outcomes of the choices they make; and view the organization from a very different perspective. When developers approach coaching in this way, coaching is transformed from being a responsibility to an honor, and developers, learners, and organizations benefit enormously.

Coaching Competency Self-Assessment

Having the ability to coach others effectively means that developers are skilled in the following six areas:

1. Being an excellent developer of people
2. Knowing how to accelerate the learner's growth
3. Being able to create a productive relationship with the learner
4. Knowing how to implement an effective development process
5. Being able to align the coaching efforts with organizational requirements
6. Being able to achieve lasting results

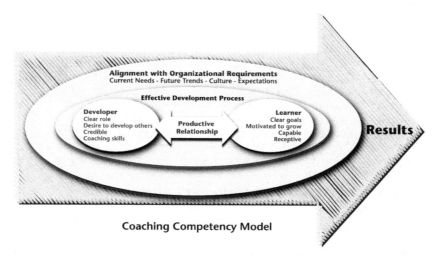

Coaching Competency Model

Several of the competency areas listed have subelements within them. As you read the information about coaching competencies in the chart on pages 232–234, take a moment to assess your current skills as a coach. Doing so will help you recognize your coaching strengths and determine the areas needing further development. For each component that follows, please rate yourself on a scale of 1 to 5 (1 = low, 5 = high).

Coaching Competency Self-Assessment

1. Being an excellent developer of people

A clear role

Understanding your role as that of either manager, mentor, or coach and knowing the behaviors required for that particular role; adhering to the behaviors and confidentiality boundaries inherent in that specific coaching role; and holding employees ultimately accountable for their own development

1 2 3 4 5

Desire to develop others

Believing that development is an investment in the employee's and organization's future; demonstrating through word and action that employee development is among the highest organizational priorities; truly enjoying the challenge of developing others; taking a sincere interest in helping others fulfill their aspirations; and learning as much from the coaching experience as the learner does

1 2 3 4 5

Credibility

Being perceived as highly competent and professional; having experiences similar enough to the learner's that the learner believes the coaching guidance will be useful; willingly sharing knowledge, experiences, and insights; having a successful track record in developing others; being equally task- and people-oriented; and demonstrating integrity that includes a solid ethical orientation

1 2 3 4 5

Coaching skills

Being skilled at identifying and assessing key talent and high potentials; being able to coach learners with different learning styles and a wide variety of developmental needs; providing learners with ongoing positive and constructive feedback that is respectful, objective, and action-oriented; and recognizing and leveraging growth opportunities, including recommending challenging tasks and assignments for learners

1 2 3 4 5

2. Knowing how to accelerate the learner's growth

Learner's goals

Helping the learner formulate clear, actionable goals that are in the best interests of both the learner and the organization; keeping the learner focused on the central issues connected to his or her development goals; and being willing to adjust the goals or the direction of the development as needed

1 2 3 4 5

Learner's motivation

Knowing a variety of effective ways to activate the motivation of individuals with different needs and personality styles; being able to access the learner's motivation at different stages in the coaching process; and using effective techniques to challenge and support the learner's desire to grow

1 2 3 4 5

Learner's capability

Accurately assessing the learner's current and future competence   1 2 3 4 5
in relationship to his or her development goals; identifying the
learner's mental models, emotional responses, and behaviors that
support or detract from the achievement of the development goals;
and keeping track of the learner's progress and effectiveness in
enhancing his or her capabilities

Learner's receptivity

Behaving in a variety of ways that encourage the learner's   1 2 3 4 5
receptivity to the coaching process; recognizing when learners
are receptive to the coaching and when they are not, and having
effective strategies for enhancing their receptivity; and identifying the
learner's psychological and behavioral defenses to development and
using these to help the person increase his or her rate of learning

3. Being able to create a productive relationship with the learner

Following the learner's pace and developmental needs rather than   1 2 3 4 5
pushing one's own agenda; creating an ongoing open dialogue
about the effectiveness of the coaching experience; being willing
to adjust direction as the situation requires; being approachable
and warm rather than distant and aloof; establishing a relationship
in which both learner and developer feel trusted and respected;
and using the relationship and interactions to enhance the growth
of both learner and developer

4. Knowing how to implement an effective development process

Being available for frequent coaching discussions; following   1 2 3 4 5
a flexible yet systematic coaching process; collaborating with the
learner on the creation of a compelling development plan; and
providing ongoing feedback to support the plan's implementation

5. Being able to align the coaching efforts with organizational requirements

Understanding how organizations operate, including   1 2 3 4 5
organizational elements such as strategy, structure, and politics;
being sensitive to the specific organizational culture of the learner
and its implications for the success of the learner; aligning the
learner's development to the organization's goals, expectations,
and processes; and ensuring that the pace of the coaching meets
the organization's ongoing and future business needs

6. Being able to achieve lasting results

Understanding what the learner needs in order for the results   1 2 3 4 5
of the coaching to have long-lasting results; and assisting the learner
in developing an individualized change strategy that will enable
the person to actualize the coaching goals

Total   _____ / 60

Reflect on your coaching skills by answering the following questions:

Which competency area is your strongest skill set?

How can you leverage this strength without overusing it?

Which competency area is your weakest skill set?

What can you do to develop stronger skills in this area?

Short-Term Coaching

Short-term coaching is particularly useful in certain situations: The learner is new to coaching and wants exposure to the developer and/or the coaching experience before he or she commits to long-term coaching; the coaching goal is sufficiently precise and narrow in scope that it can be achieved in a short time period; or the learner has a limited window of opportunity in which to develop in the agreed-upon coaching area. Short-term coaching will not be useful if the coaching goal is beyond the scope of what can be achieved in a short time frame, or if the learner is either too low in self-mastery or has insufficient skills and/or on-the-job experience to achieve the coaching goal within the allotted time period.

Although there are a variety of excellent short-term coaching methods, the Change Strategy Formula[1] is straightforward, logical, and highly flexible.

Change Strategy Formula
$$D \times V \times P > R = C$$

D = desire and demand for the change; dissatisfaction with the status quo
V = vision for the change
P = plan and process for achieving the change
R = resistance to change
C = change the learner most desires, the goal to be achieved

Focus first on **C**, and have the learner define a clear goal for the coaching, one that is precise, measurable, and stated in positive terms rather than negative language. For example, "To be less anxious at work" is imprecise, difficult to measure, and negatively phrased and should be rephrased as, for example, "To feel consistently confident when I present project reports in front of the

---

[1] The Change Strategy Formula is an adaptation of the Formula for Change created by Dick Beckhard and David Gleicher in the 1960s.

senior management team." During this discussion and all others, make sure to document every comment.

Next, proceed to **D**, followed by **V** and **P**. For each of these elements, have the learner assign a numerical score from 0 to 5 (0 = low; 5 = high), then have him or her explain exactly why this score was given. When the learner explains the score for **D**, ask probing questions to elicit the learner's depth of desire, the external demands for this change, and the dissatisfaction the learner or others feel about the situation as it is. For **V**, determine whether the learner can articulate the vision fully and imagine him- or herself completely engaged in this new behavior. For **P**, verify that the learner has a concrete and viable plan and process already in place in order to achieve the vision (**V**) and accomplish the change (**C**).

Third, proceed to **R** (resistance); have the learner give it a numerical score from 0 to 5 and explain the reasons behind the score. Many learners are surprised to find that they themselves have resistance to the change they say they want, or that some people around them may not support them in their desire to grow.

Fourth, complete the calculation. Notice that multiplying **D**, **V**, and **P** means that if any of these three elements is 0, the entire left side of the equation is 0. When this is the case, no change will occur. However, if the left side of the equation is greater than the **R** or resistance score, change is likely; the greater the score on the left side relative to the **R** score, the greater the speed and magnitude of the change.

Finally, reflect on the scores and the documented information under each element of the Change Strategy Formula. It will be clear what needs to be done to accelerate the learner's progress toward the change goal. For example, if **D** is low, coaching needs to focus on the learner's motivation. If **V** is the lowest element, spend more time helping the learner create a new vision. If **P** has the lowest value, work on a development plan that engages the learner. If **R** is too high, spend time exploring the nature and cause of the resistance and how to overcome it. During this analysis, it will become obvious that each element of the formula affects other elements. For example, if **V** is given a high score, the value for **D** may also increase.

The elegance of the Change Strategy Formula methodology is that it is diagnostic, strategic, practical, and stimulating and works with individuals of all Enneagram styles. In addition, the Change Strategy Formula methodology also works well in conjunction with the level-based self-mastery approaches and the four coaching challenges described earlier in the book.

Crisis Coaching

Crisis coaching is required when the learner is in crisis—that is, something extremely serious is occurring in that person's personal or professional life that is causing him or her severe duress. Even if the learner and developer are already engaged in short-term or long-term coaching, crisis coaching requires a different approach.

To understand crisis coaching, it can be helpful to examine examples from other disciplines. In economics and international relations, a crisis is an extremely unstable situation in which the consequences appear so ominous that they pose a strategic threat of great magnitude. In literature, a crisis occurs when the story's most significant conflict reaches a turning point, a struggle emerges between opposing forces, and information is revealed that has been partially or entirely unknown; all of this precedes the plot's ultimate climax. In psychology, crisis refers to a breakdown in which the usual patterns of functioning and coping behaviors no longer work. And in medicine, a patient in crisis exhibits an intensification of symptoms so extreme that the patient may be about to take a dramatic turn for the worse.

Because learners in crisis experience most or all of the above, developers need to proceed carefully, cautiously, and quickly in order to support and guide the learner. The Crisis Coaching Method box on page 238 provides the developer a clear structure for doing this.

CRISIS COACHING METHOD

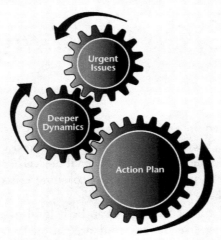

Respond to the urgent issues
1. Listen attentively.
2. Address immediate problems when possible; give advice carefully.
3. Be calm, compassionate, and clear.

Deal with the deeper dynamics
4. Identify root causes.
5. Deal with the learner's deeper concerns.
6. Provide hope and relief.

Create a sustainable action plan
7. Create a focused, concrete plan of action.
8. Design a support system.
9. Refer the learner to additional resources as needed.

Respond to the urgent issues

1. Listen attentively.

Listening with an open mind and heart is the most important gift a developer can offer. Individuals in crisis need to talk about what is disturbing them and can often determine what they need to do on their own by telling their story to another person, knowing that someone cares enough to give them their full attention, and learning more about themselves as they talk. In addition, learners may need clear, practical, and wise advice from the developer so that they don't do something precipitous that they will later regret. Unless they listen fully to learners in crisis, developers may give premature suggestions that are ill advised.

2. Address immediate problems when possible; give advice carefully.

Individuals in crisis need developers to help them solve immediate and urgent problems, and learners may feel so confused and anxious that they rely on the developer's advice and guidance more than usual. This dependency is normal. However, developers must advise cautiously, because learners are the ones who must live with the choices and accept the consequences.

3. Be calm, compassionate, and clear.

When people are in crisis, they are usually in great turmoil, full of emotions, and confused. In order to provide a countervailing and constructive force to the learner's intensity and anxiety, the developer needs to be inordinately calm, visibly compassionate and empathic, and clear-sighted.

Deal with the deeper dynamics

4. Identify root causes.

Although crisis coaching does not usually involve enough time to deal with the root causes of the learner's dilemma, it is important for developers to help learners identify the key factors involved and how these are related. Learners gain greater insight into the dilemma and can then work with the developer to formulate an approach they can take to explore the root causes and dynamics on their own, either by engaging in long-term coaching or obtaining other types of outside help. However, learners are not ready to do this level of analysis until they have resolved or reduced their anxiety about the most urgent issues. Similarly, they cannot develop a plan of action to address the critical issues until they understand the issue's root causes and underlying dynamics. Otherwise, learners end up addressing the problem's symptoms, not its cause.

5. Deal with the learner's deeper concerns.

Individuals in crisis are deeply concerned about their situation. Developers can guide the learner through a discussion of which outcomes are likely to occur, which are just possibilities, and which are unlikely to manifest. In addition, developers can help learners differentiate between factors over which they have some control and those they cannot affect, then explore viable actions for the factors that learners can influence. Finally, when individuals are in crisis, their most fundamental Enneagram style–based needs and anxieties get triggered and become hyperactive. Unfortunately, a highly anxious state is not conducive to resolving a crisis. Developers should notice these concerns and anxieties when they appear and help learners acknowledge these deeper feelings. Learners need to realize that they cannot afford to let their fears drive their behavior or get in the way of the more pragmatic actions they need to take. These deeper concerns for individuals of each Enneagram style include the following:

Ones	Feeling deeply wrong
Twos	Feeling unworthy
Threes	Having no intrinsic value
Fours	Feeling deeply deficient
Fives	Feeling empty and drained
Sixes	Having absolutely no certainty or support
Sevens	Feeling not whole and solid
Eights	Feeling dead inside
Nines	Having no significance

When learners are in crisis, their primary defense mechanisms (described in Chapters 3 through 11) can become overactivated and dysfunctional or may cease to function altogether, leaving the person in a highly vulnerable and undefended state. If the learner's defense mechanism seems to be in overdrive, developers can use Enneagram style–specific defense mechanism challenges. In most instances, it is safest to start with an indirect challenge, since learners in crisis are more sensitive and highly vulnerable.

In addition, learners in crisis may blame other people and circumstances for their problems or issues as another coping strategy they use in addition to their primary defense mechanism. This way of externalizing responsibility for what is occurring provides the learner with temporary relief as well as with an outlet for his or her anger. However, it also puts the learner in a victim's role, a position from which individuals rarely learn the important lessons that crises often provide. In addition, people in victim roles have a narrow view and a limited range of constructive options. When learners start to perceive themselves as victims, developers should listen just long enough for the learner to feel heard, then get the learner's attention by saying something like this: "Many external factors are involved in this. However, when you focus primarily on these, you end up feeling like everything is being done *to* you, which means that very little can be done *by* you."

6. Provide hope and relief.

Learners need some hope that the situation can get better and that the developer can help them make this so. The activities in Chapter 12, Transformation, can be useful. In addition, developers can use a technique from a methodology called Appreciative Inquiry to provide the learner some relief.

Appreciative Inquiry focuses on the positive rather than the negative, thus energizing instead of depleting the learner. When in crisis, most individuals focus on the negative and often forget about the positive elements in their lives as well as the strengths and skills they possess. A simple, well-phrased question such as this can provide insight and relief: "Can you tell me about a time when you were in a difficult situation, yet you were able to summon strengths and skills to resolve this in ways you couldn't have anticipated?"

Create a sustainable action plan

7. Create a focused, concrete plan of action.

While it is not realistic to develop a plan of action that will solve all of the issues related to the learner's crisis, it is essential to have a plan for how the learner is going to resolve the issues. Without a concrete plan, the learner will remain highly anxious, and the specific problem is unlikely to go away. Even if the crisis becomes less acute, something similar is likely to reappear at a later date.

8. Design a support system.

Although everyone can benefit from having an ongoing support system that provides comfort, constructive confrontation (for example, from people who care about us enough to tell us the truth), and resource referrals when needed, learners in crisis need these even more. Developers can help learners think about the support systems they currently have, the kinds of support provided, and what more might be needed.

9. Refer the learner to additional resources as needed.

Learners in crisis may have needs beyond what the developer can or should provide, and these may be in place of or in addition to continuing the coaching relationship. For example, learners may need referrals to a therapist, a substance abuse counselor, or a lawyer. In addition, there is an excellent book available for anyone going through difficult times: *When Things Fall Apart* by Pema Chodron. Short, practical, philosophical, and compelling, Chodron's book offers a way to understand life's most stressful times as well as techniques for dealing with tumultuous situations.

Long-Term Coaching

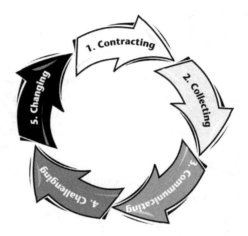

COACHING STAGE 1

Contracting involves one or more initial discussions between the developer and the learner. During these conversations, each gets to know the other better in his or her respective roles and the two discuss their expectations, define the coaching goals, clarify the time commitments required as well as the frequency and duration of the coaching meetings, and discuss what data about the learner would be useful to gather from others and how this will occur. Ultimately, the developer and learner reach a collaborative and mutually agreed-upon coaching plan. This is the optimal stage at which to introduce the Enneagram to learners who are not familiar with it. Sharing this knowledge at Coaching Stage will enable both of you to use the Enneagram's insights throughout the coaching process.

The effectiveness of contracting is fundamental to a successful coaching experience, preventing many problems and misunderstandings that can occur later in a coaching relationship. Ineffective contracting always creates future misunderstandings and negatively affects the trust between the developer and the learner and the success of the coaching.

COACHING STAGE 2

Collecting refers to gathering objective and useful organizational information that is directly related to the
coaching goals. Many developers make the mistake of
obtaining coaching-related data only from the learner.

The drawback to this approach is obvious: Most people do not see themselves
in an unbiased way. People often perceive themselves based on their intentions rather than their actual behavior, and they often emphasize the aspects
of themselves that make them the hero or victim in the story rather than the
villain or perpetrator. People also overestimate their strengths and under-
emphasize the areas in which they feel less capable, or vice versa. For these
reasons, it is important to gather information from multiple sources *in addition to* collecting data from the learner. Many avenues exist for collecting additional data: interviews, focus groups, surveys, performance reviews, 360°
feedback reports, video or audiotapes, written communications, and direct
observations or real-time experiences that occur in the coaching meetings.

When collecting data through surveys, interviews, or focus groups, ask
questions that are as neutral as possible; doing so provides more objective and
balanced data and prevents the skewing of responses in a positive or negative
direction. For example, a question such as "Please describe this person's leadership style" is far better than "What leadership problems does this person
have?" When asking non-neutral questions, it is important to ask for both
positive and negative responses—for example, asking both "What are this
leader's greatest strengths?" and "What are this leader's key development
areas?"

Finally, the anonymity of those who provide data is crucial to the trust
between the developer and the learner. If the developer breaks the confidentiality of a respondent, the developer not only breaches the confidentiality of
that person but erodes the trust between the developer and the learner. The
learner thinks, *If the developer would breach someone else's confidentiality, how
can I assume the same won't be done to me?*

COACHING STAGE 3

To effectively **communicate** the data collected, developers need to organize the data for maximum impact
and structure the data-feedback meeting with the
learner in such a way that he or she will be most receptive to the information.

How to Organize the Data

When determining how to best organize the data, the following five areas need to be addressed:

1. Quantity of data collected
2. Consistency of data
3. Coaching goals
4. Insight-based information
5. Learning style of learner

The amount of time allotted to the meeting should *not* be a factor in determining how to organize the data; in fact, ample time should be prescheduled for the data-feedback meeting—a minimum of two hours and as long as a full day.

1. Quantity of data collected

When a large quantity of data has been generated, the information needs to be crystallized down to a manageable size for the learner. The most common way to do this is to organize the data into main themes, coupled with a sampling of actual—and, of course, anonymous—quotes.

2. Consistency of data

When the data are reasonably consistent, the developer can organize the information in a simple and straightforward way. With less consistent data, more data must be shared, including the nuances of the issues involved.

3. Coaching goals

All data should directly relate to the learner's coaching goals; data that do not are usually excluded.

4. Insight-based information

The developer needs to share information that leads to action. There are four types of information:

- *Data:* the raw information that has been collected
- *Knowledge:* the patterns based on the raw data
- *Insight:* the kernels of truth that emerge from the patterns of knowledge
- *Wisdom:* the right action a person should take based on insight

The data collected should be organized and shared at the level of knowledge and insight. When information is organized in this way, the learner acknowledges the patterns, gains insight with the help of the developer, and then makes an informed decision to act.

5. Learning style of learner (auditory, visual, or kinesthetic)

Information is best communicated using the learner's preferred learning style. Learners with an auditory style prefer to hear the information; visual individuals want to see information, often preferring graphs and illustrations to words; kinesthetic learners want direct and thorough discussions of the information and prefer written materials and conversations that include the implications for action—but not a prescription for action—they can take as a result of the information.

Verbal cues often indicate an individual's primary mode, especially the nouns and verbs the person most commonly uses. Following are three examples of how one person might describe the same successful work project, depending on which modality he or she uses.

LEARNING STYLES

Auditory
"I knew that the project was successful when I *heard* all the feedback from my boss. He *told* me that the clients *raved* about how well it had gone and would *call* us back when the next project comes up for bid."

Visual
"I knew that the project was successful when I *saw* the *look* on my boss's face. He *appeared* to be thrilled. In fact, he couldn't stop *smiling*. The client's reaction was better than anything I could ever have *pictured*."

Kinesthetic
"I knew that the project was successful when my boss *came* to my office and *sat* down. He said that he had made the right decision by *putting* me on this project. The *sense* I got from him was that the client would *use* us again in a minute."

If the primary learning and processing mode of the learner is not known, the best alternative is to organize the data so that they appeal to all three learning modes—auditory, visual, and kinesthetic. In addition, most people have a secondary mode in addition to their primary one, so a bimodal approach usually reaches two of the three preferred learning styles of the person receiving the feedback.

How to Structure the Data-Feedback Meeting

Most data-feedback* meetings are divided into two parts: *preliminary discussion items* and *primary discussion items.* The specific items are shown in the Data-Feedback Meeting Agenda box below.

DATA-FEEDBACK MEETING AGENDA

Preliminary Discussion Items
1. Establish rapport
2. Review the initial coaching goals and the data collection methodology
3. Reiterate the confidentiality agreements
4. Ask the learner about any concerns

Primary Discussion Items
1. Present the data
2. Discuss the data and prioritize the most important issues
3. Discuss next steps

Preliminary Discussion Items

The four preliminary discussion items establish the context for the data-feedback meeting and give the learner the opportunity to discuss any concerns before reviewing the actual data. How best to establish rapport depends on the learner's Enneagram style. An offer of something to drink and a sincerely stated question (such as "How are you?") often suffice, but a few Enneagram styles need slight adjustments. In particular, Nines usually need more time than other styles to discuss a topic of mutual interest, as this relaxes them, whereas Fives and Eights prefer less time for rapport-building, wanting to get to the data as quickly as possible.

Primary Discussion Item 1: Present the data

There are two questions to consider when determining how to present the data during the meeting:

- Should the data be given to the learner all at once without discussion, or is it more effective to give the data to the learner in distinct sections, with discussion after each section?
- Should a print copy of the data be given to the learner, and if so, when?

Data and *data-feedback,* as used here, refer to the information shared, not the raw data.

The answer to the first question depends on a number of factors: the length of the data to be shared; the extent to which the learner needs to hear all the information before he or she understands its full meaning; and the learner's preference. In most cases, however, learners need to be encouraged to make comments or ask questions rather than being passive recipients of the data.

The answer to the second question is more straightforward. In almost every data-feedback meeting, the developer verbally explains the data rather than having the learner read it silently. This allows the developer to amplify certain parts of the information and to adjust his or her remarks in response to the learner's comments and nonverbal behavior. When learners receive a print copy of the data at the beginning of the meeting, most will read the information—even reading far beyond what the developer is communicating—rather than listen to the developer. Thus, it is better to give the learner a print copy either section by section—if the data are being presented in this way—or at the end, so he or she can review it after the meeting and reflect on its meaning.

Primary Discussion Item 2: Discuss the data and prioritize the most important issues

When learners are totally silent during the feedback portion of the meeting, it means they are unhappy with the data, are thinking about something that was communicated earlier in the meeting, or are being overly passive and possibly resistant. For these reasons, it is important for the developer to elicit some reactions early on and to pay close attention to changes in the learner's tone of voice or body language. When the learner has been silent for a period of time or when these voice and physical changes occur, ask *"How are you reacting to this?"*

The most important discussion between the developer and learner comes after all the data have been communicated. Developers can start the conversation by asking these two questions:

- *What parts of the data do you agree with?*
- *What do you disagree with or not understand?*

Knowing what the learner agrees and disagrees with helps the developer know the feedback areas that will be relatively easy for the learner and those that will be challenging. When discussing areas of disagreement, developers can use one or both of the following tactics:

- *If you don't think this information is accurate, please tell me what you think is correct from your perspective.*

- *Even if you think the information is not accurate or fair, these are some people's perceptions. What do you think might cause someone else to have these perceptions?*

During the conversation, the developer needs to elicit the learner's thoughts and feelings about what has been presented and discussed. Some learners appear to be responsive to the data yet are actually discounting its importance. Others may overemphasize a small critique as if it were of great importance and magnitude. The learner's Enneagram style affects the person's dexterity and clarity in discussing his or her true reactions. For example, Threes, Fives, and Sevens may need developers to elicit their reactions and help them feel comfortable discussing feelings, while Twos, Fours, and Sixes may need developers to help them sort out and clarify the abundant feeling responses they are experiencing. The Body Center styles—Eight, Nine, and One—can usually discuss thoughts and feelings in equal measure, but they need the developer to make them spend the time to do this before they move to action.

Once the data have been discussed, the next task is to prioritize the key issues. This is usually done collaboratively. Many criteria can be used to set priorities, among them issues directly related to the coaching goals, themes that have some urgency for the organization or the learner, and areas that excite and/or distress the learner.

Primary Discussion Item 3: Discuss next steps

Finally, the meeting needs closure. This involves clarifying what the next steps will be for the learner and developer—for example, topics and logistics of forthcoming coaching meetings, new goals or revisions of earlier goals as a result of the data, and any actions the learner or developer should take as an outgrowth of the data-feedback meeting.

Some developers and learners may want to proceed directly to Coaching Stage 4 (Challenging) and Coaching Stage 5 (Changing) as part of the data-feedback meeting. This can work well with some learners, especially those who have already made great strides through their coaching experience and are highly motivated to change. However, with most learners, allowing some time away to consider what has been said and what they want to do in response is highly beneficial. This is referred to as "soak time," a period that allows for reflection and integration. In addition, some learners may appear agreeable and even compliant during the feedback discussion, then return later with strong negative reactions or misinterpretations of what was said. For these reasons, it is generally advisable to separate communicating the data from challenging growth and planning for the changes needed.

COACHING STAGE 4

After the learner has received the feedback data and prioritized the issues raised, the next step in the coaching process is the **Challenging** stage. While some learners may wish to skip the Challenging stage and

proceed to the Changing stage at this time, it is not recommended that the learner move directly to action.

There are several reasons not to skip the Challenging stage. First, both learners and developers need time to discuss what was learned during the Communicating stage. New ideas, contrasting feelings, larger perspectives, and answers to important questions usually emerge during the Challenging stage. Second, the Challenging stage is essential for motivating the learner to engage in sustained growth. All learners need to ask themselves: *Do I really want to change my behavior?*

While challenging someone may not initially sound like supportive behavior, it can become a turning point for many learners when it is done with respect and compassion. In the coaching context, *challenging* refers to actions on the part of the developer that get the learner's attention and cause him or her to really take stock of behaviors. Four high-impact challenges for individuals of all nine Enneagram styles are included in Chapters 3 through 11.

COACHING STAGE 5

One of life's hard lessons is that no one can really *change* someone else. We can suggest, encourage, support, reward, cajole, and even try to force someone to change, but these tactics rarely work unless the individual truly wants to be different.

Sometimes, the greatest gift a developer can give learners is helping them gain self-knowledge and self-acceptance. Through the coaching process, individuals learn to know themselves better and to understand how they interact with others. Deep self-knowledge and true self-acceptance are rare phenomena and can be the most positive outcomes of any coaching experience. Paradoxically, when individuals come to the conclusion that they really are okay—accepting both their foibles and their strengths—they actually become far more open to personal and professional development.

By the time the coaching relationship reaches the final stage, **Changing**, the learner has more often than not already begun the process of change, *if* the following criteria have been met:

1. The contracting was clear, complete, and renegotiated as needed.
2. The data collection process asked the right people the right questions.
3. The data were communicated effectively, organized to suit the learner's goals and learning style, and delivered through an honest dialogue between the developer and the learner.
4. The learner felt constructively challenged by the developer.

The majority of learners will have begun to change in varying degrees prior to this final stage of coaching—for example, setting clear goals that matter to them, receiving some feedback that had a strong impact on them, or having increased self-awareness as a result of coaching or personal growth. During the final stage, Changing, the developer's job is to help learners focus their efforts to accomplish the following tasks:

1. Reconfirming goals
Learners need to make certain that their initial goals are the most important ones for their development. The developer can ask the learner: "Considering all you have learned, what do you really want to change?"

2. Identifying criteria for success
Learners need to define when their goal or goals will have been reached so they will know when it is time to acknowledge their success. For example, "to give effective public presentations" can mean giving a speech to 50 or 500 people without feeling anxious, giving PowerPoint presentations without relying on notes, going on television and receiving rave reviews, and many other things. The developer can ask the learner: "Given your development goal, how will you know when you have achieved it?"

3. Creating an effective and viable development plan
Learners need to create a simple, practical, and stimulating development plan if they are going to accomplish their development goals. This plan needs to include the precise goal desired, the development activities that will be conducted to accomplish this goal, the related success criteria, and the support required to implement the plan successfully. An effective and enriching development planning process is described in Chapter 12, Transformation.

Resources

Enneagram-Based Development Activities

Bringing Out the Best in Yourself at Work: How to Use the Enneagram System for Success by Ginger Lapid-Bogda (McGraw-Hill, 2004).

> Divided into chapters based on applications of the Enneagram—communication, feedback, conflict, teams, leadership, and personal transformation. Each chapter includes three detailed development activities for individuals of each style, plus activities for everyone.
> *Available at all major online and retail bookstores.*

The Enneagram Development Guide (2007).

> Over 300 pages of development activities (over 50 activities for each Enneagram style) for leaders and individual contributors on every business application of the Enneagram, plus deep-level activities for personal transformation.
> *Available at TheEnneagramInBusiness.com Store.*

The Enneagram Learning Portal

> The Enneagram Learning Portal on TheEnneagramInBusiness.com website has an abundance of Enneagram business information and development activities for individuals of each style. A special section (Interactions at Work) describes how the styles work together, the manager-employee dynamics, and the performance review, with developmental activities to improve these interactions.
> *Available by subscription only at TheEnneagramInBusiness.com Learning Portal.*

What Type of Leader Are You? Using the Enneagram System to Identify and Grow Your Leadership Strengths and Achieve Maximum Success by Ginger Lapid-Bogda (McGraw-Hill, 2007).

> Divided into chapters based on leadership competencies—Drive for Results, Strive for Self-Mastery, Know the Business: Think and Act Strategically, Become an Excellent Communicator, Lead High-Performing Teams, Make Optimal Decisions, and Stretch Your Leadership Paradigms. Each chapter contains three detailed development activities for leaders of each style, plus activities for everyone.
> *Available at all major online and retail bookstores.*

Enneagram Training Materials

Over 25 different full-color training tools for use in the following organizational applications of the Enneagram: communication, feedback, conflict, teams, leadership, self-mastery, decision making, strategic thinking, and transformation, as well as basic typing tools.

> *All tools available at TheEnneagramInBusiness.com Store.*

Enneagram Training Programs

Certification Programs (Train-the-Trainer Programs)

Two different programs for coaches, consultants, trainers, and managers are offered in locations throughout the world: *Bringing Out the Best in Yourself at Work* (6 days) and *What Type of Leader Are You?* (6 days).
Information and dates available at TheEnneagramInBusiness.com Events Calendar.

Coaching Program

A five-day training program focused on the coaching concepts and techniques from *Bringing Out the Best in Everyone You Coach: Use the Enneagram System for Exceptional Results.*
Information and dates available at TheEnneagramInBusiness.com Events Calendar.

Enneagram Books

The Enneagram: Understanding Yourself and the Others in Your Life by Helen Palmer (HarperOne, 1991).

Palmer knows the Enneagram system as well as any contemporary Enneagram teacher, and her use of real stories and examples and insights makes this worth reading.

Ennea-type Structures: Self-Analysis for the Seeker by Claudio Naranjo (Gateways Books & Tapes, 1991).

Claudio Naranjo is credited with bringing the Enneagram work of Oscar Ichazo to the United States and other parts of the world and has combined his Enneagram expertise with his vast work as a psychiatrist and teacher of Gestalt therapy.

The Essential Enneagram: The Definitive Personality Test and Self-Discovery Guide by David N. Daniels and Virginia A. Price (HarperOne, 2009).

A description of the nine styles from a Stanford University psychiatrist and major Enneagram teacher. Daniels explains the psychological aspects of each type so they can be easily understood.

The Wisdom of the Enneagram: The Complete Guide to Psychological and Spiritual Growth for the Nine Personality Types by Don Richard Riso and Russ Hudson (Bantam, 1999).

> The best-selling of all Enneagram books, *The Wisdom of the Enneagram* is accessible and thorough, providing a solid foundation for understanding the nine styles.

Coaching Books

Action Coaching: How to Leverage Individual Performance for Company Success by David L. Dotlich and Peter C. Cairo (Jossey-Bass, 1999).

> Action coaching is particularly useful for those who do executive coaching and work with high-level leaders in organizations.

Appreciative Coaching: A Positive Process for Change by Sara L. Orem, Jacqueline Binkert, and Ann L. Clancy (Jossey-Bass, 2007).

> A coaching application of the positive questioning approach Appreciative Inquiry, the book is filled with affirmative questions to ask coaching clients.

Coaching: Evoking Excellence in Others by James Flahrety (Butterworth-Heinemann, 2005).

> The founder of New Ventures West, a coaching certification company that uses the Enneagram for the personal development of its students, offers a variety of techniques that enable coaching clients to expand and transform the way they view themselves and their worlds.

Spiritual Books

The Enneagram of Passions and Virtues: Finding the Way Home by Sandra Maitri (Tarcher, 2005).

> Maitri clearly explains the sometimes difficult-to-understand spiritual dimensions and transformations of the Heart Center.

The 9 Dimensions of the Soul: Essence and the Enneagram by David Hey (O Books, 2007).

> As a student of Faisal Muqaddam, Hey explains the spiritual aspects of each Enneagram style in a way that reads like poetry.

The Spiritual Dimensions of the Enneagram: Nine Faces of the Soul by Sandra Maitri (Tarcher, 2001).

> Maitri explains the spiritual dimensions and transformations of the Head Center. In this book, she writes in a spiraling rather than linear way that some have difficulty understanding, so it is best to start by reading her *Enneagram of Passions and Virtues* first.

When Things Fall Apart: Heart Advice for Difficult Times
by Pema Chondron (Shambhala, 2005).

> This book is a gem and particularly useful for people in crisis. Chodron
> draws from the Buddhist tradition and includes suggestions and activities
> that make a real difference.

Index

"Impassive Body," The, 197
learner motivation, 203, 211
narcotization, 207–8, 215
paradox, 209–10, 213
self-mastery level and range, 203–5, 211
subtypes, 200
    one-to-one subtype, 200
    self-preservation subtype, 200
    social subtype, 200
typing questions, 201
wings, 200–201, 213–14
workplace behaviors, 197, 198–99

O'Donnell, Rosie, 181
Ones
    arrow lines, 46–47, 60
    body center as center of intelligence, 43
    challenges
        body center, 55–56, 59
        defense mechanism challenge, 53–55, 58–59
        head center, 52–53, 58
        heart center, 53–55, 58–59
        transformative paradoxical challenge, 56–57, 59
        "what if?" challenge, 52–53, 58
        "why would you want to do that?" challenge, 55–56, 59
    coaching approaches, level-appropriate, 49–51, 58
    coaching case study, 57–59
    coaching goals, 48–49, 57
    coaching overview, 47–57
    coaching techniques, 51–57, 58–59
    "Controlled Body," The, 43
    core beliefs, 43
    defense mechanism, 53–55, 58–59
    development activities, 59–61
        communication, 61
        conflict, 61
        core issue, 60
        expansion through wings and arrows, 60
        leadership, 61
        teams, 61
    development motivators, 49, 57
    emotional patterns, 43, 44

famous Ones
    Clinton, Hillary, 45
    Gandhi, Mahatma, 45
    Seinfeld, Jerry, 45
    identifying, 43–47
    learner motivation, 48–49, 57
    paradox, 56–57, 59
    reaction formation, 53–55, 58–59
    self-mastery level and range, 49–51, 57–58
    subtypes, 46
        one-to-one subtype, 46
        self-preservation subtype, 46
        social subtype, 46
    typing questions, 47
    wings, 46, 60
    workplace behaviors, 43, 44–45

Palmer, Helen, xviii
paradox. See transformative paradoxical challenge
projection, 149–50, 154

rationalization, 169–71, 174–75
reaction formation, 53–55, 58–59
repression, 72–74, 77–78
Riso, Don, xviii, 15

Schwarzenegger, Arnold, 181
Seinfeld, Jerry, 45
self-mastery level and range. See individual Enneagram style, self-mastery level and range
Sevens
    arrow lines, 162–63, 176
    challenges
        body center, 171–72, 175
        defense mechanism challenge, 169–71, 174–75
        head center, 168–69, 174
        heart center, 169–71, 174–75
        transformative paradoxical challenge, 172–73, 175
        "what if?" challenge, 168–69, 174
        "why would you want to do that?" challenge, 171–72, 175
    coaching approaches, level-appropriate, 165–67, 174
    coaching case study, 173–75
    coaching goals, 164–65, 173

ABOUT THE AUTHOR

Ginger Lapid-Bogda, Ph.D., a consultant, trainer, and coach with over 35 years of experience, works with Fortune 500 companies, nonprofits, and service organizations in the areas of strategy development, executive leadership, change management, high-performing teams, and cultural transformation. Her clients include Apple Computer, Clorox, Disney, Federal Reserve Bank, Genentech, Hewlett Packard, Whirlpool, and numerous law firms and nonprofit organizations.

Since Ginger began integrating the Enneagram with her work in organizations, she has become a world-class leader in using the Enneagram in business to foster individual and team effectiveness and to create viable, flexible, innovative, and responsible organizations. Ginger has written three seminal Enneagram-business books that have been translated into more than ten languages; has certified over 500 professionals worldwide to use the Enneagram in their professional work; provides state-of-the-art Enneagram-business training materials that are available in English, Spanish, French, German, Portuguese, Thai, Korean, Czech, and Danish; and conducts Train-the-Trainer programs on her books *Bringing Out the Best in Yourself at Work: How to Use the Enneagram System for Success* (McGraw-Hill, 2004) and *What Type of Leader Are You?* (McGraw-Hill, 2007). In addition, she offers Coaching with the Enneagram programs around the world, based on her most recent book, *Bringing Out the Best in Everyone You Coach: Use the Enneagram System for Exceptional Results* (McGraw-Hill, 2010).

An award-winning speaker and author, an expert consultant and facilitator, and a member of National Training Labs (NTL) and Organization Development Network (ODN), Ginger works with Enneagram in Business professionals across the globe, offering local and global services to companies ready to respond to the challenges of the 21st century. In addition, her Enneagram in Business website (*www.TheEnneagramInBusiness.com*) provides information about how the Enneagram is being used in a wide array of applications, industries, and countries. The Enneagram Learning Portal offers e-learning opportunities for individuals and companies that want to use the Enneagram in greater depth. Ginger can be reached at *ginger@TheEnneagramInBusiness.com*.

CPSIA information can be obtained
at www.ICGtesting.com
Printed in the USA
BVHW041459130619
550873BV00007B/91/P

9 780071 637077